A FALCON GUIDE®

Hiking
New York

Second Edition

Rhonda and George Ostertag

FALCON®

GUILFORD, CONNECTICUT

An imprint of The Globe Pequot Press

A FALCON GUIDE ®

Cover photo, interior photos, and maps: George Ostertag

ISSN 1536-6278
ISBN 0-7627-2242-8

Manufactured in the United States of America
Second Edition/Third Printing

 Text pages printed on recycled paper.

Contents

Acknowledgments

We would like to acknowledge the trail associations and individual volunteers who blaze and maintain the trails, the preservationists who work to save New York State's prized natural and cultural areas, and the many landowners who have allowed the state trail system to grow and endure. We would like to thank the individuals who helped with our research and volunteered their ideas or faces to this book, and we would like to thank our East and West Coast base camps for freeing us to do our work.

Legend

Interstate Highway	**81**	Viewpoint	⊙
State or Other Principal Road	**000**	Point of Interest	★
Paved Road		Campground	▲
Gravel Road		Bridge	
Unimproved Road	= = = = = ▷	Cabins/Buildings	■
Trailhead/Parking	Ⓟ	Peak/Elevation	9,782 ft.
Main Trail(s)		Falls	
Climbing Route		Pass/Saddle	) (
Alternate/ Secondary Trails/ Cross Country Trails		Lookout Tower	
River/Creek		High Rock	
Lake		Cliffs	
Ditch		Trail Shelter	△
Wetlands		Mine / Quarry	✕
Picnic Area		Gazebo	●
Railroad Tracks		Spring	
		Scale	0 0.5 1 Miles
		Map Orientation	N

Overview Map

A. Thousand Islands–Seaway Region
B. The Adirondacks
C. Niagara Frontier
D. Chautauqua-Allegheny Region
E. Finger Lakes
F. Central-Leatherstocking Region
G. Capital-Saratoga Region
H. Catskills Region
I. Hudson Valley
J. Long Island

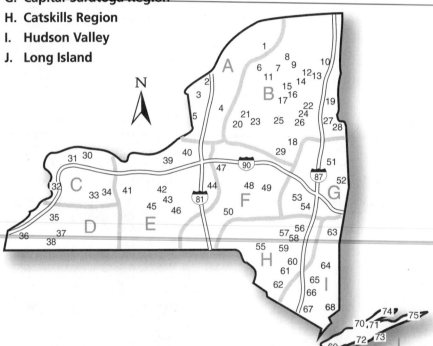

Introduction

New York State extends a premier outdoor playground, featuring thousands of miles of trail ranging from short nature walks to lengthy canal and rail trails to outstanding rugged wilderness hikes. Pacing off these routes, hikers discover a winning diversity of landscape, a seemingly limitless natural offering, and a rich geologic and cultural history that indelibly etch New York State in the journal of one's memory.

The trails described in this book explore many of the state's premier parks, forests, mountains, gorges, flatlands, swamps, beaches, and private reserves. Hikers will travel past dazzling waterfalls and daunting cliffs, bag summits and tag valley floors, but mostly they will get to know New York. Although some of this treasury is well known, great expanses remain little tapped.

This guidebook features a statewide sampling of nature walks, day-length hikes, and backpacking trips (where available)—a collection to challenge, excite, and engage. Despite the East's early settlement, New York still revels in open spaces and untarnished vistas.

If the New York trail system has one failing, it would be the design of its peak trails. Many charge straight at the summit, creating runoff channels and broad erosion scars. Hikers should take a role at the forefront of conservation and support, rather than thwart, the land management agencies in their efforts to reroute and improve these trails. Switchbacks, contours,

Eastern hardwood forest.

1

and other design features help retain the integrity of the land. Our adventure should not come at the price of the land or the enjoyment of future generations.

WEATHER

For the most part, New York offers three-season hiking, with many hiking trails serving dual roles as winter cross-country ski routes and snowshoe trails. Spring and fall offer a preferred mix of mild temperatures and low humidity. Summers can bring extremes in both categories, as well as dramatic afternoon thunder and lightning storms.

Like much of the East, New York endures a tormenting mosquito and black fly season. Less troublesome in dry years, the insects can attain unbearable numbers in wet years. June through much of July, insects may keep hikers at bay, especially in the Adirondacks and in New York's lowlands and swamp country. Wildflower devotees learn to wear netting and a smelly armor of insect repellent.

TERRAIN

The advance and retreat of four glacial masses over a period of two million years sculpted the face of New York State, gouging north-south lakes, scouring valleys, and depositing rock debris.

The state boasts a diversity of terrain and habitat that can inspire and fulfill for a lifetime. The coastal influence and pine barrens habitat of Long Is-

East Branch Ausable River, Adirondack Mountain Reserve.

land, the highlands and valley plain of the Hudson River, the beauty and folklore of the Catskills, the quartzite ledges of the Shawangunks, the finger-gouged lakes and east-west gorges of the Finger Lakes Region, the flat ridges and V-shaped valleys of the Allegany Hills, the Great Lakes and Saint Lawrence River country, and the prized peak-and-lake terrain of Adirondack Park spread a buffet suitable for the gods.

Outcrop vistas, grand waterfalls, clear-coursing streams, lakes, beaver ponds, marshes, rolling hardwood forests, alpine stands of fir and spruce, meadows, and desert plains season the journey. Hikers encounter the paths of past presidents and literary giants, soldiers, and farmers. The sparks of independence and the tide of the Industrial Revolution brush the terrain.

LAND OWNERSHIP

While this book concentrates primarily on public land offerings, trails across private, trust, and conservancy lands extend one's hiking opportunity. Hikers assume full responsibility for their own well-being when they cross onto private lands; they also consent to heed posted rules. Keep to the trail, leave gates as they were found, and police your own actions as well as those of any trail illiterates who may have passed before you. "Pack it in, pack it out."

The text will indicate if and where a trail traverses private land. Occasionally, land ownership changes or a landowner may withdraw the privilege of through-travel; respect such closures. Privately operated resorts or reserves may charge fees or suggest donations.

The Nature Conservancy (TNC), a nonprofit organization devoted to the protection of biodiversity, opens its trails to the public for hiking, nature study, and photography. Please note that straying from the trail, hiking with pets, collecting, smoking, picnicking, camping, building fires, swimming, and bicycle riding are forbidden activities in these preserves.

With a mission to conserve and preserve the land and its habitats and inhabitants, TNC extends hiking privileges only where and when they are compatible with this primary objective. Donations help defray the cost both of maintaining existing preserves and acquiring new ones.

A separate nonprofit entity in the Shawangunks, Mohonk Preserve, similarly protects in perpetuity a tract of prized land in its natural form. This preserve offers hiking and like pursuits and has its own rules and fees.

Trails traversing lands managed by state, county, and federal agencies shape the core of this book. Of the state-operated properties, state park sites (overseen by the New York State Office of Parks, Recreation and Historic Preservation) typically show greater grooming and development and possess more facilities, although the trails may not necessarily reflect the same level of civility. Some are overgrown and poorly marked. At most state parks expect to pay a seasonal entrance fee. Many hikers find that the New York State Empire Pass, an annual day-use pass, easily pays for itself.

The New York State Department of Environmental Conservation (DEC) manages the vast acreage of state-owned lands. State forests account for much of New York's open space; these lands provide planted stands and woods for selective harvests and multiple-use recreation. Backcountry shelters and privies, trail registers, and parking lots are the basic facilities. The state forest preserves found at Adirondack Park and in the Catskills feature vast expanses of protected woodlands closed to harvest and other revenue-making enterprises but open to various recreational pursuits. Wildlife management areas primarily promote and sustain waterfowl and wildlife populations, with hunting and fishing, bird-watching, and hiking being compatible recreations. Multiple-use areas serve a gamut of year-round recreational users.

TRAIL MARKINGS

Most of the trailbeds throughout New York are worn rather than cut into existence. With the predominance of deciduous forest, some manner of trail blazing—either paint, diamond, or disk markers—guides hikers along these routes. A double-blazing pattern typically warns of a change in direction. Often the top blaze is offset to the right or left to indicate the direction of the turn.

As the intervals between blazes can vary greatly, familiarize yourself with the blazing frequency. An uncommonly long lapse between blazes may indicate that you have strayed off course. Autumn hikers need to be especially alert, as leaves can conceal the tracked path.

The DEC uses color-coded and user-coded disks to mark its routes. In several areas the agency offers independent trail systems for foot, horse, and mountain bike use.

Trail marker.

Several fine long-distance routes crisscross the state, including the white Appalachian Trail, the blue Northville-Placid Trail, the yellow- or white-blazed Finger Lakes Trail, the aqua Long Path, and the orange Conservation Trail. On some private lands, blaze patterns may exist for one-directional travel only; consult a mapboard or flier before plotting your course. Cairns and stakes are other manners of marking a route.

THE VOLUNTEER COMPONENT

Devoted, energetic volunteers and established hiking organizations, such as the New York–New Jersey Trail Conference, the Adirondack Mountain Club (ADK), the Appalachian Mountain Club (AMC), the Finger Lakes Trail Conference (FLTC), and the Long Island Greenbelt Trail Conference, keep the New York State trail system maintained, promoted, and growing. Hikers should support these groups through membership as well as through the purchase of their maps and materials. Typically, the maps produced and sold by the volunteer organizations hold the most current information on the lay of the trail, land ownership, shelters and facilities, and obstacles.

Hikers likewise owe an enormous thanks to the legion of private landowners who allow trails to cross their lands. Many trails would slip from existence without their cooperation.

How to Use This Guide

We have structured the book to aid in the trail-selection process. First, to ease page flipping for trail comparisons, we have grouped the trails according to ten commonly accepted geographic regions. Second, a summary table heads each write-up, presenting the trail at a glance for a quick measure of its overall interest. Information bullets sketch the trail, its general location, specialness, length, difficulty, maps, special requirements or concerns, season, and a source for more information. The "Key points" and elevation profiles further help readers visualize a trail. Although the handful of key points allows a quick check on progress, the listing cannot replace the hike text for guiding you along the trail. At the end of the summary, readers will find detailed directions to the trailhead. Turn to Appendix D for the complete address and phone number for each named information source.

"The hike" component of the text describes the progress of the trail, drawing attention to special features and alerting readers to obstacles and potentially confusing junctions. Mentions of habitat changes, seasonal surprises, sidelights, and discoveries flesh out the tour. Where appropriate, for a balanced view we have mentioned flaws and disappointments.

The maps included within the text are not intended to replace more-detailed agency maps, road maps, state atlases, and/or topographic maps, but they do indicate the lay of the trail and its attractions to help readers visualize the tour.

AN EXPLANATION OF SUMMARY TABLE TERMS

Distance measures for the trails represent pedometer readings. Backpacking excursions—sometimes dictated by distance, sometimes by attraction—are left to the hiker's judgment and the rules of the appropriate managing agency, landowner, or private trust.

The subjective classification of "easy," "moderate," or "strenuous" takes into consideration overall distance, elevation change (the difference between the elevation extremes), cumulative elevation (how rolling a trail is), trail surface, obstacles, ease of following, and its difficulty relative to the other hikes in the book.

We deliberately excluded estimated hiking times, as personal health and physical condition, party size, the interest of the trail, weather, and a trail's condition all influence time on the trail. Gain a sense of your personal capabilities and hiking style, and judge the time yourself based on the distance, the elevation change, the difficulty rating, and what you glean from the text. Customize the hikes to fit your needs; you need not continue just because a description does, nor must you stop where it stops. Interlocking loops, side trails, and alternative destinations await.

Fungi at Tug Hill State Forest.

Azalea blooms, Mianus River Gorge Preserve.

Outdoor Primer

Whether wilderness trekking brings about a revitalizing experience or turns into an ordeal depends largely on one's preparation. Nature does not come without some inherent risks and discomforts, but learning to anticipate and mitigate the downside clears the way to great outdoor fun.

PREPARATION

Ten essentials. Outdoor experts have assembled a list of "ten essentials," the cornerstone to safe backcountry travel. These are (1) extra food, (2) extra clothing, (3) sunglasses, (4) knife, (5) candle or chemical fuel to ignite wet wood, (6) dry matches, (7) first-aid kit and manual, (8) flashlight with bulb and batteries, (9) maps for the trip, and (10) compass.

Dress. The amount and the types of clothing worn and carried on a hike depend on the length of the outing, the weather conditions, and one's personal comfort. Layering is key to comfort; select items that can serve more than one purpose. A long-sleeved shirt may be layered for warmth, lends sun protection, hinders mosquitos, and protects against ticks. A lightweight raincoat may double as a windbreaker. Choose wool for cold, wet, or changeable weather conditions; it retains heat even when wet. Choose cotton for dry summer days. For their weight, hats are invaluable for shielding eyes, face, and top of the head and for preserving body heat.

Footgear. While sneakers may be passable for nature walks, boots give comfort and protection on long hikes and uneven terrain. Sock layering, with a light undersock worn next to the foot and a second wool sock worn atop, helps prevent rubbing, cushions the sole, and allows for the absorption of perspiration. Avoid socks with a large cotton content; they are cold when wet and slow to dry.

Food. Pack plenty, as hiking demands a lot of energy. Pack foods that will not spoil, bruise, or break apart in the pack. Maximize the energy value for the weight, particularly when backpacking. Food fends off fatigue, a major contributor to accidents on the trail.

Equipment. The quantity and variety depend on the length and nature of the hike and on the season, but a good pack for transporting gear is essential. A day pack with padded straps, a reinforced bottom, and side pockets for water bottles works for most short outings. For overnight outings, select a backpack that has a good frame and balance and supports the weight without taxing hips, shoulders, or neck.

As high-quality backpacks represent a major investment, newcomers should first try renting one. You cannot evaluate a pack in the store with only a few sandbags for weight. A trail test delivers a better comfort reading, plus it demonstrates how well the unit packs with one's personal gear. Most good backpacking stores with a rental program will allow the charge of one rental to be applied to the purchase price of a new pack; ask the manager. Appendix A offers a checklist of other commonly carried items.

Map and compass. All hikers should become familiar with maps and know how to read them in conjunction with a compass. Maps provide an orientation to an area, suggest alternative routes, and aid in planning and preparing for the journey.

Become familiar with the United States Geological Survey (USGS) topographic maps. While most of these quads for New York State are too dated to show the lay of the trail, they still provide information about the steepness and flatness of the terrain, whether a site is treed or open, waterways, and the works of man. The USGS offers two sizes: the 7.5- and the 15-minute series.

New York State Department of Transportation (DOT) maps, based on the USGS 7.5-minute series, provide the same information but lack color to indicate vegetation.

Remember that true north does not equal magnetic north. For New York State the declination is about 14 degrees west. Search the map border for the declination.

TAKING TO THE TRAILS

Pacing yourself. Adopt a steady, comfortable hiking rhythm, take in the surroundings, and schedule short rests at regular intervals to guard against exhaustion.

Crossing streams. Cross at the widest part of a watercourse, where the current usually is slower and the water more shallow. Sandy bottoms suggest a barefoot crossing; fast, cold waters and rocky bottoms require the surer footing of boots.

Shed your socks before mounting a boot-clad wade. That way, once across, you will have a dry sock layer to help protect and keep your feet warm in the wet boots; wool socks show their thermal value. The discomfort of hiking in wet boots is minor compared with the alternative—a dunking. For frequent stream crossings or for hiking streambeds, lightweight sneakers earn their portage.

Hiking cross-country. For safe cross-country travel, one must have good map and compass skills, good survival skills, and good common sense. Steep terrain, heavy brush, and downfalls physically and mentally tax hikers, increasing the potential for injury. This, of all hiking, should not be attempted alone. Even know-how and preparation cannot fully overcome the unpredictability of nature and human fallibility.

Hiking with children. For young children, choose simple destinations and do not insist on reaching any particular site. Allow for the difference in attention span and energy level. Enjoy the passing of time, and share and encourage children's natural curiosity, but come prepared for sun, mosquitos, and poison ivy. Discuss what to do should you become separated; even small ones should carry some essential items: a sweater, water jug, and food.

Chautauqua Creek.

Red eft, Allegany State Park.

A WILDERNESS ETHIC

Trails. Keep to the path. Shortcutting, skirting puddles, and walking two abreast all contribute to erosion and the degradation of trails. Report any damage to the appropriate agency.

Permits and registration. In a few areas, land agencies issue trail or camp permits to help monitor and manage the trails and minimize overuse. Check under the heading of "Special concerns" in the trail summary table. On DEC lands, single-site stays of longer than three days and camping parties that exceed ten in number require permits. To protect the integrity of the wild, keep your party size small.

The DEC has an extensive trailhead registration program. Take the time to sign in and out and comment on the condition of the trail and its markings. The collected information figures into the allotment of funds for trail improvement and expansion.

Pets. Owners should strictly adhere to posted rules for pets. Controlling your animal on a leash is not just a courtesy reserved for times when other hikers are present; it is a responsibility to protect the wildlife and ground cover at all times.

Camping. Zero-impact camping should be everyone's goal. Select an established campsite and do not alter the ground cover, bring in logs for benches, bang nails into trees, or dig drainage channels around the tent. The clues that a hiker passed this way should be minimal.

Where no preestablished campsite exists, select a site at least 200 feet from the water and well removed from any trail. Avoid delicate meadow and alpine environments, and do not degrade lakeshore, waterfall, overlook, or other prized sites with a camp.

Reduce comforts (as opposed to necessities). Carry a backpacker's stove for cooking; when a campfire is unavoidable, keep it small. Snags and live trees should never be cut.

Sanitation. For human waste disposal, select a site well away from the trail and at least 300 feet from any water body. Dig a hole 8 inches deep in which to bury the waste. This biologically active layer of soil holds organisms that can quickly decompose organic matter. If the ground prohibits digging a hole of the specified size, dig as deep as possible and cover well with gravel, bark, and leaves.

Use tissue sparingly; for shorter excursions carry a zip-seal plastic bag for packing out soiled tissue. Burying often results in the tissue becoming either nest-building material for rodents or unsightly garbage scattered by salt-seeking deer.

Litter. "Pack it in, pack it out." This includes aluminum foil, cans, orange peels, peanut shells, cigarette butts, and disposable diapers. For nature to reclaim an orange peel takes six months, and a filter-tip cigarette butt requires ten to twelve years. Disposable diapers have become an incredible nuisance and a contaminant in the wild. Burying is *not* a solution.

Washing. Washing of self or dishes should be done well away from the lake or stream. Carry wash water to a rocky site and use biodegradable suds sparingly. Despite their benefits and ecological-sounding names, these soaps still present a threat to water.

SAFETY

Water. Water is the preferred refreshment; carry a safe quantity from home on all excursions, as wilderness sources dry up or may become fouled. Know that caffeine and alcohol are diuretics, which dehydrate and weaken you.

Treat water taken from wilderness sources when it is to be used for drinking or for washing foods or utensils for eating. *Giardia lamblia,* a waterborne organism that causes stomach and intestinal discomfort, finds a home in even the most remote, clear streams. Bring water to a full boil for at least five minutes. Water purification systems that remove both debris and harmful organisms offer a satisfactory alternative to boiling. As these filters come in varying degrees of sophistication, make certain the selected system strains out harmful organisms. Iodine tablets offer less protection—and no protection against *Giardia*—and are not considered safe for pregnant women.

Getting lost. Prior to departure, notify a responsible party of your intended destination, route, and time of return. Then keep to it and notify your contact upon your return.

If lost, sit down and try to think calmly. No immediate danger exists, as long as one has packed properly and followed the notification procedure. If hiking with a group, stay together. Short outward searches for the trail, returning to an agreed-upon, marked location if unsuccessful, is generally considered safe. If near a watercourse, following it downstream typically delivers a place of habitation or a roadway where help may be sought. Aimless wandering is a mistake.

Blowing a whistle or making loud noises in sets of three may summon help. If it's late in the day, prepare for night and try to conserve energy. Unless one has good cross-country navigational skills, efforts are best spent conserving energy and aiding rescuers by staying put and hanging out bright-colored clothing.

Modern aids such as global positioning system (GPS) receivers, cell phones, and walkie-talkies can reduce the risk of becoming lost or can speed rescue.

Hypothermia. This dramatic cooling of the body occurs when heat loss surpasses body-heat generation. Cold, wet, and windy weather commands respect. Attending to the Ten Essentials, eating properly, avoiding fatigue, and being alert to the symptoms of sluggishness, clumsiness, and incoherence among party members remain the best protection. Should a party member display such symptoms, stop and get that person dry and warm. Dry clothing, shared body heat, and hot fluids all help.

Heat exhaustion. Strenuous exercise combined with summer sun can lead to heat exhaustion, an overtaxation of the body's heat-regulatory system. Wearing a hat, drinking plenty of water, eating properly (including salty snacks), and avoiding fatigue are safeguards.

Poison ivy, oak, and sumac. The best way to avoid contact with these and other skin-irritating plants is to learn what they look like and in what environments they grow. Consult a good plant identification book. New vaccines and creams can provide some relief, but science has yet to conquer these irritating plant oils. If you suspect you have come in contact with one of these plants, rinse off as soon as possible and avoid scratching, as it spreads the oils.

Ticks, stings, and bites. Again the best defense is knowledge. Learn about the habits and habitats of snakes, bees, wasps, ticks, and other "menaces" of the wild and how to deal with the injuries they may cause. Also become aware of any personal allergies and sensitivities you or a party member might have.

Lyme Disease, transmitted by the tiny deer tick, has become a serious concern in the East, but it need not deter you from the outdoors. Hikers come into contact with these ticks amid grasses and shrubs; the ticks do not drop from trees. Wear light-colored long pants and long-sleeved shirts, and keep your layers tucked into one another. This will help you identify any ticks and keep them on the outside of your garments. While hiking, make frequent checks for the unwanted hitchhiker. Once at home, shower and search skin surfaces thoroughly and launder hiking clothes directly.

Should a tick become attached to the skin, remove it by drawing evenly on the body, disinfect the bite with alcohol, and monitor over the next few weeks. Look for a red bull's-eye swelling at the site of the bite; also be alert to inexplicable muscle pain, tiredness, or flulike symptoms. Consult a physician immediately should any of these symptoms occur.

Poison ivy, Bashakill Wildlife Management Area.

Bears. The black bears in the East represent more nuisance than threat. Use common sense; do not store food near camp—especially not in the tent. If clothes pick up cooking smells, suspend them along with the food from an isolated overhanging branch well away from camp. Sweet-smelling creams or lotions also should be avoided.

Hunting. While most public lands open to hunters do not prohibit hiking during hunting season and few have any record of conflict, we would still advise fall hikers to point their boots toward lands and trails where hunting is not allowed. If you hike where hunting occurs, wear bright orange clothing and keep to the trail.

Trailhead precautions. Unattended hiker vehicles are vulnerable to theft and vandalism, but the following steps can minimize the risk:

- Whenever possible, park away from the trailhead at a nearby campground or other facility.

- Do not leave valuables in the vehicle. Place keys and wallet in a button-secured pocket or remote, secure compartment in the pack, where they will not be disturbed until your return.

- Do not leave any visible invitations; stash everything possible in the trunk, and be sure that any exposed item advertises that it has no value.

- Be suspicious of loiterers; do not volunteer the details of your outing.

- Be cautious about the information you supply at the trailhead register. Withhold information such as license plate number and duration of stay until you are safely back at the trailhead.

Backcountry travel includes unavoidable risks that every traveler assumes and must be aware of and respect. The fact that a trail or an area is described in this book is not a representation that it will be safe for you. For while the book attempts to alert users to safe methods and warn of potential dangers, its scope is limited. Time, nature, use, and abuse can quickly alter the face of a trail. Let independent judgment and common sense be your guide.

For more detailed information about outdoor preparedness, consult a good instructional book or enroll in a class on outdoor etiquette, procedure, and safety. Even the outdoor veteran can benefit from a refresher.

Lady's Slipper.

Thousand Islands– Seaway Region

This Upstate New York region features an exciting terrain at the Canadian border uniting Thousand Islands, the St. Lawrence River Seaway, the eastern shore of Lake Ontario, and the low-lying forests west of the Adirondacks. The hikes visit gorge and gulf features, racing waters, a pristine beach, an island splendor, and a unique "alvar" habitat. Vistas applaud lake, river, and Canadian shore. The changeable weather associated with the Great Lakes brings an added intensity to this rich and varied stage.

1 Stone Valley Trail

General description:	This moderately difficult wooded trail rounds an exciting 3.2-mile stretch of the Raquette River.
General location:	In the towns of Colton, Parishville, and Pierrepont.
Special attractions:	Waterfalls, rapids, chutes, scoured potholes, gorges, islands, and overhanging cliffs; hemlock–beech forest; cathedral pines; tannery ruin.
Length:	7.8-mile loop, including spur.
Difficulty:	Moderate.
Maps:	*Stone Valley: A Cooperative Recreation Area* pamphlet sponsored by Niagara Mohawk Power Corporation (generally available at the trailhead registers or from the St. Lawrence County Planning Office).
Special concerns:	Be alert to the possibility of rapidly rising water. In winter expect icy spots and some risky stretches where an icy slip could land you in the river.
Season and hours:	Year-round, but best spring through fall; twenty-four hours.
For information:	Saint Lawrence County Planning Department.

Key points:
- 0.0   Northwest trailhead; hike south.
- 1.0   O'Malley Brook Overlook spur.
- 2.0   Lucy's Hole.
- 3.8   Colton; cross road bridge.
- 7.1   Lenny Road.
- 7.8   End at northwest trailhead.

Finding the trailhead: From the intersection of New York 56 and New York 68 at the southern end of the hamlet of Colton, go north on NY 56 for 3.6 miles and turn right (east) on Browns Bridge Road/Saint Lawrence County 24. Go 0.5 mile and turn right to reach the northwest trailhead parking lot

Stone Valley Trail

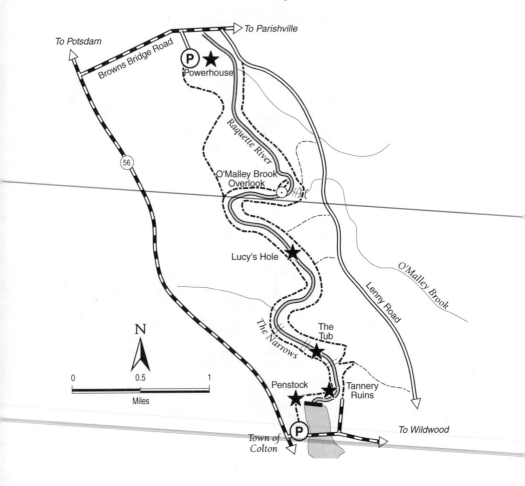

near the powerhouse in 0.1 mile; this site offers the best parking. Find additional access in Colton at the Raquette River bridge.

The hike: From the northwest trailhead off Browns Bridge Road, the trail travels lands owned by Niagara Mohawk Power, Saint Lawrence County, and the town of Colton. Arrows, blue trail markers, and small plaques explaining the geologic and cultural history of the area mark the route. Be cautious where the path is canted and eroded and on log crossings.

Follow the marked service road leaving the southwest corner of the parking lot. In 0.1 mile turn left, finding the trail register and brochures. Round the site of the Niagara Mohawk Powerhouse and turn south, away from the facility, following service roads and grassy tracks. The trail passes through

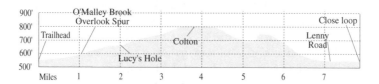

open woods, bramble-shrub clearings, and plantations. Wildflowers spangle the way, while deer tracks riddle the soft dirt.

Be alert for a marker pointing hikers left along an old woods road at 0.6 mile. The path descends and rounds toward the river, crossing a drainage where some creative stepping may be needed in addition to the corduroys to escape getting wet.

At a mile the trail forks; bear right. In a few feet a sign on the left indicates O'MALLEY BROOK OVERLOOK. This 0.5-mile round-trip side tour travels a pine–maple slope overlooking a series of beaver dams on a river tributary before reaching a Raquette River overlook and beach. Across the river you will see 15-foot O'Malley Brook Falls. The side trail ends, swinging a small loop on the river flat.

Past this overlook spur, the true river hike begins, rolling along the wooded slope for a grand upstream tour. Where hikers first meet the tannin-colored river, it flows broad and slow, coursing between rock and fern banks. Upstream it cuts a more volatile figure as the trail undulates between shore level and 100 feet above the stormy water.

Raquette River.

At 2 miles pass Lucy's Hole, or The Gut, a deep pool with a brightly painted geometric design adorning the rock of the far shore. The song of the river follows the trail as it drifts from the waterway.

Past three moss-mantled boulders make a steep ascent and descent to reach the lower end of The Narrows. Here, long bedrock fingers squeeze the water into channels of river fury. Upstream 15- to 18-foot falls, tilted bedrock slabs, worn chutes, and potholes capture the imagination. Side drainages arriving as waterfalls add to the bonanza. Above The Tub (a 12-foot-diameter river pothole hidden by a stone lip), another set of falls dazzles the eye, dropping 25 feet over a 100-foot distance.

As the Raquette River becomes gorgelike nearing the power company dam, the trail veers away from the river, climbing above the stone ruins of a tannery. Cross the footbridge over a penstock (a water conduit) and turn left on the dirt road, entering Colton near the town museum (3.75 miles).

For the loop, cross the road bridge over the Raquette River and take the first left, following a paved road past the Colton Fire Department. At the road's end (4 miles), find a small parking lot. Here two millstones represent the site's hydropower history and usher hikers back onto the foot trail. River angles and the orientation of the bedrock present an entirely new perspective for the return downstream journey.

From a small ridge, the trail angles downhill, skirting a soggy meadow bottomland that separates the path from the river. At the upcoming intersection with a woods road, turn left. At 4.4 miles, the trail curves right, edging a bedrock slab at the river. Steel anchor pins in the rock harken back to the nineteenth century, when lumberjacks floated logs to downstream mills.

By 4.6 miles the trail rolls alongside the river; side trails branch right to Lenny Road. At 4.8 miles view several large potholes riddling the bedrock ridge that forms The Tub; spring floods transform this rock into a roaring cataract of churning stones. The east shore path grows canted, more rootbound, and less civilized than it was for its first mile, and chutes and channels characterize the waterway.

Departing The Narrows (5.2 miles), the trail makes a steep uphill charge, remaining along the upper slope to 5.6 miles, where it plunges back to the river. East shore plaques identify marble outcrops (common in the Adirondack lowland), glacial erratics, and fossils.

Past Lucy's Hole, additional deep pools characterize the next 0.1 mile. Frog, hummingbird, toad, and grouse forge an acquaintance. At 6 miles comes the next uphill charge. Where the trail next descends, cross O'Malley Brook as it cascades beneath the cathedral pines.

From the O'Malley Brook footbridge (6.3 miles), cross a woods flat on a dirt road to pick up the trail on the left. The trail now hugs or travels a terrace 50 feet above the river. At 6.6 miles is an aspen gnawed half-through by beaver. Deciduous trees offer shade, and easy river access exists throughout.

The foot trail comes to an end at Lenny Road at 7.1 miles. Go left on Lenny Road to Browns Bridge Road, turning left to cross the river. Again turn left to close loop at the trailhead parking lot at 7.8 miles.

2 Wellesley Island State Park

Overview

Wellesley Island State Park introduces the beauty of the Thousand Islands to the land-locked traveler. Once farmed, this island shows mixed deciduous woods, abandoned field and pasture, rocky shores, and hilltop knolls. Panoramas take in the Saint Lawrence River, Thousand Islands, and Canadian shore.

In the southwestern portion of the park, a 600-acre peninsula and nature preserve holds 10 miles of interlocking trails that welcome short excursions. The featured hike for this park, the Round-the-Peninsula Trail, stitches together several of the named paths for a first-rate depiction of the island, its terrain, and locale.

General description:	This rolling tour travels the perimeter of the peninsula, serving up outstanding Saint Lawrence River–Thousand Islands views.
General location:	On the Saint Lawrence River.
Special attractions:	Vistas, fishing, steep cliffs and knolls, beaver ponds, glacial potholes, wildflowers, nature center.
Length:	4.4 miles round-trip, including pond detour.
Difficulty:	Easy.
Maps:	*Welcome to Minna Anthony Common Nature Center* brochure.
Special concerns:	Fee access to park.
Season and hours:	Spring through fall, dawn to dusk.
For information:	Wellesley Island State Park.

Key points:
- 0.0 Nature Center trailhead.
- 0.6 Sand Cove.
- 1.9 Spur left for pond loop.
- 3.1 East Bay Trail.
- 4.4 Ending fork: left to nature center; right to parking.

Finding the trailhead: From Watertown, go north on Interstate 81 for 26 miles and take exit 51 for Wellesley Island State Park (after the Thousand Islands Toll Bridge). Following the signs, turn right in 0.1 mile, and again turn right onto Jefferson County 100 in another 0.5 mile. Go 0.5 mile more and turn right onto Cross Island Road. The park entrance is in 1.6 miles. Follow the signs to the nature center for the trails.

The hike: The Round-the-Peninsula Trail unites five shorter interlocking nature trails that tour the peninsula. Enjoy views of Eel Bay,

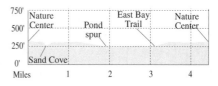

Wellesley Island State Park

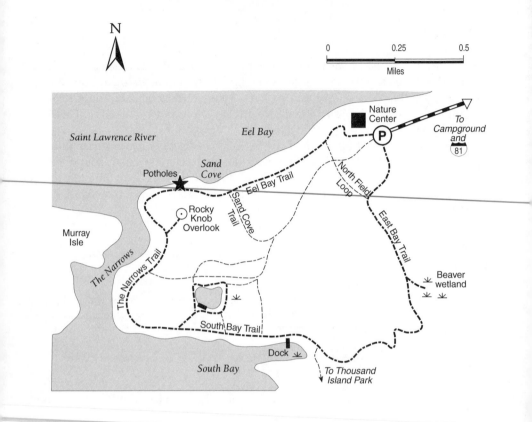

The Narrows, South Bay, and the islands of the United States and Canada. In turn, mixed forest, oak-grassland, wetland, and field frame the way.

Pursuing the signs for Eel Bay Trail, round the west side of the Minna Anthony Common Nature Center (museum) on the paved Friendship Trail, an interpretive trail with raised-letter plaques. Past the geology wall fashioned of rocks found in the Saint Lawrence Valley, bear left. Maple, hickory, ash, aspen, birch, and mixed oaks overlace the trail and filter looks at Eel Bay. At 0.1 mile go right for Eel Bay Trail, which begins at the end of the pavement, crossing over the North Field Loop Trail.

Travel is on a bluff some 50 feet above the bay, passing through tall woods with a full canopy. A jeweled lighting dances off Eel Bay as the Saint Lawrence River spreads away big, wild, and blue, bustling with recreation and transportation vessels.

At 0.5 mile the trail curves left, descending to Sand Cove. Where the Sand Cove Trail arrives on the left, continue forward for the peninsula tour. To the right rests the cove with its thin sandy beach edged by box elder and willow.

St. Lawrence River, Wellesley Island State Park.

The trail next rolls uphill to travel a semiopen bench above the water; outcrops sloping to the water prove popular with anglers and daydreamers. More views await where the trail travels atop a 70-foot cliff at 0.8 mile. Stairs again draw travelers closer to the bay and the clear, rocky-bottomed water. Where hilltop Rocky Knob Overlook comes into view, a spur trail to the right descends to the glacial potholes. The upper pothole measures 3 feet wide and 15 feet deep; the lower one is about a third that size.

The peninsula tour resumes following The Narrows Trail, with an early look at the watery channel separating Wellesley Island and Murray Isle. Where the trail tops out after a rocky ascent, a detour left finds Rocky Knob Overlook. The site holds benches and locator boards, pointing out the Thousand Islands neighborhood, including Mosquito, Big Gull, and Little Gull Islands, Eel Bay, and the Canadian islands to the north.

At 1.25 miles an outcrop offers an open view of The Narrows; stairs then descend the slope. Bear right, keeping to The Narrows Trail, which rolls up and over the next hill. Where the trail next bottoms out, a 100-foot spur heads right to a shoreline outcrop offering a farewell look at The Narrows.

Before long, the trail parallels South Bay, passing amid an oak-grassland. At the 1.9-mile junction, the Pond Spillway Trail heads left, adding a pond visit. The Round-the-Peninsula tour continues straight on the South Bay Trail.

To add the pond detour, ascend along the outlet ditch 0.1 mile to the small round pond and the 0.4-mile trail encircling it. Counterclockwise, the trail travels the open grassy bank. Observations include drowned snags, a marshy edge, and perhaps an irritable beaver sounding alarm with a thunderous beat of its tail. Gases percolate up through the waters. As the trail skirts a smaller lily pond, it curves left past picnic tables and a usable privy. A blind offers looks at the beaver lodge before the loop ends. Grouse, frog, porcupine, and kingfisher are other possible encounters.

Resuming the Round-the-Peninsula tour (2.5 miles), the South Bay Trail offers a wider path, advancing with mild undulations, touring a wooded plateau 15 feet above the water. Opportunities to shorten the loop branch to the left; stay on the South Bay Trail for the full tour. At 3.1 miles wooden steps descend to a viewing dock overlooking a mosaic of open water, lily pads, and cattail marsh. In case the stairs are in disrepair, be watchful of your step.

Ahead, the Round-the-Peninsula Trail turns left, now following the East Bay Trail through moister woods. The path heading straight soon leaves the park. Deer commonly crisscross paths with hikers as the East Bay Trail steadily ascends to 3.5 miles, where it tops out and curves left, rolling and meandering but trending downhill. Maple, oak, and white pine dominate the forest mix.

Although this section of trail is newer and less tracked, red disks with central white arrows point the way. At 3.75 miles the trail overlooks a large snag marsh parted by a boardwalk. The trail then dips and crosses side-by-side logs over a drainage, coming to a T-junction. Here a 100-foot detour to the right adds a visit to the previously admired wetland pond. The boardwalk journeys to a central dry island in the shallow pond, where beaver lodges, open water, buttonbush, duckweed, cattails, and snags create a rich stage.

En route to the museum, the trail crosses a boardwalk to follow a wider, more-defined trail. At 4.25 miles bypass North Field Loop and traverse a field. The next junction offers an opportunity to visit yet another beaver swamp, a 0.5-mile round-trip detour to the right. Ahead, the East Bay Trail forks; conclude the hike by going right to the parking lot or left to the museum.

3 Chaumont Barrens Preserve

Overview

At this Nature Conservancy preserve, discover the unusual habitat of a rare alvar landscape—an austere barrens with a naturally occurring linear-vegetation scheme. In North America only a pocketful of alvar sites occupy an arc swinging from northwest Jefferson County in New York through Ontario, Canada, into northern Michigan. Chaumont Barrens represents the premier site in New York State.

This harsh landscape holds a textured mosaic of tufted grassland, juniper-shrub flats, evergreens, mixed deciduous woods, and cracked bedrock. Aerial photographs best reveal the site's odd linear vegetation pattern. Intense glaciation, recurring cycles of flood and drought, and strong winds together shape this severe but intriguing land.

General description:	An easy self-guiding loop examines the mystery and beauty of this globally significant habitat.
General location:	14.5 miles northwest of Watertown, off Jefferson County 125.
Special attractions:	Limestone bedrock fissures, marine fossils, rare native grasslands, rubbly moss gardens, shrub savannas, spring and autumn wildflowers, bird-watching.
Length:	2-mile loop.
Difficulty:	Easy.
Maps:	Preserve brochure.
Special concerns:	Keep to the trail, using stepping stones where available, and beware of cracks, fissures, and hidden holes. Leave pets at home, and obey The Nature Conservancy's (TNC's) rules and closures that protect this fragile treasure. Summer temperatures may reach extreme highs, so carry water.
Season and hours:	Early May through mid-fall, dawn to dusk. Exact dates depend on the flooding cycle.
For information:	The Nature Conservancy, Central and Western New York Office.

Limestone fissures, Chaumont Barrens Preserve.

Chaumont Barrens Preserve

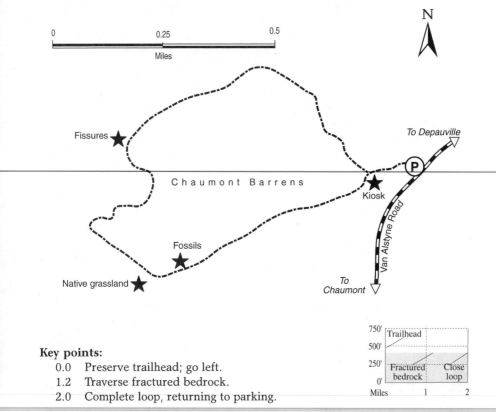

Key points:

0.0   Preserve trailhead; go left.
1.2   Traverse fractured bedrock.
2.0   Complete loop, returning to parking.

Finding the trailhead: From Interstate 81 at Watertown, take exit 47/Coffeen Street, and follow New York 12F west for 2 miles. Turn right (north) on Paddy Hill Road/NY 12E crossing over the river and turning left, staying on NY 12E all the way to the village of Chaumont (8.4 miles from the NY 12F junction). In Chaumont take the first right on Morris Track Road/Jefferson County 125; go 3 miles and turn left on unsigned Van Alstyne Road, just beyond a small cemetery on the right. A board with an arrow indicating CHAUMONT BARRENS points out the turn. The preserve entrance and parking are on the left in 1.1 miles; closures are posted at the parking lot.

The hike: An excellent brochure helps visitors identify the habitats and the plant and animal life found at the preserve. The simple 2-mile loop suggests a slow, respectful tour.

The trail starts to the left of the Chaumont Barrens sign, passing through a juniper flat and a pine-hickory corridor and alongside early examples of limestone fracturing (4 to 6 inches wide and 1.5 feet deep). At the interpretive kiosk at 0.1 mile, find panels describing the preserve habitats, trail brochures, and the start of the loop. A left begins a clockwise tour.

The trail is mostly open, passing through a complex of juniper, shrub, and grassland dotted by oak, pine, hickory, and a few snags. A varied tapestry of texture, layers, and color addresses the eye, while the clicking of summer insects entertains the ear.

At 0.5 mile the trail skirts a glacial erratic; at 0.7 mile the limestone bedrock comprising the trail reveals long, segmented fossils of a predatory cephalopod—a primitive marine animal. Elsewhere, discover coral and wormhole fossils. Next, overlook a rare remnant ten-acre prairie grassland, with sketchy tufts of native grasses, sedges, and wildflowers; some of these plants occur nowhere else in New York.

The trail then briefly travels a mixed woods of cedar, spruce, and aspen before crossing the Calcareous Barrens, with open, fractured bedrock, boulders, grasses, juniper, and runty cedar. As one overlooks the barrens, another native grassland sweeps away to the far right. The trail then returns to woods. In places, hikers might notice where trees sprout in a line along the fissures, hinting at the linear arrangement seen from the air.

Scarlet tanager, hawk, warbler, deer, toad, and snake can divert attention. Foxes find the more remote fissures suitable for dens. At 1.2 miles the trail crosses a broad, block-fractured bedrock plate. Again, worm burrows and other fossils can be detected; milkweed and wild rose grow from the cracks. Habitat changes occur in quick succession. Open hickory-deciduous woods yield to grassy flats, which yield to shrubs, which yield to shady woods.

At 1.6 miles an old dirt road advances the loop, passing from an open cedar-deciduous woods through a shrub and wildflower grassland, bringing the loop to a close at the kiosk. Return to the parking lot as you came (2 miles).

4 Inman Gulf Hiking and Nature Trails

General description:	Three nature and hiking trails line up end-to-end for a single rim tour, overlooking 5 miles of Inman Gulf.
General location:	About 10 miles south of Watertown.
Special attractions:	Sheer shale walls, a waterfall, the ancient river drainage, diverse forests, wildflowers, fall foliage, interpretive plaques, wildlife.
Length:	5.5 miles one-way (11 miles round-trip).
Difficulty:	Easy.
Maps:	Inman Gulf Trail flier.
Special concerns:	Beware of unstable edge; keep to trail.
Season and hours:	Spring through fall, dawn to dusk.
For information:	New York State Department of Environmental Conservation, Region 6.

Mushrooms, Tug Hill State Forest.

Key points:

Finding the trailhead: From the intersection of New York 177 and U.S. Highway 11, go east on NY 177 for 6.4 miles and turn north onto Lowe Road at Tremaines Corners. In 1.4 miles bear left and continue 0.2 mile more to Williams Road/Old State Road. There turn east (right) on Williams Road, going another 0.2 mile to reach parking area 1, with space for a half dozen vehicles. Four additional parking lots farther east along Williams Road offer opportunities to shorten the tour or alternative starting points.

The hike: Inman Gulf extends 9.6 miles between Barnes Corners and the Sandy Creek confluence in Rodman. Sidewinding through its depths, Gulf Stream alter-

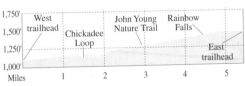

nately displays sections of riffles and still, black pools. A west-to-east (upstream) tour along the south rim offers a restful woods walk, with overlooks of the impressive chasm that measures 250 feet deep. Trail disks, paint blazes, and cairns at various places mark the tour.

Inman Gulf Hiking and Nature Trails

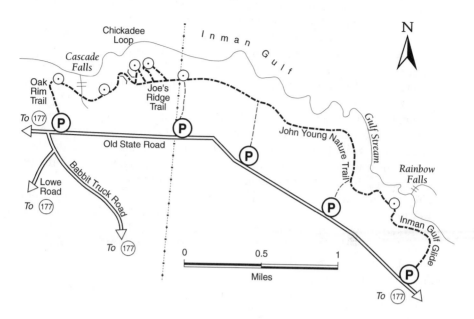

The yellow-marked Oak Rim Trail launches the hike, journeying north from parking area 1 through a pine-deciduous forest; jewelweed replaces the woods flora in the moister pockets. At 0.4 mile reach the gulf rim, snaring a quick, restricted look at Inman Gulf. A better view lies just ahead, where a bench seat presents the best up-canyon view of the entire tour. This banner look features the fluted cliffs and steep wooded walls of Inman Gulf, meeting in a "V," with a back rim peeking through the pointed gap. Wooden plaques identify trees along the route.

Next, with a rock-hopping crossing, follow a drainage downstream. Cascade Falls plummets in a steep cataract over tiered rock and races into the gulf. At 0.7 mile pass beneath an ancient red oak, reaching a broad, tree-framed down-canyon view. A congestion of thin-trunked deciduous trees enfolds the tour, as it passes yet another prized vista and bench. Views prove particularly stirring when the gulf dons fall color.

Tread carefully where an open, crumbling shale nose protrudes into the gulf. As the tour progresses, views across the gulf and into its twisting belly urge hikers onward. Hemlocks often claim the rim; oaks cling to the cliff's edge, and mixed deciduous trees fill the gulf. As the trail drifts away from the rim, follow a drainage, descending among ash, maple, black cherry, and pine to cross a footbridge.

At the bridge (1.4 mile) hikers may continue straight ahead or take the red-marked Chickadee Loop, a 0.2-mile side tour that returns to the Oak Rim Trail east of the bridge. Chickadee Loop ascends a small side ridge and point for a gulf vista that showcases a tight downstream bend and the steep shale cliff of the north wall.

Where Chickadee Loop rejoins the main (yellow) trail, hikers again have an option of either following the main trail or taking another side tour, the blue-marked Joe's Ridge Trail, which heads left. This 0.3-mile side loop passes through a natural mineral lick, where deer commonly gather, to ascend yet another thin pull-apart ridge (perhaps isolated by the ancient Gulf Stream). This side tour likewise offers a front-row seat to Inman Gulf, while the main trail gets lost in the cheap seats.

The rim-hugging tour resumes with stolen glances through the hemlock boughs and later through the branchwork of oak, beech, and aspen. At an open utility corridor (2.25 mile), find an unobstructed look at the gulf. Cross the width of this clearing to continue the rim tour; a right turn, hiking out the corridor, leads to Williams Road and parking area 2.

The rim tour shows gentle gradients, while brightly colored mushrooms and virtually colorless Indian pipe sprinkle the forest floor. At 2.9 miles the red-marked John Young Nature Trail replaces the Oak Rim Trail as host for the tour. Steep plunging cliffs give admirers a sinking-stomach thrill.

At 3.3 miles pass through a depression formed in the Ice Age, when the Gulf Stream flowed near the top of the forest plateau. Gulf views become more teasing. To the right a bench swing invites unburdening of the pack for a quiet forest moment. Aspens fill out the canopy, and interpretive plaques come more often as the trail drifts away from the rim.

At 3.9 miles the blue-marked Inman Gulf Glide brings home the tour. It briefly follows an overgrown woods road, crossing a drainage to return to the rim. Plush green vegetation claims the southern wall. At 4.4 miles a tree-framed look at Rainbow Falls halts steps. Rainbow Falls is a 60- to 80-foot white veil spilling from a treed drainage on the north wall. When full, the falls rages. Deer, owl, toad, and raven offer surprise encounters.

At 4.7 miles a lower terrace distances the trail from the gulf. Where deciduous trees again win dominance, pass within 15 feet of the rim. At 5 miles the trail curves away from the gulf, passing through a plot of mature, planted white and red pine. Round-trip hikers may choose this point to turn around. Jewelweed, brambles, and berries along with ash and dogwood frame the trail's exit at parking area 5 (5.5 miles).

5 Lakeview Natural Beach Hike

General description: This hike offers a relaxing stroll along a limited-access natural barrier beach on Lake Ontario.

General location: 20 miles southwest of Watertown.

Special attractions: Natural white-sand beach and spit; protected vegetated dunes; Floodwood Pond; seabirds.

Length: 6.5 miles round-trip.
Difficulty: Easy.
Maps: None.
Special concerns: No swimming, picnicking, camping, fires, or radios. Access to the natural beach is via Southwick Beach State Park, a fee area.
Season and hours: Spring through fall.
For information: New York State Department of Environmental Conservation, Region 6.

Key points:
- 0.0 Start at Southwick Beach State Park.
- 0.2 Enter Natural Beach Area.
- 3.2 Floodwood Pond; backtrack north.

Finding the trailhead: From Interstate 81, take exit 40 and go west on New York 193 for Southwick Beach State Park, reaching the entrance in 8.3 miles. For a beach hike alone—and better parking—start at the state park's beach parking lot. For an inland start follow the Nature Trail south from the Southwick Beach entrance station.

The hike: Ideal for exercise or daydreaming, this tour travels the northern 3-mile spit of Lakeview Wildlife Management Area (WMA). The more remote southern spit is inaccessible, save by boat.

The selected hike heads south from the Southwick Beach State Park bathhouse and concession building. During the heyday of the 1920s, this beach bustled with bathhouses, a midway, dance hall, roller coaster, and ballfield. Now, a much quieter developed beach for swimming and sunbathing abuts the natural spit of the WMA.

The compressed, fine-grained sandy strand embellished by wave-deposited lines of duckweed and tiny mussel shells beckons. Mornings, the cottonwood trees shading the campground above the beach toss long shadows across the strand.

At 0.25 mile leave the developed state park, entering the signed Lakeview Wildlife Management Area—Natural Beach Area, where a low berm or flattish dune backs the beach. Cottonwoods still claim the back swale. At 0.5 mile a boardwalk traverses the dune, marking the arrival of the Nature Trail.

The rhythmic lapping and tranquil blue of the lake water provide a soothing backdrop for the walk. Storms rolling across the Great Lakes churn out a much more exciting stage. A low, flat lake terrain sweeps away to the horizon, as treed shorelines curve away north and south. Across the broad blue expanse, a power plant spews steam.

Bonaparte gulls bob in the shallows and race along shore, as terns cut and dive into the water after silvery fish. By 0.75 mile the dunes grade higher into humps stabilized by trees and vegetation. Some of the dunes reach 30 feet high but have little loose sand other than that on the low seaward brow

Lakeview Natural Beach Hike

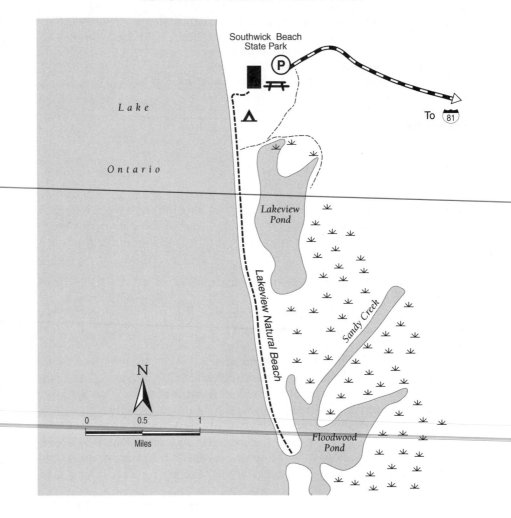

and between the discrete bunches of dune grass. At times small yellow bee-tles cling to everything, including the hiker who lingers too long.

Fish carcasses picked bare by gulls and the occasional flotsam from a boat alone mar the clean wilderness strand. Makeshift wind shelters dot the beach.

At 3.1 miles come to the river outlet of Floodwood Pond; across the out-let stretches the inaccessible southern spit. Driftwood-strewn sands and beachgoing red-winged blackbirds precede the outlet. Among the weathered gray wood, discover tiny cottonwoods taking root or the dizzying tracks of shorebirds. By hiking the outlet upstream, hikers may extend the tour as far

Lakeview Natural Beach.

as the mouth of the pond at 3.25 miles. Large beds of reeds characterize Flood-wood Pond. From the pond's mouth, the hike must be reversed. Backtrack north along the beach.

For hikers who instead choose to start at the Nature Trail, follow the path south, passing in turn an abandoned orchard, some impressive beech trees within a hardwood grove, and a small waterfall at the Filmore Brook crossing. The hike then turns right (west) to arrive at the beach via boardwalk, joining the tour at the 0.5-mile mark. Ask rangers about the nature trail's condition before starting, and beware of poison ivy.

The Adirondacks

For seekers of chiseled mountains, remote wooded valleys, crystalline streams, enticing lakes, and expansive views, the Adirondacks fulfill the quest. Occupying the eastern two-thirds of Upstate New York, six-million-acre Adirondack Park provides a much needed and sought-after outlet for challenge and adventure, renewal and escape. Two visitor information centers, one at Paul Smiths, the other at Newcomb, launch travelers on their way.

The Adirondack High Peaks Region, which encompasses all the peaks over 4,000 feet in elevation, receives the greatest amount of boot traffic, but superb trails explore the entire region. Venture to pristine lakes for fishing or swimming; inspiring streams, cascades, and waterfalls; wildflower-dotted beaver meadows; whisper-quiet forests; and stirring vistas of the lake-forest tapestry. The majestic High Peaks can be admired from virtually every corner, and this northern locale treats visitors to one of the showiest fall color changes to be found anywhere.

6 Grass River Wild Forest Hike

General description:	This hike traces the east shore of the wild river, overlooking a waterfall, deep pools, rapids, and cascades.
General location:	15 miles south of Canton.
Special attractions:	Waterfall, picturesque river, mixed forest, wildlife, solitude, colorful fall foliage.
Length:	3 miles round-trip.
Difficulty:	Easy.
Maps:	None. Look for mapboard where trail enters state land.
Special concerns:	An easement through private property accesses this trail; respect this landowner's rights and any posted notices.
Season and hours:	Spring through fall.
For information:	New York State Department of Environmental Conservation (DEC), Region 6.

Key points:
- 0.0 Grass River Wild Forest trailhead.
- 0.6 Lampson Falls viewing.
- 1.5 Site of former bridge; turn around.

Finding the trailhead: From Cranberry Lake Village, go west on New York 3 for 19.9 miles. There turn north toward DeGrasse on Saint Lawrence County 27 (DeGrasse Fine Road). Bear right in 0.8 mile; go another 7.6 miles

Grass River Wild Forest Hike

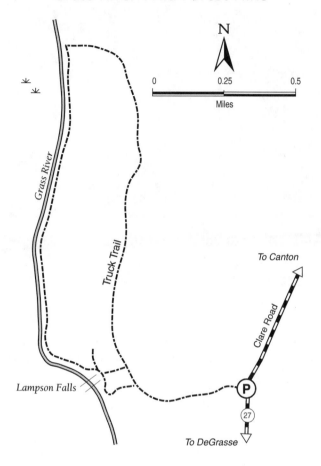

and turn right at a T-junction in DeGrasse, remaining on County 27. Go 4.3 miles from DeGrasse to find the DEC sign for Grass River Wild Forest on the left. Park along the road shoulder away from the gate.

The hike: This hike incorporates the walkable designated trail that explores Grass River and its enfolding forest preserve.

Round the gate and hike west through private property, keeping to the dirt truck trail for 0.2 mile. The wooded lane offers a pleasant stroll with blue jays, squirrels, and grouse as co-travelers. Where yellow DEC blazes replace the orange ones of the private landowner, look right for the map-board that indicates existing and proposed routes.

Continue west via the road, touring amid transition woods and magnificent conifers, coming to a Y-junction at 0.4 mile; either way leads to the river.

Lampson Falls, Grass River Wild Forest.

A right on the truck trail followed by a quick left on the foot trail leads to the pool at the base of the falls. Go left at the fork to add an upstream and side view of Lampson Falls.

Where the left option, in turn, forks (0.5 mile), the main foot trail turns right (downstream). The path ahead quickly dead-ends where the river flows broad, black, and deep above the falls. To continue downstream, pass through an herb-and-forb clearing, entering the woods where a well-tracked footpath descends the east bank. The 60-foot plunge of Lampson Falls churns and sheets over a 60-foot-wide outcrop before spilling to a black pool.

Where the trail bottoms out at a small boardwalk (0.6 mile), the two river-access routes merge. Mount the reinforced steps, ascending the steep slope to the north. Midway uphill, turn left to round an outcrop for a frontal view of the falls and the continuation of the river trail. Atop the rise you will find a scenic white pine flat, campfire ring, and privy.

The outcrop point holds the first red marker and an end to the confusion of footpaths that accompany the falls. Here Grass River glides over bedrock, reaching a second black pool. Pine, maple, and hemlock bring spotty shade, while poison ivy claims niches in the rock.

The trail rolls, alternately traversing the river-plain meadow and hemlock-deciduous shore. Hobblebush, fern, sarsaparilla, whorled aster, clintonia, oxalis, and bunchberry bring a burst of green. Spurs branch to shore.

A quiet-flowing river hosts travel from the falls to the site of the one-time hiker bridge (1.5 miles), where a scenic rock island parts the river and launches riffles. In late August the birds begin to flock, and the tips of the maples flash a showy red–orange. Where the trail dead-ends at the river, the truck trail from 0.4 mile arrives on the right, and an informal trail continues north (downstream) along the east shore. Future plans call to develop this trail, extending the hike north to Harper's Falls on the North Branch Grass River.

Meanwhile, hikers may opt to retrace the east shore route or hike the truck trail south to the junction at 0.4 mile, both equidistant. From there, turn east to return to the vehicle.

7 Floodwood Loop

General description:	This easy woodland loop in the Adirondack Lakes Region strings together prized canoe waters.
General location:	17 miles northeast of the hamlet of Tupper Lake.
Special attractions:	A network of glacial ponds, with rock and pine-clad islands; mature conifer–deciduous woods; water lily blooms mid-July to August; loons, osprey, herons, frogs, and fish.
Length:	7.7-mile loop, plus another mile of canoe-carry spurs.
Difficulty:	Easy.
Maps:	Adirondack Mountain Club, Adirondack Northern Region map.
Special concerns:	None.
Season and hours:	Spring through fall.
For information:	New York State Department of Environmental Conservation, Region 5.

Key points:

0.0	Western trailhead; head south.
0.5	Middle Pond junction.
1.8	Floodwood Passage Bridge junction.
6.2	Polliwog–Little Polliwog Ponds canoe carry.
7.8	Floodwood Road (eastern trailhead); turn left.
8.7	End loop at western trailhead.

Finding the trailhead: From Tupper Lake travel east on New York 3 East/New York 30 North to the split-off in 5.3 miles. There take NY 30 north for 8.6 miles and turn left (west) on Floodwood Road, bearing left at the fork. The eastern trailhead lies 2.1 miles west of NY 30, the western trailhead 3 miles west. The final 2.3 miles are unpaved; the western trailhead has better turnout parking.

The hike: By taking full advantage of the canoe carries, this hike visits the shore of seven large ponds and the waters of Fish Creek. Orange and yellow snowmobile markers point the way. The final 0.9 mile is on Floodwood Road.

Floodwood Loop

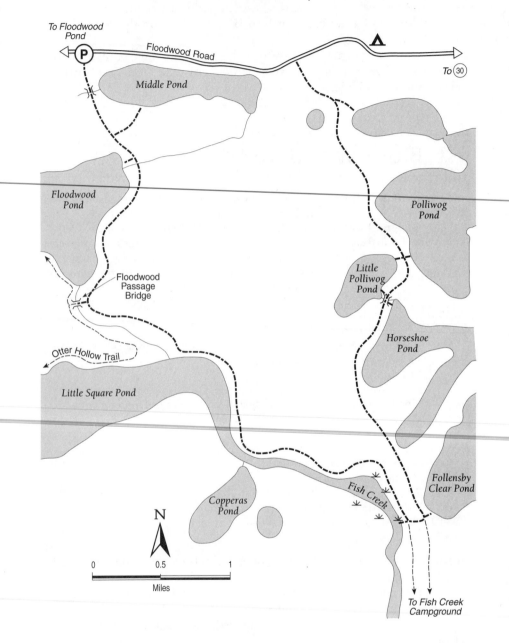

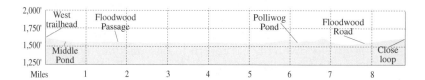

	West trailhead	Floodwood Passage				Polliwog Pond	Floodwood Road		

2,000'
1,750'
1,500'
1,250'
Middle Pond ... Close loop

Miles   1   2   3   4   5   6   7   8

Head south from the western trailhead. Beech, birch, maple, and hemlock overlace the cushiony path, while ferns, hobblebush, oxalis, and club moss decorate the floor. A mild gradient, diffused lighting, and scenic snags and logs contribute to the relaxation of this counterclockwise tour.

As the trail descends to a footbridge crossing, it presents a quick peek at Middle Pond. At the 0.5-mile T-junction, find the first canoe carry heading left to Middle Pond in 0.1 mile; the loop journeys right. Middle Pond presents a charming forest-rimmed crescent, a conifer-clad island, and vast mats of lily pads. Approach quietly; turtles sun on the logs.

The loop resumes, bypassing an enormous, mossy boulder coming to the second canoe carry at 0.8 mile. Go right 250 feet to view Floodwood Pond.

The loop trail then drifts from shore, exploring an engaging woods, where logs ease the crossing of Middle Pond outlet. At 1.6 miles sphagnum moss claims a typically soggy site. Past a campsite overlooking the steep bank of Floodwood Pond, bear left for the loop; side paths branch to shore.

At the marked junction for Floodwood Passage Bridge, detour right; straight continues the loop. Aspen and pine frame the way to this lengthy

Middle Pond, Adirondack Park.

39

bridge across the Floodwood–Little Square Ponds passage. Log-riddled and flowing with aquatic plants, the tranquil, muddy-bottomed stream hosts schools of fish and the occasional canoe. Otter Hollow Trail travels the opposite shore; for Floodwood Loop, return to the junction and go right.

From the loop at 2.4 miles, look across Floodwood Passage to see a couple of beaver lodges. Occupying a point on Little Square Pond, a campsite and privy serve both land and water travelers. A marshy peninsula and lily-pad shallows lend character to the long rectangular pond; berry bushes and sheep laurel adorn the shore. At a camp flat and fire ring at 2.6 miles, bear right. Trail markers disappear for a spell, but the path remains good.

Hemlocks weave in and out of the mix, bringing richer shade as the trail flattens for the next 1.5 miles. At a three-pronged junction at 3.9 miles, a right turn yields a boardwalk access to Fish Creek. Straight leads to Fish Creek Campground, and left leads to Follensby Clear Pond and the loop. Fish Creek is a broad, slow, marshy-sided water, with sheep laurel, cranberry, and pitcher plants along shore.

En route to Follensby Clear Pond, quickly come upon another trail intersection. To the left lies the loop; to the right, a second trail journeys south to Fish Creek Campground. The canoe carry straight ahead leads to Follensby Clear Pond, a huge water body, with rounded peninsular shores and islands. Conifers dominate its skyline; motorboats disturb its calm.

From the intersection the loop swings north for the return leg, traversing low glacial ridges. In places, snags open up the cathedral. The deep blue ahead belongs to Horseshoe Pond.

At 4.9 miles the trail dips to a spruce bog before resuming its rolling tour through mixed woods. At 5.3 miles come within striking distance of Horseshoe Pond, but no formal access exists until the footbridge for Little Polliwog Pond outlet. North of the outlet bridge lies a junction. A left finds not-so-tiny Little Polliwog Pond, with a marshy far end and jail-like look to its rim of pine snags.

Northbound, the loop travels the ridge between Little Polliwog and Polliwog Ponds, reaching the canoe carry between the two at 6.25 miles. To the left lies an open-water look at Little Polliwog Pond; to the right a beautiful hemlock avenue ushers hikers to Polliwog Pond, a much larger water body.

At 6.65 miles a drowned 20-foot segment of the loop proves tricky to skirt. At the 7.2-mile junction, a spur to the right leads to an isolated arm of Polliwog Pond; the loop continues left, coming to a fork in 0.2 mile. Straight leads to an open-water view of Middle Pond, while a right leads to Floodwood Road (7.8 miles). Turn left on this lightly used dirt road to close the loop at 8.7 miles.

8 Jenkins Mountain Trail

General description:	This trail explores forest, glade, and glacial drift before attaining a summit vista.
General location:	Adirondack Park Visitor Interpretive Center at Paul Smiths, 15 miles northwest of the village of Saranac Lake off New York 30.
Special attractions:	Vistas, mixed forests, meadow openings, beaver pond, wildlife sightings, fall foliage.
Length:	8.2 miles round-trip.
Difficulty:	Moderate.
Maps:	Paul Smiths Visitor Interpretive Center (VIC) Trail System flier.
Special concerns:	None.
Season and hours:	Summer and fall only; during the wet season, the trail remains closed to protect the bed from damaging wear and erosion. Building hours: 9:00 A.M. to 5:00 P.M. daily, except Thanksgiving and Christmas. Trails: daylight hours.
For information:	Paul Smiths VIC.

Jenkins Mountain view, Paul Smiths VIC.

Jenkins Mountain Trail

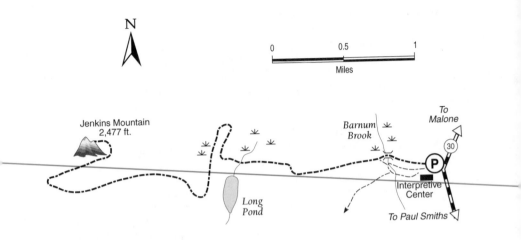

Key points:
- 0.0   From VIC entrance road, head west on service road.
- 0.4   Cross Barnum Brook.
- 1.8   Foot trail replaces road.
- 4.1   Summit outcrop; return by same route.

Finding the trailhead: From the New York 30–New York 86 junction (26 miles north of the hamlet of Tupper Lake, 13 miles west of Saranac Lake), go north on NY 30 for 0.9 mile and turn left (west) to enter the VIC.

The hike: Paul Smiths VIC boasts a fine collection of nature trails, but for those with an appetite for greater challenge and a quest to get above it all, the site's Jenkins Mountain Trail may better fill your time.

Uphill from the parking lots, this blue-blazed trail follows the gated service road west off the VIC entrance road for 1.75 miles. The road offers a good walking surface and mild grade. Maple, beech, birch, and the occasional conifer shape a semifull canopy; hobblebush and brambles claim the road shoulder.

Locator boards for cross-country skiers and 0.5-mile incremental markers assist hikers. At 0.4 mile the route crosses over Barnum Brook; to the right the brook shows a snag-pierced marsh. The path heading left along the brook's west shore leads to Barnum Brook Trail; keep to Jenkins Mountain Road.

Past a privy, a foot trail replaces the service road, traversing a glacial-drift ridge that parts a fern glade from a beaver pond. Beech, maple, and birch clad the ridge. A beaver lodge, a neatly constructed dam, and the north summit of Jenkins Mountain contribute to views.

Round the point of the glade and continue advancing along and over similar low glacial ridges. Sarsaparilla, fern, and club moss accent the rock-studded forest floor. A few black cherry trees appear in the forest ranks. After crossing a small drainage, the trail enters a long straightaway at the base of Jenkins Mountain. Deer, songbirds, woodpeckers, and fingertip-sized toads divert attention.

At 3.25 miles the trail ascends fairly steeply, taking a switchback between boulders and outcrop ledges. Where the trail hugs the line of Jenkins Mountain Ridge, the grade moderates. Stepping stones assist travel through a small jewelweed meadow.

Just beyond the 4-mile marker, the summit outcrop presents a 180-degree southwest panorama, with tower-topped St. Regis Mountain claiming center stage. The Adirondack high peaks, Long and Black Ponds in the valley bottom, and a rolling wooded expanse complete the view. Fog may lift from the ponds and paint the drainages between the mountains, enhancing the view. Return as you came for an 8.2-mile round-trip.

9 Adirondack Park Visitor Interpretive Center at Paul Smiths, Nature Trails

Overview

Paul Smiths is one of two visitor interpretive centers operated by the Adirondack Park Agency and serving travelers to New York State's six-million-acre Adirondack Park; the other is in Newcomb. At Paul Smiths four superb nature trails encourage one to lace on the hiking boots and go exploring. Seasonally, the nation's first Native Species Butterfly House beckons a detour.

General description:	Four easy, interlocking interpretive trails travel mature mixed forest, pine forest, and wetland habitats.
General location:	15 miles northwest of the village of Saranac Lake off New York 30.
Special attractions:	Bird-watching, diverse forests, insect-eating plants, nature discovery.
Length:	The trails range between 0.6 mile and 1.3 miles in length.
Difficulty:	Easy.
Maps:	Paul Smiths Visitor Interpretive Center (VIC) Trail System flier.
Special concerns:	None.
Season and hours:	Spring through fall for hiking. Building hours: 9:00 A.M. to 5:00 P.M. daily, except Thanksgiving and Christmas. Trails: daylight hours.
For information:	Paul Smiths VIC.

Adirondack Park Visitor Interpretive Center at Paul Smiths, Nature Trails

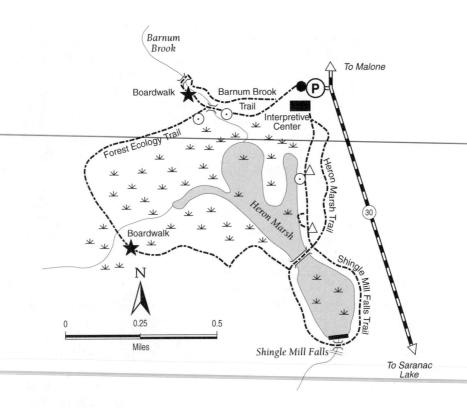

Key points:

Barnum Brook Trail:

    0.0   VIC entry trailhead.

    0.3   Pass Forest Ecology Trail.

    0.6   Complete loop, ending at trailhead.

Forest Ecology Trail:

    0.0   Start at midpoint of Barnum Brook Trail.

    0.9   Boardwalk.

    1.3   End at Shingle Mill Falls Trail; backtrack or head left for VIC.

Heron Marsh Trail:

    0.0   VIC backdoor trailhead; hike counterclockwise.

    0.2   Observation platform.

    0.4   Pass Shingle Mill Falls Trail near pontoon bridge.

    0.8   End at VIC.

Shingle Mill Falls Trail:

    0.0   Start off Heron Marsh Trail at pontoon bridge.

    0.3   Shingle Mill Falls.

    0.6   Complete loop.

Finding the trailhead: From the New York 30–New York 86 junction (26 miles north of the hamlet of Tupper Lake, 13 miles west of Saranac Lake), go north on NY 30 for 0.9 mile and turn left (west) to enter Paul Smiths VIC.

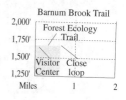

The hikes: The nature trails may be toured independently or woven together for longer loops. They pass over bark shavings, with boardwalks and observation decks. Interpretive panels help inform travelers.

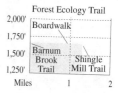

Starting at the gazebo to the right of the VIC's entry walk, **Barnum Brook Trail,** a 0.6-mile barrier-free loop, travels a wide earthen trail and a handsome boardwalk and bridge spanning the tea-colored water of Barnum Brook. A dial-a-tree identification wheel and species identification tags introduce a stunning woods of big pines, maple, birch, black cherry, beech, red spruce, and balsam fir. Observation decks overlooking Heron Marsh and the mirror-black outlet pool of Barnum Brook win over travelers. Quotes from Theodore Roosevelt bridge time and the sentiments of naturalists.

From the loop's midpoint, hikers may access the 1.2-mile **Forest Ecology Trail,** which edges Heron Marsh, touring mixed conifer-deciduous woods and offering an overlook. Interpretive plaques introduce geology, habitat, and natural processes. A 900-foot boardwalk traversing bog and fen habitats wins praise. Initially, tamaracks line the walk; elsewhere, sphagnum moss, alder, sedges, cattail, heath,

and insect-eating bladderwort, pitcher plant, and sundew engage botanists and photographers. Where the Forest Ecology Trail comes to a junction, go left to meet the Shingle Mill Falls Trail near the pontoon bridge (1.3 miles). Either backtrack or turn left to return to the VIC.

Out the back door of the VIC, the **Heron Marsh Trail,** an 0.8-mile loop, offers an alternative launch pad for the Paul Smiths nature trail system. A counterclockwise tour takes visitors along the shore of extensive Heron Marsh, while side loops and spurs lead to marsh vantages and an observation platform. Birders will want to travel with scopes, binoculars, and identification books. An ascent through mature mixed conifers and young deciduous woods returns hikers to the center.

Forming a figure-eight with the Heron Marsh Trail, the 0.6-mile **Shingle Mill Falls Trail** rolls along the wooded rim of the open water of Heron Marsh. The long pontoon bridge spanning the wetland neck may either begin or end the tour; cow lilies, pickerelweed, and cattail-sedge islands contribute to views. At the bridge near Heron Marsh Dam, hikers overlook Shingle Mill Falls.

Heron Marsh boardwalk, Paul Smiths VIC.

Spilling over a natural bedrock sill, the falls powered early-day mills. Bittern, heron, osprey, and a variety of ducks number among the winged sightings. Beaver-felled trees ring shore.

10 Poke-O-Moonshine Trail

General description:	This hike climbs an eastern Adirondack peak, passing through mixed woods and topping outcrops before reaching the rocky summit and fire tower.
General location:	Some 7 miles south of Keeseville off U.S. Highway 9.
Special attractions:	Granite-gneiss cliffs, mixed forest, lean-to, fire tower, and Lake Champlain–High Peaks views.
Length:	2.4 miles round trip.
Difficulty:	Moderate.
Maps:	Adirondack Mountain Club, Adirondack Eastern Region map.
Special concerns:	Day-use or campground fee charged; hikers may avoid this fee by parking along the road shoulder of U.S. 9 outside the no-parking zone that abuts the state campground, but be careful when doing so.
Season and hours:	Late spring through fall.
For information:	New York State Department of Environmental Conservation, Region 5.

Poke-O-Moonshine Mountain summit outcrop, Adirondack Park.

Poke-O-Moonshine Trail

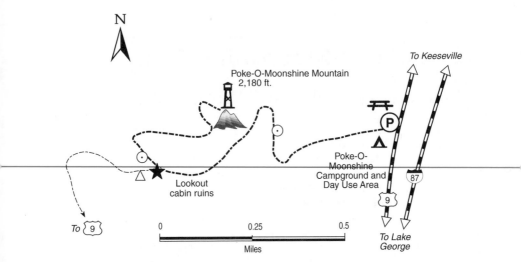

Key points:
- 0.0   Trailhead near campsite 14.
- 0.7   Ruins of one-time lookout cabin.
- 1.2   Summit tower; turn around.

Finding the trailhead: From the junction of New York 9N and U.S. Highway 9/New York 22 in Keeseville, go south on U.S. 9 for 7.2 miles, turning west to enter Poke-O-Moonshine State Campground. From Interstate 87 take exit 33 and go south on U.S. 9 for 3.1 miles to reach the campground. The trail heads west near site 14 at the south end of the campground.

The hike: This sometimes steep, eroded trail scales the wooded flank of Poke-O-Moonshine Mountain, which owes its peculiar name to a dichotomous profile of fractured cliff and summit rock slabs. To the Algonquin Indians these features suggested a descriptive name, combining the words *pohqui,* meaning "broken," and *moosie,* meaning "smooth." Through time and general use the name corrupted into "Poke-O-Moonshine." Peregrine falcons and rock climbers coexist in this rocky realm.

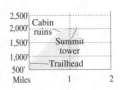

The trail charges steeply up the mostly shady slope, cloaked in sugar maple, birch, and beech. Oaks rise among the bigger trees—rare interlopers in the Adirondacks. Side trails branch away, rounding below the cliffs to the right. Sarsaparilla and a few ferns dot the rock-studded forest floor. Although boots have broadened the trail, the slope retains its soil.

At 0.2 mile veer left at the base of a cliff, topping a ledge for an early view of the highway corridor below and the ridges stretching east to Vermont.

48

White pine, hemlock, striped maple, and oak prefer these rockier reaches. A variety of bird whistles, pipes, and caws vie with the roadway drone.

The trail now moves inland from the edge of the cliff and so should hikers. The effects of weathering combined with a canted surface can cause hikers to lose their footing. The trail narrows, exhibiting a more moderate grade. Soon it follows a drainage crowded with nettles, trillium, and red-flowering raspberry. As the drainage steepens, so does the trail.

At 0.6 mile a formidable cliff rises beyond the trees to the right. In a saddle clearing, a rock fireplace and old foundation hint at the one-time lookout cabin. Skirt the site to the left to reach the present overnight lean-to and privy. The trail to the fire tower bears right at the ruins, ascending the eroded, spring-soaked slope. Infrequent red markers point the way.

Just above the saddle, come upon a bald outcrop sloping up to the left. It affords fine views west of ski-run streaked Whiteface Mountain, as well as a ragged skyline of rounded and conical peaks. For overnight hikers staying at the lean-to, the outcrop proves ideal for stargazing, especially during the annual Perseid meteor showers, which peak August 11 or 12.

Additional outcrops follow, but they neither improve upon nor significantly alter the view. The trail advances via brief ups and level stretches. At 0.95 mile top and follow the ridge to the right. After cutting through a corridor of low-stature white birch and striped maple, come out on the summit outcrop at the tower.

Although currently abandoned, the fire tower is scheduled for adoption and rehabilitation by a "Friends" group. Their endeavors should result in the saving of a landmark and, possibly, the reopening of the tower to the public, both as a vantage and as a visitor center. The tower rises five flights, allowing for a 360-degree view.

The long, shimmery platter and dark-treed islands of Lake Champlain dominate the view to the east-northeast; Whiteface Mountain rises to the west. Smaller lakes, rural flats, and the ridge and cliffs of Poke-O-Moonshine Mountain complete the panorama. Below, mountain ash joins the tapestry of green.

Should the tower be closed at the time of your visit, the bald summit slab still warrants the journey, adding dimension and drama to the eastern view, overlooking the peak's plunging cliffs and broken-rock tiers. Lichen and mineral leaching streak the cliffs green, orange, and black. When ready to surrender the view, return as you came.

11 High Falls Loop

General description: This clockwise loop into Five Ponds Wilderness traverses a diverse area of marsh, hardwood forests, conifers, and blowdown, visiting the Dead Creek Flow of Cranberry Lake, High Falls, and the Oswegatchie River drainage. The loop is advanced via levee, foot trail, old truck grade, and beaver bypasses and dams.

General location: Cranberry Lake Region, Adirondack Park.

Special attractions: Cranberry Lake and Oswegatchie River accesses and views, High Falls, beaver-modified marshes and creeks, hardwood forest, the blowdown legacy from the great windstorm of 1995, spurs to overnight shelters, wildflowers, wildlife sightings, fall color.

Length: 16.8-mile loop.

Difficulty: Strenuous, with beaver-caused flooding.

Maps: Adirondack Mountain Club, Adirondack Northern Region map.

Special concerns: Come prepared for biting insects; netting and repellent recommended. Avoid after heavy rains or during high water. Find pit toilets at the overnight shelter sites at Janack's Landing and High Falls. Designated campsites likewise serve the route. There is no camping within 150 feet of road, trail, or water, except at designated sites.

Season and hours: Best in late summer and fall.

For information: New York State Department of Environmental Conservation, Region 6.

Key points:

- 0.0   Eastern trailhead; follow Plains Trail.
- 3.1   Janack's Landing junction.
- 4.0   Cat Mountain junction.
- 7.0   High Falls.
- 8.4   Sand Lake Trail junction.
- 11.8 Stone bridge.
- 16.2 Barrier/western trailhead.
- 16.8 End at eastern trailhead.

Finding the trailhead: From the junction of New York 3 and County 61 (the Wanakena turnoff), 8 miles west of Cranberry Lake and 6 miles east of Star Lake, turn south on County 61 and proceed 1 mile, twice keeping right to cross the Oswegatchie River bridge and continue east on South Shore Road. Locate the western trailhead (the High Falls Truck Trail) on a southbound dead-end road in 0.1 mile, its trail parking next to tennis courts in another 0.1 mile, and the eastern trailhead (Plains Trail) 0.4 mile farther.

High Falls Loop

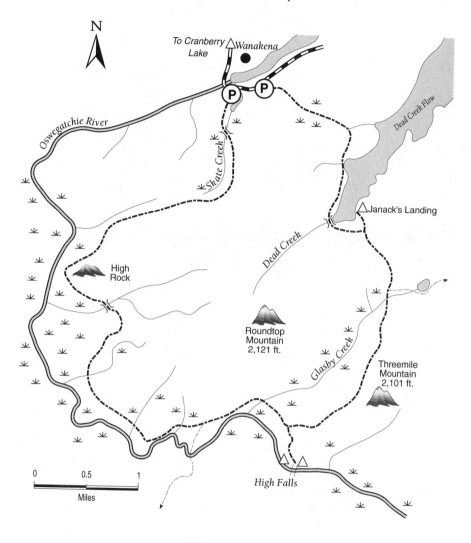

High Falls, Adirondack Park.

The hike: A clockwise loop follows the Plains Trail, tracing a former logging railroad grade for easy walking. Young forest frames the route along with wind-snapped trees. At 0.2 mile the trail parts a beaver marsh; some watery links may require stepping over or negotiating via coupled logs. The snag skyline, blackwater reflections, and clumps of greenery add to viewing; lively bird-song serenades the ear. The grade narrows to a brown ribbon.

Where the maples are untouched, find a rich, shady cathedral. By 1.5 miles the grade is edging Dead Creek Flow, part of Cranberry Lake. Open water views alternate with treed buffers. Loon and heron may visit the lake arm. Although the scenery suggests a leisurely Sunday pace, the mosquitoes may call for double-time. Spans bridge the inlet flows for dry footing, except where beaver-raised waters overflow the log passages.

At 3.1 miles reach the next register and trail junction. A 0.2-mile detour left leads to the grassy point of Janack's Landing and its overnight shelter on the peninsular knoll. Rustic boardwalk and trail lead to the landing and its engaging lake view. Lady's slippers seasonally decorate the forest floor.

Keeping to the loop, proceed forward and gradually ascend, passing within a mixed-age woodland of maple, cherry, and birch. In less than a mile arrive at the next junction. Here the yellow-marked trail heads left toward Cat Mountain; the red-marked loop arcs right, easing down to the Glasby Creek crossing en route to High Falls.

The creek shows scenic cascades and beaver-broadened segments as the trail traces the east shore in an easy-to-follow bypass along the base of

Threemile Mountain. The route can be hot and humid, with an open sky-line, snags, thick shrubs, and briers. Continue downstream, crossing back over the creek atop a beaver dam at 5.5 miles; wet feet are unavoidable. White pines grow nearby.

A blowdown rubble zone next claims the loop. Although the trail itself is clear, hikers can marvel at the power of the event that took place in 1995. Remain in the disrupted area until the High Falls junction at 6.6 miles. Head left 0.4 mile to add a visit to the falls, keeping left (upstream) at the fork. High Falls is a 20-foot-high cascade near the head of Oswegatchie River. The tannin-colored water spills between and over the bulging and sloped out-crops of pink granite, streaked by varnish and mottled by lichen. Away from the riotous falls stretches tranquil river. Set back in the woods is a shelter.

Backtrack to the High Falls Junction and resume the loop by turning left on a truck trail (High Falls Truck Trail), passing through scenic woods of white pine and mixed hardwoods before entering a tamarack-pine area and, later, grass meadow. Glasby Creek threads through the meadow and is crossed by a plank bridge. While following the Oswegatchie River downstream, gain overlooks and enjoy more setting changes.

Where the levee of the truck grade parts two more beaver ponds, water can again spill over the boot, but generally the old route allows fast, dry travel. At 8.4 miles is the Sand Lake Trail junction; its blue-marked course heads left. Remain on High Falls Truck Trail, as the Leary Trail to the right was not reopened after the windstorm. A few faded, remnant red disks may mark the route. More levee and beaver sites follow, and designated campsites are passed where the trail overlooks a horseshoe bend on the Oswegatchie.

By 11 miles, the red DEC markers make a more regular appearance as the truck route passes through forest-transition habitat, with clues to the blow-down seldom absent. The passage remains remarkably clear of logs. In about another mile cross an old stone bridge at a canted-bedrock waterfall on an Oswegatchie tributary. At the upcoming truck trail junction (12.2 miles), keep right for the red-marked loop.

As the hike completes its passage along the vast Oswegatchie River marsh, it skirts High Rock. After the grade trends northward, the route crosses a pair of brooks and slow-moving Skate Creek to emerge at the barrier and register for the western trailhead (16.2 miles). Round the gate and follow the drive north to South Shore Road in 0.1 mile. There, turn right (east) and proceed 0.5 mile to the eastern trailhead, completing the loop at 16.8 miles.

12 Van Hoevenberg Trail

General description:	This demanding all-day or overnight hike arriving from the north offers the shortest approach to Mount Marcy—at 5,344 feet, the highest point in New York State.
General location:	Adirondack High Peaks Region, 12 miles southeast of Lake Placid.
Special attractions:	Spectacular High Peaks panorama, rare arctic-alpine habitat, wildlife, scenic brooks, lake, lean-tos, visitor information center.
Length:	14.8 miles round-trip.
Difficulty:	Strenuous.
Maps:	Trails in the High Peaks pamphlet; Adirondack Mountain Club, Adirondack High Peak Region map.
Special concerns:	Adirondak Loj charges for parking; its lots sometimes fill in summer. Expect a rock scramble for the final 0.5 mile to the summit. Come prepared for chill winds and cool summit temperatures, and be alert to weather changes. Camp only at the lean-tos or designated tent sites, properly storing food away from bears. Camping and fires above 4,000 feet are prohibited. Find privies near the camp areas.
Season and hours:	Year-round, spring through fall for hiking.
For information:	New York State Department of Environmental Conservation, Region 5.

Key points:

- 0.0   Loj trailhead; follow blue trail.
- 2.2   Cross wooden Marcy Dam.
- 4.2   Cross Marcy Brook.
- 6.4   Saddle junction; bear right.
- 7.4   Summit; return by same route.

Finding the trailhead: From the junction of New York 73 and New York 86 in the village of Lake Placid, go east on NY 73 for 3.2 miles and turn right (south) on Adirondak Loj Road. Go 5 miles to reach the entrance station for the Loj. Find the trailhead at the opposite end of the lower parking lot from the High Peaks Visitor Information Center.

The hike: From the register follow the wide, well-trampled blue-marked trail, passing through a mixed conifer-deciduous forest and crossing over the Mr. Van Ski Trail. Ongoing improvements have reduced the mire and erosion that once characterized the Van Hoevenberg Trail. Reinforced steps, foot planks, levees, and stepping stones number among the changes.

Van Hoevenberg Trail

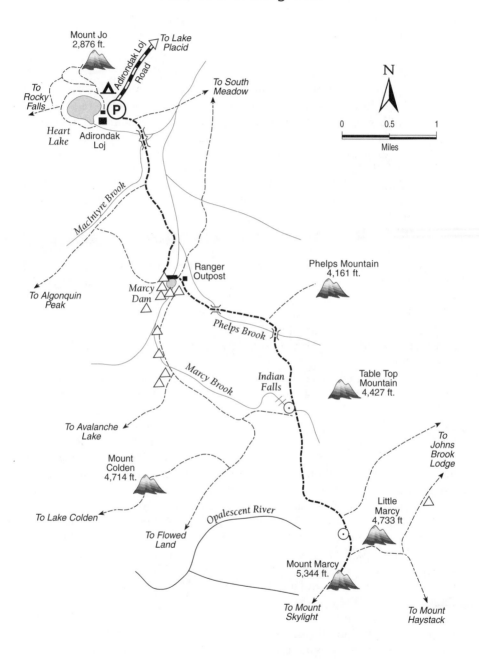

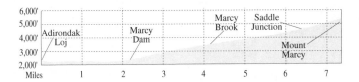

Passing through a stand of planted pines, cross the footbridge over Heart Lake outlet, followed soon after by the footbridge over MacIntyre Brook. At 0.5 mile enter state land and wilderness. Despite the popularity of this hiker highway, wildlife sightings still reward the early-morning traveler. Owl, deer, bat, and even a pine marten may surprise you.

At the 1-mile junction bear left, staying on the blue trail; the yellow trail leads to Algonquin Peak. Maple, birch, small beech, hobblebush, and striped maple enfold the tour. In another mile ascend along rushing Marcy Brook, sequestered deep in a draw; here campsites occupy the woods of balsam fir and birch.

At 2.2 miles cross scenic wooden Marcy Dam. Campers suspend foodstuffs from it, but beware, the bears have figured out this game. Cross-pond views feature Mount Colden; Avalanche, Phelps, and Table Top Mountains; and the slope of Wright Peak and Algonquin. Over the shoulder looms Whales Tail Mountain. Six lean-tos and a ranger station bring bustle to the area.

Bear right from the dam, pursuing the blue markers along shore. In 500 feet go left for Mount Marcy; to the right is the trail to Avalanche Lake and Lake Colden.

Following the rocky terrain of Phelps Brook upstream, find the high-water bridge at 2.5 miles; during low-water cross 500 feet upstream via the rocky streambed itself. The tour continues upstream on the opposite shore, but Phelps Brook slips from sight. At the junction with the red Phelps Mountain Trail, continue forward; dense spruce and fir narrow the aisle.

At 3.5 miles cross a bridge back over Phelps Brook, finding a steeper climb and larger rocks. Shortly the trail turns away from the brook, while a winter-use trail continues upstream. Small-stature trees weave an open cathedral. Stone steps and short log ladders add to the trail.

Bypassing an area of designated camp flats, cross Marcy Brook (4.2 miles) upstream from Indian Falls. Upon crossing, take an immediate right on the foot trail heading downstream. In 100 feet exit onto a broad outcrop plane washed by the brook. From the head of Indian Falls, where the water spills through a cliff fissure, find a striking look at Algonquin and the MacIntyre Range.

Resume the hike to Marcy, continuing away from the creek and skirting campsites. At the junction at the 3,600-foot elevation, bear left with the blue disks, temporarily enjoying a more relaxed grade. Bunchberry, moss, and whorled aster carpet the ground. Corduroys cross a spring-muddied area to reach a steep rocky ascent with stones aligned as stairs. Overhead, clouds whip past.

Mount Marcy summit view, Adirondack Park.

In a high meadow find the first view of imposing Mount Marcy. A better view follows, capturing the ridge to Little Marcy, silver snags piercing the fir mantle, and the open summit outcrop. Tiny-appearing hikers wind skyward. This eye-opener also alerts hikers to the hefty climb still ahead. At the 5.8-mile junction, Keene Valley lies to the left; go right for Marcy.

Canted exposed outcrop alternates with corduroy as the trail draws into an alpine opening with boulder seating addressing Mount Marcy. With the climb, views build, previewing the summit attraction. At the saddle junction at 6.4 miles, bear right; yellow paint blazes and the occasional cairn point out this final leg to the summit.

En-route views suggest a breather; close-by Haystack proves particularly arresting. An arctic–alpine habitat claims the upper reaches of Marcy, so keep to the prescribed route, now a rock scramble to the top. From the summit plaque (7.4 miles), one last scramble tags the ultimate high point. The view is nothing less than glorious, humbling onlookers. During summer months, a steward watches over Marcy, educating hikers about this sensitive site.

The first recorded ascent came in 1837. To the Indians the mountain was known as *Tahawus* or "Cloud Splitter," an apt name. Views sweep the regal MacIntyre Range, the ridges north to Canada, the Green Mountains of Vermont, lakes Champlain and Placid, Boreas Ponds, and Lake Tear-of-the-Clouds, the highest lake source of the Hudson River. The Hudson–Saint Lawrence River Divide passes over the top of Mount Marcy; crystals and lichen adorn the rock. Return as you came.

13 East Branch Ausable River Loop

General description:	Within a private Adirondack reserve, this rolling tour travels the east and west shores of a pristine river drainage, with side trips to an overlook and waterfall.
General location:	19 miles southeast of Lake Placid.
Special attractions:	Old-growth hemlocks, overlooks and valley floor vistas, scenic river and side brooks, waterfalls.
Length:	9.1 miles round-trip, including side trips (10.5 miles with the road distance to and from trailhead parking).
Difficulty:	Moderate to strenuous.
Maps:	Adirondack Mountain Club, Adirondack High Peaks Region map.
Special concerns:	All hikers entering the reserve must register. No pets, fires, camping, or bicycles on Lake Road, and only reserve members may fish or swim. The reserve has protected this site since 1897, so do your part. Visitors must park away from the Ausable Club and not block the area road with shuttle drop-offs and pickups.
Season and hours:	Spring through fall, daylight hours.
For information:	Adirondack Trail Improvement Society; New York State Department of Environmental Conservation, Region 5.

Key points:

0.0	Watchman's Hut trailhead.
3.3	Leach Bridge.
4.2	Indian Head.
5.3	Rainbow Falls.
6.8	Beaver Meadow Falls.
9.1	End at watchman's hut.

Finding the trailhead: From Keene Valley go south on New York 73 East for 2.8 miles and turn right (west) on an unmarked gravel road opposite the marked trailhead for Roaring Brook Trail to Giant Mountain. Find the trail parking lot on the left in 0.1 mile; because it often fills, hikers may need to park along the shoulder of NY 73 (at their own risk). Do not park anywhere along the gravel road.

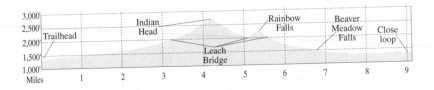

East Branch Ausable River Loop

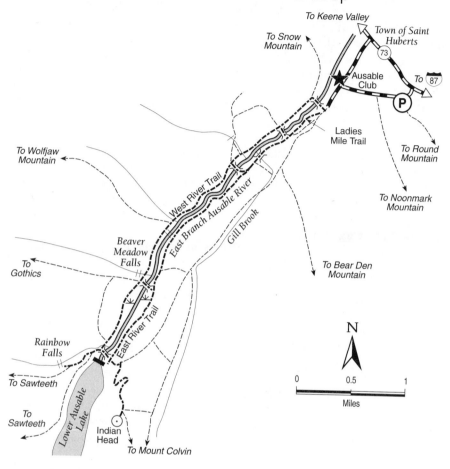

Hike west on the unlabeled road (surface later changes to pavement) to reach Ausable Club (0.5 mile). Turn left and descend the road between the tennis courts. Beyond member parking, reach the register and watchman's hut at 0.7 mile.

The hike: For an east bank–west bank tour, hike the dirt road past the watchman's hut and round the rustic wooden gate to Adirondack Mountain Reserve. In 100 feet turn right, following the Ladies Mile Trail, marked by a tiny wooden sign; keep an eye out for it. This footpath travels hemlock-beech woods, crosses small drainages, and bypasses a woodshed coming to a loop junction (0.2 mile); go right to reach and follow the river upstream. Orange "ATIS" (Adirondack Trail Improvement Society) markers point the way.

The East Branch is a clean-coursing mountain water, reflecting the hues of the rocks it bathes. Upstream, the river reveals a variety of personalities. At 0.4 mile, where the Ladies Mile Trail loops left, continue straight to reach the river trails in 500 feet. Keep to the east shore for a clockwise tour; a footbridge spans the East Branch to West River Trail.

Along the elevated bank, hemlock and hardwood enfold the tour; a few mossy stones stud the trail. Periodically, the trail veers away from and above the river. At 0.75 mile young spruce appear in the forest. After crossing the footbridge over gravelly Gill Brook, turn left following this side brook upstream to another reserve road and trail junction.

Cross the road and ascend within a high-canopy forest of maple and beech. The trail rounds below an isolated outcrop, gaining views of Wolfjaw Mountain, and travels an old-growth hemlock plateau, drawing some 200 feet above the river. From the plateau travel the slope's rim before making a quick, difficult descent along the steep wooded flank.

On the lower slope find an overlook of a double river falls at 1.8 miles. In a pinched gorge the upper 20-foot falls feeds a lower 6-foot falls, with a surging channel between and a dark pool at the exodus. Where the trail returns to the elevated riverbank, look for a pair of room-sized boulders. At the 2.2-mile junction bear right keeping to the east bank; to the left is the main reserve road. Briefly the trail parallels a blue pipe that draws river water for the club.

At 2.3 miles bear left for the East River Trail; the path to the right finds a river bridge to Beaver Meadow Falls. The rolling tour now overlooks the meadow shore and gray cliff of the west bank; upstream views feature the irregular skyline of Sawteeth and the Gothics. A railing eases descent where erosion and outcrops have made this a split-level trail.

Beaver Meadow soon claims the river bottom, braiding the stream. At 2.8 miles is Bullock Dam, a plank-topped log stretched the length of the river. Despite the infrequency of the ATIS markers, the trail remains easy to follow. Birch and spruce line the route.

At 3.3 miles Leach Bridge crosses the river below the dam at the outlet of Lower Ausable Lake. The lake waters and boathouse are closed to the general public, and shore access is limited to the marked trails. Cross the bridge for the loop. To visit Indian Head for a lofty vantage, remain on the east shore. Ascend sharply left, turn right near a storage shed, and ascend 50 yards on gravel road to come out on the main reserve road (3.4 miles).

Go left on the main reserve road for 500 feet, finding the marked trail to Indian Head on the right. Where a spur descends to the private boathouse area, stay left, contouring and switching back up the rocky deciduous-clad slope. At 3.6 miles a 115-foot spur heads right to Gothics Window, a tree-framed look at the rugged Gothics and high-peak amphitheater. The main trail continues climbing, with short ladder segments overcoming the steepest stretches.

At a three-way junction on the ridge (4.1 miles), go right 0.1 mile, topping Indian Head—a broad, flat outcrop with a spectacular view surpassed only by the view from the Indian's brow below. Nippletop, Colvin, the beautiful

Lower Ausable Lake, Adirondack Mountain Reserve.

curved platters of Upper and Lower Ausable lakes, Sawteeth, the Gothics, and Wolfjaws compose the pristine stage. The view honors the forward-thinking reserve members from the 1890s, who protected this raw beauty.

Return to Leach Bridge (5.1 miles) and cross the river, viewing the rock profile of Indian Head and the Mount Colvin–Sawteeth gateway at the head of Lower Ausable Lake. By turning left at the west shore junction, hikers add a 0.5-mile round-trip spur to Rainbow Falls. At the dam bear right and, shortly after, again bear right to find sheer cliffs, the 150-foot misty shower of Rainbow Falls, and a greenery-filled box canyon. When sun touches the mist, a rainbow spectrum autographs the picture.

Upon return to Leach Bridge (5.6 miles), follow the West River Trail downstream and bypass the trail to Lost Lookout, for a demanding shore-line hike removed from the river. The route weaves in and out and steps up and over rocks below the cliffs. A spruce-hardwood complex shades travel. The trail eases as it crosses a beech flat and raised dike. Views east span the alder meadow to Bear Den–Dial Mountain ridge. Cross a couple of drainages and bypass a ladder ascent to the Gothics to reach Beaver Meadow Falls along-side the trail (6.8 miles). This attractive 80- to 100-foot falls splashes over a tiered cliff, broadening at the base.

Cross the brook downhill from the falls for an easier tour. Deciduous trees dominate with a few interlopers. A different perspective on the double falls on the East Branch precedes the trail's drift from the river into a realm of old-growth hemlock.

Stay on the West River Trail, crossing a paired-log bridge over a pretty brook with a 10-foot falls spilling through a slot in the rocks. A forest gap offers a look at Noonmark, and the 7.5-mile vista presents a limited look at Noonmark–Dial Ridge.

Descend the trail's steep ridge, remaining above the river, which is also dropping. Where the trail bottoms out, veer left coming to a junction (8 miles). Downhill to the right is Canyon Bridge, the largest of the river footbridges; stay on the West River Trail. Spurs branch left to Pyramid Brook and a falls mostly swallowed by the rocks. To see this falls requires a 0.4-mile round-trip detour; for this description, forgo the side trip.

Downstream, the trail again travels at river level, bypassing yet another river bridge. The West River Trail now merges with the Nature Trail (brochures available at the watchman's hut); tags identify the vegetation. Three-hundred-year-old hemlocks grace the hike, which now rolls along a side channel of the river.

Cross the river bridge at 9 miles, turn left (downstream), and veer right into woods. Within a developed area, cross over a drainage for a gentle as-cent to return to the watchman's hut (9.1 miles). To return to the car, ascend through the club grounds and turn right.

14 Indian Pass–Lake Colden Loop

General description:	This grueling boulder-and-mud obstacle course passes through typical Adirondack splendor: mixed forests, pristine waters, and inspiring views. Beware, though—the loop includes the notoriously difficult Cold Brook Pass.
General location:	MacIntyre Mountain Range, Adirondack Park.
Special attractions:	Wallface Cliff and High Peaks views, chill-blue lakes, crystalline brooks, challenge and adventure; springboard to Mount Marcy and other peak/lake destinations.
Length:	15.9-mile loop.
Difficulty:	Strenuous backpack; extremely strenuous day hike.
Maps:	Adirondack Mountain Club, Adirondack High Peaks map.
Special concerns:	Steely determination, stamina, a sure foot, and good backcountry skills. Avoid during high water, and respect property rights of private landowners.
Season and hours:	Best in summer and fall.
For information:	New York State Department of Environmental Conservation, Region 5.

Key points:

    0.0   Upper Works trailhead.
    0.4   Loop junction; head left.
    4.4   Summit Rock vantage.
    7.2   Cold Brook Pass.
    9.4   Pass Lake Colden Dam.
    10.9 Calamity Pond/Spur to Henderson memorial.
    12.5 Cross Calamity Brook suspension bridge.
    15.5 Close loop; return to trailhead.

Finding the trailhead: From the New York 30–New York 28N junction in Long Lake, go east on NY 28N for 18 miles. There turn left on Essex County Road 2 (seasonally maintained), bearing left at the intersection in 0.4 mile. In another 0.8 mile turn left on County 25 toward Tahawus, following the road to where it dead-ends at Upper Works trailhead (another 9.5 miles). As trailhead parking and the beginning and ending trail miles represent state easements on private land, keep to the trail.

The hike: Take the cabled-off gravel road next to the trail register, following the Upper Hudson River upstream, crossing over it at 0.25 mile. Cedar,

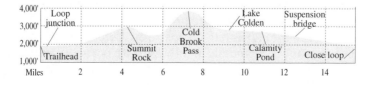

Indian Pass–Lake Colden Loop

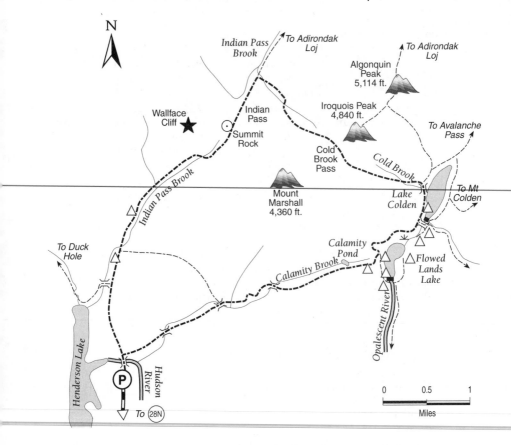

spruce, birch, and beech frame the corridor; a beaver pond lies beyond the trees to the left. At the 0.4-mile loop junction, go left for a clockwise tour, following yellow disk markers. Still traveling logging roads, bear right at 0.75 mile.

A descent offers tree-filtered peeks at Henderson Lake. The trail now crosses a brook and travels worn log corduroys and soggy road stretches. At 1.5 miles bear right traveling the slope above Indian Pass Brook, coming to a junction; for the loop continue straight ahead. Red disks now point the way to Indian Pass. A few big spruce, fir, and snags weave among the deciduous trees; hobblebush, clintonia, sarsaparilla, and ferns dress the floor.

Hike past brookside Henderson lean-to on a well-traveled though minimally marked footpath. Where the trail exits a small brushy passage, a sign points upstream (right) to a bridge crossing. In another 200 feet bear left to cross the attractive three-plank-wide bridge.

The gentle-grade trail turns left (downstream) before veering into woods, where it becomes more rootbound and rocky, with boot-swallowing organic mud. At 2.7 miles pass the Wallface lean-to and privy to parallel Indian Pass Brook upstream along the west shore, stone-hopping side brooks at regular intervals. Jewelweed and dogwood dot the banks.

By 3.7 miles the cliff of Wallface looms beyond the leaves and conifers wane from the mix. Below a camp flat on the west shore comes the crossing of Indian Pass Brook. The trail now weaves and ascends among gigantic boulders—some the size of barns, others with cavelike overhangs.

At 4 miles the red trail turns right, charging at an angle up the slope; keep an eye out for markers. A wooden ladder provides a leg up as the trail briefly rounds to the back side of the bouldery slope. At the base of a second ladder (4.3 miles), uneven-sized logs braced against a split boulder offer the intrepid a means to scale the rock for a stirring view of Wallface. Rival, more-accessible views are but a minute away at Summit Rock.

Wallface, an Adirondack landmark, presents a western profile with sheer cliffs, broken ledges, and spire-topped conifers. Views of the southern drainage of Indian Pass Brook toward Henderson Lake and Mountain complete the Summit Rock offering.

The trail ahead remains extremely rugged and steep, passing camp flats, crossing brooks, and allowing a look at a 100-foot side waterfall. At 4.9 miles ease down a steep rock crease for a rock-hopping tour amid the rushing water of Indian Pass Brook. Here the trail and northern brook drainage are generally one and the same. In this tailbone-cracking terrain, give full attention to the rocks.

Where a footpath again follows the east shore of Indian Pass Brook, find a trail junction at 5.5 miles and turn right, following the yellow-marked trail to Lake Colden. After an uphill plod, dip back down to follow a side brook upstream. Again rocks and conifer-birch woods characterize travel. Brook crossings tie together the trail fragments, showcasing crystalline waters, falls, cascades, and deep pools. For brief periods the trail departs the brook, exploring woods.

At 6.4 miles climb steeply to cross the next brook over, traversing a conifer-birch forest where Iroquois Peak may be glimpsed. After topping Cold Brook Pass (7.2 miles), the trail flattens, giving way to a plank boardwalk across wet pockets and meadow openings. Views are of Mounts Marcy and Colden. Blue gentian dots the meadow.

Before long, a demanding rock-hopping and oozing-mud descent advances the loop; the young trees trailside provide an anchor for the slip-sliding traveler. At 8.25 miles comes a crossing of Cold Brook—another Adirondack classic beauty comprising chutes, cascades, and siren pools. Again, sections of rocky-brook travel stitch together the trail segments.

By 8.6 miles the trail's steep character subsides, giving way to a rolling tour. At the junction at 8.9 miles, follow the blue trail to the right, crossing a footbridge and traveling atop stones, pallets, and hewn logs to round the Lake Colden shore. Cross-lake views find Mount Colden with its sheetlike cliff and rocky crest. Length-of-the-lake views present a picturesque mountain gateway shaped by Mount Colden and Avalanche Mountain.

Trail ladder near Summit Rock, Adirondack Park.

Near the end of the lake, a pair of prized lean-tos occupy a treed point. At Lake Colden Dam (9.4 miles) go straight for the loop; a detour onto the dam adds a grand-farewell lake view.

Red markers again lead the way, with logs aiding passage through a beaver-grown wetland. At the footbridge look downstream to find the wetland-meadow corner of Flowed Lands Lake, with views of the blue platter reserved for later. Conifer and birch claim the way.

The route remains rolling, rocky, rooted, and muddy. Flattish stones brought in by trail crews aid hopscotch travel. At 10.6 miles cross an old diversion channel, coming to a junction with two Calamity lean-tos and a picturesque view of the open water and rimming marsh of Flowed Lands Lake. Go right for the loop.

At the alder rim of Calamity Pond (10.9 miles), a path to the right leads to the 6-foot-tall marble monument honoring David Henderson, who helped open up the Adirondacks and who died on this site in an accidental shooting in 1845. The loop resumes left with more mud and more stone-and-plank crossings, plus a meadow crossing at 11.2 miles. Maples reappear as the moderate-grade trail descends parallel to but away from Calamity Brook.

At 12.5 miles turn right, cross Calamity Brook on a suspension bridge, and continue following the brook downstream through a deciduous-conifer forest. At 12.8 miles a couple of scenic camp flats lie to the left, the last ones before private land.

The trail improves as it follows a well-drained road bed. After 13.25 miles travel is on private land; keep to the marked trail. At 14 miles go left, crossing Calamity Brook via footbridge to travel a wide logging-road easement to close the loop at 15.5 miles, and to return to the trailhead at 15.9 miles.

15 Northville–Placid Trail

General description:	This difficult long-distance route through the rugged splendor of the Adirondacks takes an average of two to three weeks to hike.
General location:	From Northville to Lake Placid.
Special attractions:	Wilderness solitude; lakes, rivers, and brooks; colorful fall foliage; spur trails to ponds and peaks.
Length:	132 miles one-way; 121 miles one-way, when forgoing the southern road miles and starting at Upper Benson (the selected hike).
Difficulty:	Strenuous.
Maps:	Adirondack Mountain Club, Northville–Placid Trail map.
Special concerns:	Through-hikers need to work out the logistics of getting adequate food and supplies, plan what to do in case of an emergency, and arrange for transportation at the end of the trail. Expect rocky,

difficult conditions; strong map and compass skills ease travel. Because beaver activity may force route adjustments, be alert while tracking blazes.

Season and hours: Late spring through fall.
For information: New York State Department of Environmental Conservation, Region 5.

Key points:

0.0	Southern (Upper Benson) trailhead; head north.
15.9	Whitehouse Crossing; cross suspension bridge.
22.2	Cross New York 8.
24.2	Piseco Post Office.
34.8	Spruce Lake; travel east shore.
40.3	West Canada Lakes.
55.8	Follow Cedar River Road north.
57.1	Wakely Dam.
63.7	Leave Cedar River Road.
69.4	Cross NY 28/30 at Lake Durant.
73.0	Tirrell Pond; travel west shore.
79.6	Central Plateau.
84.2	Cross NY 28N; hike Tarbell Road north.
84.9	Follow Long Lake's east shore.
96.7	Shattuck Clearing.
97.4	Cold River.
108.7	Duck Hole.
114.2	Spur to Wanika Falls.
121.0	End near Averyville Road–Old Military Road intersection.

Northville–Placid Trail, Adirondack Park.

Northville–Placid Trail

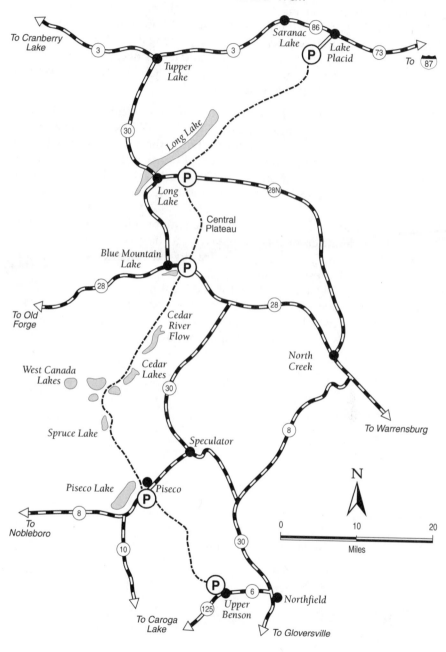

Finding the trailhead: From Northville go 4.1 miles north on New York 30 and turn west on Northville–Lake Placid Trail (Hamilton County 6), a paved road. Following the signs in 5.6 miles, turn right on a dirt road and quickly take a second right. In 0.6 mile near Trailhead Lodge, turn left on Godfrey Road to reach the trail register in 0.5 mile; parking precedes the trail on the right. Find the northern terminus at the junction of Averyville and Old Military Roads. Reach the junction by going south on Old Military Road from NY 86 or west on Averyville Road from the village of Lake Placid.

The hike: Built in 1922 by the Adirondack Mountain Club, this blue-marked trail receives regular maintenance from the New York State's Department of Environmental Conservation (DEC). The southern two-thirds of the trail rolls to obtain a top elevation of 3,008 feet at Central Plateau, south of Long Lake, the largest water body on the tour. The northern portion twists through valleys parting trailless high peaks to end at Averyville Road near Lake Placid.

Much of the tour passes through low- and middle-elevation forests, showing easy to moderate climbs. The route typically travels along drainages, past lakes, and over low passes. Expect more rugged conditions while passing through the wilderness interior.

The trail traverses public lands for the most part. Where it crosses private lands, some logging may be witnessed; keep to the trail and respect the posted rules of private landowners. Passage is mostly along foot trail and old logging tote roads; spurs represent opportunities to view other ponds or to

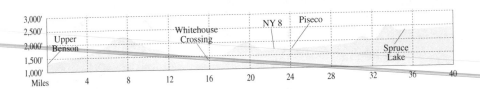

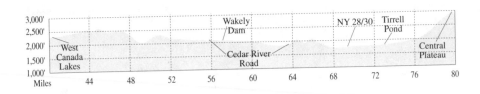

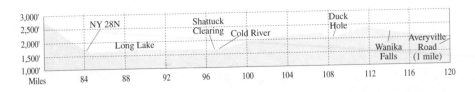

ascend peaks for vistas. Otherwise, admiration of the Adirondack Mountains comes by way of gaps in the tree cover.

Although some thirty lean-tos lie along or just off the trail—offering convenient, dry overnight waysides—a tent remains standard equipment. As lean-tos cannot be reserved, chancing that you will be the first to arrive and claim the lean-to for the night is both unwise and an unnecessary wilderness risk. Secure a camping permit from the area ranger if your group number exceeds ten or if you plan to use the same campsite for more than three nights.

Three primary crossroads, NY 8 near Piseco, NY 28/30 at Lake Durant (near Blue Mountain Lake), and NY 28N near Long Lake, break the route into four disproportionate segments. From Upper Benson to NY 8 covers 22.2 miles; from NY 8 to NY 28/30 covers 47.2 miles; from NY 28/30 to NY 28N covers 14.8 miles; and from NY 28N to the intersection of Averyville and Old Military Roads covers a distance of 36.8 miles. These primary routes, along with some secondary crossroads, suggest likely resupply or exit points.

The first quarter of the tour shows gentle ups and downs, crossing branches of the Sacandaga River and numerous brooks and creeks. Beaver ponds, lakes, and meadows punctuate travel through the mostly deciduous woods of the Southern Adirondack foothills. The lakes tend to support trout.

A series of large wild lakes and virgin forests in the popular Spruce Lake–West Canada Lakes–Cedar Lakes area highlight the second leg of the tour. The remote lakes, while enchanting in beauty, remain quiet, stilled by acid rain. Scoured clean, the lakes show not a ripple nor a dragonfly. Only the mournful call of an occasional loon breaks the silence.

This long, wild stretch of the Northville–Placid Trail provides unrivaled escape from the concerns of the workaday world. Pristine West Canada Lakes Wilderness Area remained untouched until this trail opened its gates. The picturesque spruce-hardwood forests captivate travelers. Cedar River Road, a dirt access road within Moose River Recreation Area, offers another opportunity for a resupply or exit point.

Along the third trail segment, hikers find a rolling woods excursion that takes them past several lakes before claiming the hike's high point and dipping to NY 28N. Views remain limited as the hike proceeds north.

A lengthy stretch along the eastern shore of Long Lake launches the hike's finishing leg. A half dozen lean-tos dot shore, hinting at the lake's popularity. Land ownership along the lake is mixed; the trail primarily travels public lands, skirting private parcels.

From Long Lake pass through forest to reach Cold River, an exciting, crystalline Adirondack waterway guiding travelers upstream into the High Peaks area. The trail then passes lakes, following Roaring Brook and Moose Creek (side drainages of the Cold River) upstream and over a pass entering the Upper Chubb River drainage.

Reached via a short spur less than 7 miles from the finish line, Wanika Falls puts a sterling imprint on the tour. Find the last lean-to along the waterfall spur, just below the falls.

Wildlife sightings, wildflowers, autumn hues, and clues to the past all contribute to a lifetime memory of hiking the Northville–Placid Trail.

As the spatial constraints of this book limit the detail of this description, through-travelers and hikers planning short excursions along the Northville–Placid Trail should contact the DEC for its brochure, *The Northville-Placid Trail,* which offers a concise point-to-point synopsis of the trail. Because entire books have been devoted to this premier hiking trail, consult the bookshelves of your local library, bookstore, or backpacker/outfitter store.

16 Goodnow Mountain Trail

General description:	This self-guided hiking trail in the Huntington Wildlife Forest offers one of the most manageable climbs in the Adirondacks. It leads to a restored lookout tower and a partially open summit that extend grand forest, basin, and peak views.
General location:	Newcomb area, Adirondack Park.
Special attractions:	Restored 1922 lookout tower, High Peaks–Hudson River panorama, historic structures from the Archer and Anna Huntington estate, hardwood and conifer forests, fall color.
Length:	3.8 miles round-trip.
Difficulty:	Moderate.
Maps:	Newcomb 15-minute USGS quad.
Special concerns:	No camping, fires, or hunting. Dogs must be leashed. The trail is in Huntington Wildlife Forest, privately owned by the College of Environmental Science and Forestry (ESF) in Syracuse. The ESF staff maintains the tower and produces the brochure. Respect ESF rules for times of use, use of the area, and use of the tower.
Season and hours:	Year-round, spring through fall for hiking; sunrise to sunset.
For information:	College of Environmental Science and Forestry, State University of New York.

Key points:
0.0 Goodnow trailhead.
1.9 Summit lookout tower; return by the same route.

Finding the trailhead: Locate the marked trail and its parking south off New York 28N, 1.5 miles west of the Newcomb Visitor Interpretive Center and about 12 miles east of Long Lake.

The hike: This popular, well-used trail starts behind the kiosk, angling and contouring its way upslope. Beech, birch, and maple, along with a few hemlock and white pines, shape the woodland setting. Ferns

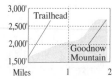

Goodnow Mountain Trail

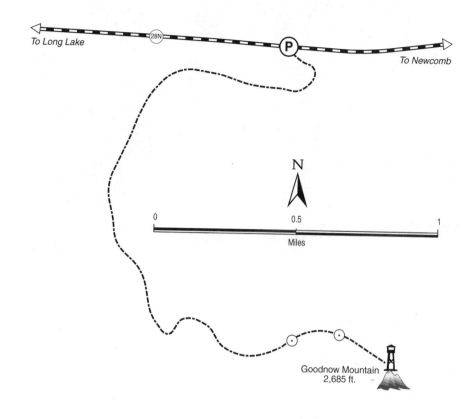

and club moss contribute to the ground cover. Beyond a mossy outcrop, a few spruce join the mix.

The trail is well designed with runoff channels, footbridges, and tiered walks and boardwalks. Arrows and interpretive posts keyed to the brochure keep hikers on track. Benches allow for pause and reflection.

Beyond the small rivulet at 0.5 mile, the trail settles into a steady climb of moderate gradient. Where the trail tops a ridge plateau at 0.9 mile, the route follows an apparent woods road (the old trail), crossing over the ridge to tour the opposite slope clad in hardwoods. When the trees drop their leaves, hikers can make out the dark outlines of neighboring peaks.

At 1.2 miles the trail crosses a small brook, signaling the start of a steeper ascent, sometimes on worn bedrock. Near a concrete foundation, gain western views out the draw. The foot trail returns as the trail traces the small saddle flat, passing an old well (reached via a spur to the right) and a horse barn. Bramble and hobblebush grow near the structures.

Cascade, Goodnow Mountain Trail.

Mossy outcrops in fern caps precede the trail's passage through a fir-spruce complex. Atop an open outcrop at 1.7 miles, bench seats extend views south-southwest, overlooking Goodnow Flowage Pond and the Upper Goodnow–Hudson River drainage. A dip to a notch precedes the final ascent to the 60-foot lookout tower perched atop its own bald outcrop (1.9 miles). The tower is nine stories high, with the crow's nest usually open to the public; heed all safety warnings. Use at your own risk, and beware of high winds.

The summit view encompasses more than twenty high peaks, including Mount Marcy and Algonquin Peak. To the northeast stretch the Santanoni Mountains; the northwest holds Kempshall Mountain. Below Goodnow Mountain rest Rich and Harris Lakes and the Hudson River. Southern views renew the acquaintances formed at the outcrop below. Altogether it's a grand mosaic of peaks, lake basins, and woods—Adirondack wilds as far as the eye can see. The historic lookout cabin below the tower served the Goodnow observers. A brief history of its use is posted at the site. Return as you came.

17 Blue Mountain Trail

General description: This quick, steep summit ascent reaches a fire tower for a cherished 360-degree Central Adirondack view.

General location: Above the east shore of Blue Mountain Lake.

Special attractions: Sweeping vistas, spruce-fir forest, fire tower, historic Verplanck Colvin benchmark.

Length: 4 miles round-trip.

Difficulty: Moderate, with some difficult rocky stretches.

Maps: Adirondack Mountain Club, Adirondack Central Region map; Trails in the Blue Mountain Lake Region brochure.

Special concerns: None.

Season and hours: Spring through fall.

For information: New York State Department of Environmental Conservation (DEC), Region 5.

Key points:

0.0 Blue Mountain trailhead; head generally east.
2.0 Summit outcrop/fire tower; return by the same route.

Finding the trailhead: From the intersection of New York Routes 28, 30, and 28N in Blue Mountain Lake Village, go north on NY 30/NY 28N for 1.4 miles and turn right (east) for the marked trailhead parking lot for Blue Mountain and Tirrell Pond Trails. Because both trails are marked by red disks, avoid taking the northbound Tirrell Pond Trail.

The hike: This highly accessible interpretive trail ascends a peak looming above the east shore of Blue Mountain Lake, providing area newcomers with a taste of the challenge and wilderness discovery of the Adirondacks. A retired fire tower sits atop Blue Mountain.

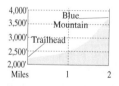

Near the start, a box at the trail register contains interpretive brochures. While normally stocked, the popularity of this trail can draw down supply. Numbered posts correspond to the brochure's write-ups. Tall maple, black cherry, and birch weave the overhead canopy, with fern, viburnum, striped maple, and brambles filling out the woods.

Following rainstorms, the worn bed of the rocky trail can become a runoff channel, but the occasional placement of side-by-side planks helps ease travel. As the trail briefly levels, big birch trees, both yellow and white, claim the way. Many of these birch germinated following the blowdown of 1950.

Where the trail crosses a brook at 0.7 mile, look upstream to find a burgundy pool and small cascade sheeting over canted rock. The trail briefly degrades to a wide, sharply ascending erosion channel. At times snags open the canopy, but the trail remains semishaded. At the next brook crossing, both forest and trail undergo a character change. A higher-elevation forest

Blue Mountain Trail

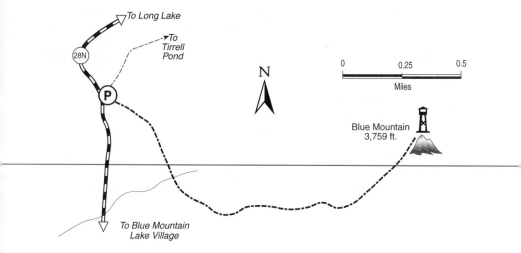

of spruce, fir, birch, and mountain ash claims the peak, while the trail narrows, steepens, and grows more rocky.

By 0.9 mile steep rock outcrops advance the trail. Along its sides grow clintonia, bunchberry, oxalis, and club moss. After rains this section can become a full-fledged creek, with racing water spilling around and over the rocks. Be watchful of your footing.

In another half mile, canted bedrock offers a more moderate climb through tight stands of picturesque fir and spruce. At 2 miles tag the bald summit outcrop, topped by the five-story steel-frame observatory and radio tower. A low ring of spired spruce restricts northward views.

The public may ascend the fire tower, but limit numbers on the structure at any one time. Erected in 1917, the tower was restored by a volunteer committee in 1994. Summit views sweep Whiteface, Algonquin, Colden, and Marcy Peaks; Blue Mountain, Eagle, Utowana, and Durant Lakes; Minnow, Mud, South, and Tirrell Ponds; and Blue Ridge—a bold terrain of forests, peaks, and lakes.

Other summit structures include a boarded-up cabin and concrete foundations from an old radar installation. Some ten paces north of the 35-foot fire tower, discover the original summit benchmark placed by Verplanck Colvin. A famous name in the New York State annals, he played a key role in opening the Adirondacks to the public. In the 1870s his men shot off bright explosions here so that the Adirondack survey teams could triangulate on this peak. Return as you came.

18 Murphy Lake Trail

General description: This easy trail accesses three sparkling lakes—Bennett, Middle, and Murphy—cradled in the quiet wooded beauty of the Southern Adirondacks.

General location: 9 miles north of Northville.

Special attractions: Fishing, camping, historic settlement site, loons, colorful fall foliage.

Length: 10.3 miles round-trip.

Difficulty: Easy.

Maps: Adirondack Mountain Club, Adirondack Southern Region map.

Special concerns: None.

Season and hours: Spring through fall.

For information: New York State Department of Environmental Conservation (DEC), Region 5.

Key points:

- 0.0   Creek Road trailhead; head north.
- 1.5   Bennett Lake.
- 2.9   Middle Lake.
- 4.2   Murphy Lake lean-to.
- 5.2   Natural dam; turn around.

Murphy Lake, Adirondack Park.

Murphy Lake Trail

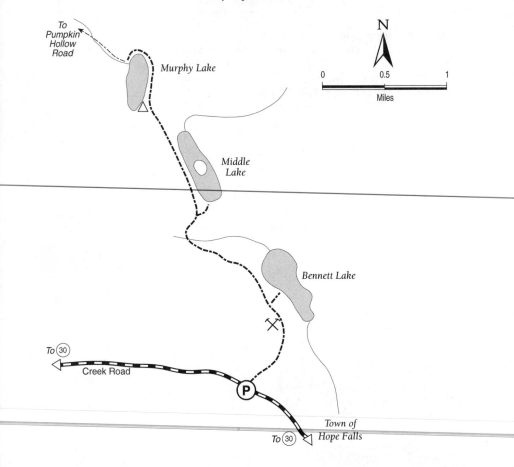

Finding the trailhead: From Sacandaga Campground and Day-use Area (3.4 miles south of Wells), go south on New York 30 for 5 miles and turn left (east) onto Creek Road. From Northville find the turn for Creek Road 3 miles north of the NY 30 bridge over the Sacandaga River. The marked trailhead is left off Creek Road in 2.2 miles; parking is on the broad road shoulder.

The hike: This trail heads north along a former road, ascending with a steady, moderate grade past the register. It probes a tall forest of white pine, hemlock, oak, maple, ash, birch, and aspen. Various ferns, sarsaparilla, and sugarscoop spot the understory. Mossy boulders and logs lend interest to the forest floor. In places the old road is worn deep into the terrain.

By 0.3 mile, hemlock, birch, and beech become the dominant species as the greenery all but vanishes from the forest floor. Where the incline flattens, big white pines shade the route and soften the road with their discarded needles. The hike next passes a remnant rock wall and rounds a barrier. This trail is closed to motorized travel save for snowmobiles; the snowmobile markers perform double duty, guiding hikers in the off-season.

The trail then dips away. At 1 mile keen-eyed travelers may discern some exposed red soil, hinting at a turn-of-the-twentieth-century ferric oxide (paint pigment) mine. Although trees and leaf mat have reclaimed the mining settlement, hikers still may notice unusual mounds, cellar holes, or rusting debris.

A pair of cairns on the right at 1.4 miles funnels hikers down a wide trail to Bennett Lake, a camp flat, and a privy (1.5 miles). The elongated oval of Bennett Lake rests below a rolling wooded ridge. Aquatic grasses and plants adorn its shallow edge, while insect chirrs enliven the air. A small boot-compressed beach offers lake access.

A moderate, rocky ascent from the Bennett Lake basin continues the hike. Toad, red eft, gray squirrel, and grouse number among the wildlife sightings. From somewhere on the lake, the haunting cry of a loon can usually be heard.

Where the trail passes between two low ridges, the comfortable earthen bed returns, and more greenery spreads beneath the trees. At 2.4 miles hikers may need to skirt a mud hole as they follow a small drainage; bridges span the larger runoffs.

At 2.8 miles the trail tops out. At 2.9 miles a side trail veers right, passing through a hemlock grove to reach a Middle Lake campsite. A muddy shoreline with a few logs for footing offers a lake perspective that presents a small island topped by white pines and a large central island that deceives visitor into thinking it is the far shore.

The primary trail contours the slope 200 feet above Middle Lake. Small-diameter trees choke out meaningful views, but the sparkling blue water provides a grand canvas for the leafy boughs. Slowly, the trail inches toward the lake. At 3.4 miles a second unmarked spur ventures 200 feet to the right, reaching Middle Lake and another campsite. A log-strewn, marshy shore again greets hikers. Views feature the north end of the big central island and a scenic rounded hill with western cliffs. Aquatic grasses, pickerelweed (arrowhead), and water lilies adorn the shallows.

The trailbed alternately shows grass, rock, and earthen stretches, as hikers continue to round Middle Lake. Prior to leaving the lake (3.8 miles), find a couple of open views. After a wooded ascent, cross a rocky drainage and curve right to reach Murphy Lake (4.25 miles), where a lean-to overlooks an outcrop sloping to the water. The reflecting waters of Murphy Lake and the enfolding, rounded, tree-mantled hills with their cliff outcrops hold a signature charm, dazzling in autumn attire.

A marked foot trail continues past the lean-to, traveling counterclockwise halfway around the lake, passing campsites, lake accesses, and coves thick with pickerelweed. The trail rolls just above shore, rounding through meadow, hemlock stand, and leafy woods. At 5.25 miles a natural rock-and-log dam at the outlet signals the end of the lakeshore trek but not the trail. A footpath descends along the outlet to a northern trailhead on Pumpkin Hollow Road 3.8 miles away (consult map for actual location, if you wish to plan a shuttle hike). For this hike, return as you came.

19 Pharaoh Mountain and Lake Loop

General description:	This all-day or overnight tour tags the summit of Pharaoh Mountain and encircles large, deep Pharaoh Lake, touring mixed forest and wetland meadows.
General location:	Eastern Adirondacks, east of Schroon Lake.
Special attractions:	Summit and shore vistas, swimming and fishing lake, expansive marsh, lean-tos, solitude, fall color.
Length:	14.5 miles round-trip.
Difficulty:	Strenuous.
Maps:	Adirondack Mountain Club, Adirondack Eastern Region map.
Special concerns:	None. Find privies near most lean-tos.
Season and hours:	Spring through fall.
For information:	New York State Department of Environmental Conservation (DEC), Region 5.

Key points:
    0.0   Crane Pond trailhead (at road's end).
    0.6   Loop junction; head right.
    2.9   Pharaoh Mountain summit.
    4.5   Pharaoh Lake.
    6.9   Outlet bridge.
    10.2 Round Split Rock Bay.
    13.9 Close loop; turn right to return to trailhead.

Finding the trailhead: From the New York 74/New York 9 junction (0.1 mile east of Interstate 87), go south on NY 9 for 0.6 mile, and turn left (east) onto Alder Meadow Road toward Schroon Lake Airport. In 2 miles bear left on Crane Pond Road and go 1.4 miles east, reaching a parking area on the left; en route, the road changes to gravel.

The road now narrows to a single dirt lane with turnouts. Drivers with conventional vehicles should go no farther than the Goose Pond trailhead, 0.8 mile ahead. Those with four-wheel-drive vehicles generally can reach the Crane Pond trailhead at road's end in another mile. You'll need to beware of

Pharaoh Mountain and Lake Loop

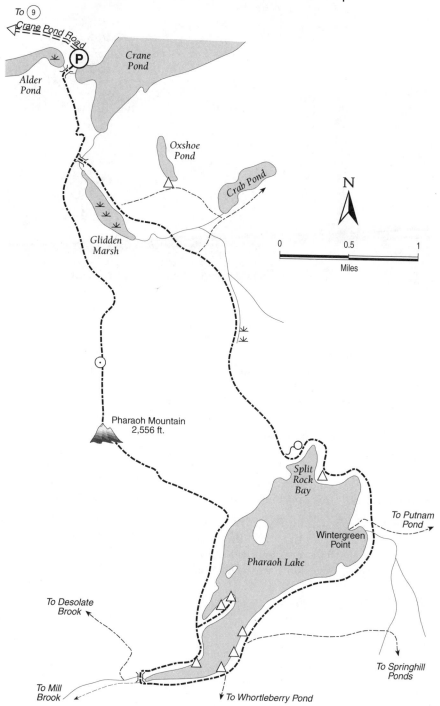

To 9
Crane Pond Road
P
Alder Pond
Crane Pond
Oxshoe Pond
Crab Pond
N
0   0.5   1
Miles
Glidden Marsh
Pharaoh Mountain
2,556 ft.
Split Rock Bay
To Putnam Pond
Wintergreen Point
Pharaoh Lake
To Desolate Brook
To Springhill Ponds
To Mill Brook
To Whortleberry Pond

Pharaoh Lake, Adirondack Park.

a steep loose-sand area, where there is evidence of spinning tires, and a beaver-flooded stretch.

Should the DEC eventually opt to close this roadway into Pharaoh Lake Wilderness, park at the large turnout on Crane Pond Road and walk the final 1.8 miles to the trailhead. While adding distance, the route offers a pleasant tree-shaded tour, paralleling Alder Creek upstream. Outcrops, a dark hollow, wetlands, and Alder Pond vary the tour. Look left at 1.5 miles for a yellow bypass trail to skirt the flood site.

An alternative approach would be to take the blue trail south from NY 74 near Paradox Lake, which comes out on Crane Pond Road 0.1 mile west of the trailhead; this approach adds 2.9 miles of travel each way.

The hike: From Crane Pond trailhead follow the red markers across a split-level bridge over the outlet linking Crane and Alder Ponds. Huge boulders punctuate the evergreen-deciduous shore. Alder Pond shows a more-vegetated water body with meadowy islands; both ponds draw canoeists.

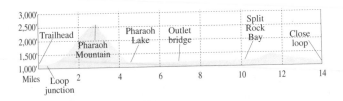

An old woods road then leads into the wilderness for an easy ascent, over-looking the wooded slope of Crane Pond. Maples and fir join the hemlock-birch mix, as do the 4-foot-diameter white pines. At 0.6 mile find the loop junction and bear right, staying on the red trail for a counterclockwise loop that tops Pharaoh Mountain first. Skirt an elbow pond of Glidden Marsh be-fore passing behind a low ridge, where a foot trail replaces the woods road. Gradually the climb intensifies.

At 2.25 miles swing right for a long angling ascent. Spruce and young fir appear as bedrock slabs now shape a more vertical charge up Pharaoh Mountain. Aspen and mountain ash interweave the open forest. Find a pre-view look northwest at Desolate Swamp, Goose Pond, and Schroon Lake.

At 2.9 miles top Pharaoh Mountain near an old mining adit. To continue the tour head south, straight across the crown. First, though, mount the sum-mit outcrops to piece together a 270-degree view. The final puzzle piece falls into place as the trail descends.

A fantastic landscape of rolling ridges, rounded peaks, and a myriad of lakes and marshes treats the eye. Atop the western outcrop (the one to the right), one of four survey markers dates back to 1896. Early in the summit descent, detour right atop yet another outcrop to complete the panoramic puzzle with a southern view of Pharaoh Lake, big and glistening, with rock islands, an irregular shoreline, and the encompassing wilderness.

Rocks and roots complicate the steep descent, which zigs and pitches south off the mountain. Corner outcrops shape short, difficult drops. Where bed-rock opens up the forest, view Treadway Mountain to the northeast.

A plank walk over a wet meadow leads to the lake at 4.5 miles. Bear right, contouring and rolling along the wooded slope and crossing rocky drainages for a counterclockwise tour. At 5.4 miles detour left, following yellow mark-ers along a peninsula to lean-tos in 0.25 mile. The peninsula's rocky end in-vites swimming, fishing, daydreaming, and stargazing.

Resume the counterclockwise tour (5.9 miles); yellow disks now mark the lake loop as well. An outcrop pushes the trail up and inland. As the trail rounds the lake, encounter additional lean-tos or the spurs breaking away to them. Pass above the shallow, pinched outlet bay to cross a footbridge. Beaver-peeled sticks can clog the brook, while frogs and mergansers may enliven the bay.

At the junction across the bridge (6.9 miles), follow the yellow markers uphill to the left, soon traveling a soft woods road. Where the trail pulls away from shore, pass through a corridor of spruce and reindeer lichen. At 7.5 miles an inviting lean-to, christened the "Pharaoh Hilton" by past guests, over-looks the lake. Beyond the shelter, the Springhill Ponds Trail heads right; pro-ceed on the lake tour, bearing left to skirt a quiet bay.

Next cross a hewn log bridging a peninsular island to shore. Here sits an-other choice shelter for overnight lodging and swimming. Cross back over the log to resume the loop, passing among mixed evergreens, birch, and sheep laurel. More outcrops lure sweaty travelers lakeside; views stretch to Pharaoh Mountain.

At a camp flat at 8.75 miles, turn right, ascending and rounding the steep rocky slope above a lily-pad bay. From a log bridge admire Wintergreen Point—the long, thin, treed outcrop separating the main lake from the bay.

At 9.2 miles bypass the trail heading right to Putnam Pond. In another 50 feet turn left on a red secondary trail to reach Wintergreen Point—a 0.2-mile round-trip detour. Past Wintergreen Point the lake trail again draws away from shore, touring a deciduous woodland with hobblebush, striped maple, and young beech; follow markers.

The trail rounds Split Rock Bay, named for a distinctive offshore feature (10.25 miles). Views southwest span Pharaoh Lake to Number 8 and Little Stevens Mountains. Cross a spring-muddied area (10.7 miles), top a small ridge for a farewell look at Pharaoh Lake, and turn right, ascending away (11 miles). The grade is steep, the terrain rocky, and the woods deciduous; yellow remains the guiding color.

Next travel the outskirts of beaver wetlands in various states of reclamation. Rock-free stretches ease a slow descent. From the junction at 12.7 miles continue straight on the yellow trail to reach the east shore of Glidden Marsh at its snag-riddled end. Ahead, lily pads, cattails, islands of grass and rock, and open water alter the marsh's appearance; Pharaoh Mountain looms to the south. Round east behind a low ridge, returning to Glidden Marsh, passing among white pine and birch.

At the blue-trail junction at 13.5 miles, continue straight for Crane Pond. Edge Glidden Marsh before dropping behind a ridge to round the west shore of a snag-riddled meadow basin. Cross the footbridge over the dark outlet of Glidden Marsh to close the loop (13.9 miles); turn right and return to the trailhead, 14.5 miles.

20 Whetstone Gulf State Park

Overview

Whetstone Creek cuts a 380-foot-deep, 3-mile-long, narrow gash into this 2,100-acre park on the eastern edge of the Tug Hill Plateau. The park trail system applauds this impressive gulf feature from its rim.

General description:	Two trails form a rim loop, allowing an overview of the geology and flora of Whetstone Gulf.
General location:	About 6 miles south Lowville.
Special attractions:	Whetstone Creek, dramatic sandstone-shale cliffs, an overlook platform, fossils, falls, and wildflowers.
Length:	Rim Loop, 6 miles round-trip.
Difficulty:	Moderate.
Maps:	State park brochure.
Special concerns:	Fee access to park. Hikers are to be off the trail by 6:00 P.M.; no one may start a hike after 3:00 P.M.

Whetstone Gulf State Park

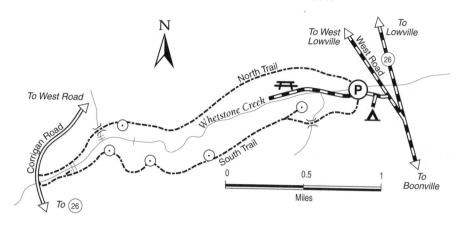

Leashed dogs are allowed on trails, but owners must present proof of each animal's rabies shot upon arrival at the park. No public access to gorge interior.

Season and hours: Spring through fall.
For information: Whetstone Gulf State Park.

Key points:
- 0.0 Near beach house, follow South Trail.
- 0.7 Lookout platform.
- 3.0 Corrigan Road; cross bridge to North Trail.
- 6.0 End loop at beach house/swimming area parking.

Finding the trailhead: From central Lowville go south on New York 26 for 6.1 miles and turn northwest (right) onto West Road/Lewis County 29. Go 0.2 mile and turn left, entering the state park. Find the trailhead near the beach house/swimming area.

The hike: The Rim Loop links the park's North and South Trails for a fine hiking circuit.

Clockwise, start on the South Trail, which begins uphill to the left from the beach house. A steep, steady ascent on a wide earthen trail passes through pine woods with oak, maple, beech, birch, and ash. Moss, Mayflower, ferns, and striped maple fill out the forest. At 0.4 mile the trail levels in a pine plantation with a maple midstory.

After a bridge crossing of a small side brook, the trail curves right toward the gulf

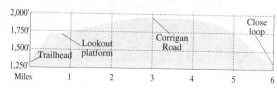

rim and a junction. The right leads to the lookout platform; the left continues the rim loop. Detour right, descending along the rim edge, which serves up forbidding overlooks of the steep forested slope. Respect the potential for danger; keep to the trail—and forget horseplay.

At 0.75 mile an open look up-canyon presents the pinched wooded gulf. From the overlook platform, which juts from the rim, views feature the north wall and span northeast beyond the rim to a pastoral valley and the flattened ridges folding to the horizon.

Return to the rim junction at 1 mile and resume the loop. Hemlock, white pine, maple, and birch shade the rim-hugging trail. Openings offer cross-gulf views of the wooded slopes, tree-filled canyon bottom, and occasional dark pool. At times aspens whisper overhead.

By 1.75 miles tree-filtered glimpses feature the dark, fluted cliffs of the north wall. Later, a short side spur to a point offers views up and out the gulf, as well as down and across. Infrequent trail disks mark the well-traveled path, and Indian pipe may be spied.

Passing through an area of small spruce and fir, the trail dips to an open view of a sheer cliff bowl where Whetstone Creek makes a hairpin turn. The cliffs now measure more than 350 feet high. The view at 2.75 miles features a 10-foot-wide falls streaming down the sheer north wall. A fast-surging Whetstone Creek announces itself below.

After a dip to cross a footbridge over a side drainage, a spur to the right leads to a furiously tumbling long cascade on Whetstone Creek as it courses through a squeezed gorge at the head of the gulf. The cascades grade from

Whetstone Gulf, Whetstone Gulf State Park.

a couple of feet high at the top to 40 feet high at the bottom. Tannin-colored water, bubbling foam, and dark weeping ledges complete the image.

Crossing a log corduroy, the trail meets dirt Corrigan Road. Turn right, cross the bridge over Whetstone Creek, and take a quick right on the North Trail for the return through a varied woods of spruce, hemlock, birch, beech, and maple. By 3.5 miles glimpse the north-wall falls and the dramatic cliffs of the south shore.

Past a side-creek footbridge, two razorback points protrude from the north wall, meeting a treed point from the south wall to shape the previously mentioned hairpin turn in the gulf. Hemlocks and deciduous trees alternately claim the way. After a drainage crossing at 4.6 miles, the descent begins.

At 5.2 miles the trail descends a thin ridge separating the gulf and a steep-sided gully. Oaks claim the gulf slope, while hemlocks fill the gully. At times the trail pitches steeply. Eyes turned toward the gulf view the park road, picnic area, and, later, the manmade swimming hole. At 5.9 miles continue straight to cross a footbridge to the swimming area parking lot, coming out downstream from the beach house to end the hike.

21 Gleasmans Falls Trail

General description: A relaxing stroll through magnificent woods and meadow clearings leads to an outcrop overlooking this falls and gorge on the Independence River.
General location: About 15 miles east of Lowville.
Special attractions: Stepped falls, Independence River Wild Forest, stone ruins, beaver pond, wildflowers, wildlife.
Length: 6.5 miles round-trip.
Difficulty: Easy.
Maps: Crystal Dale 7.5-minute USGS quad, Number Four 15-minute USGS quad.
Special concerns: Beaver activity can alter route.
Season and hours: Spring through fall.
For information: New York State Department of Environmental Conservation, Region 6.

Key points:
0.0   Trailhead; descend closed dirt road.
0.3   Cross Burnt Creek footbridge.
2.9   Cross Second Brook footbridge.
3.2   Head of Gleasmans Falls; backtrack to trailhead.

Finding the trailhead: From New York 12/New York 26 in Lowville, turn east on River Street, which becomes Number Four Road (Lewis County 26), leaving town. In 4.1 miles turn left, staying on Number Four Road for another 4.8 miles. Turn right onto Erie Canal Road, go 2.5 miles and turn left

Gleasmans Falls Trail

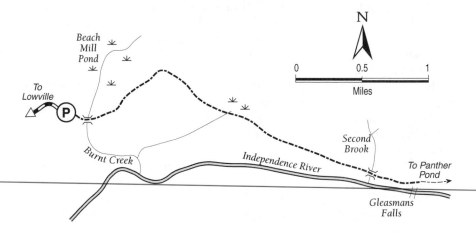

on McPhilmy Road, a single-lane dirt road. In 0.2 mile turn left on Beach Mill Road, a narrower dirt road with limited shoulder for turnouts; reduce speed. Where this road forks in 0.9 mile, stay left and go another 2 miles to reach the trailhead at road's end.

The hike: On the west-central outskirts of the Adirondack Mountains, this trail combines easy walking through majestic woods with a satisfying destination.

Follow a closed dirt road downhill from the trailhead parking lot. In 100 feet on the right, look for an old rock foundation recalling the sawmill that once operated here. Maple, aspen, and pine frame the open corridor. Soon overlook a shrubby meadow threaded by the tannin waters of Burnt Creek, the outlet of Beach Mill Pond.

With a footbridge crossing of Burnt Creek, enter the enchantment of a rich, deep hemlock forest, with yellow disk markers pointing the way. A 4-foot-wide hiker lane parts the woods; if it were once a road, it lacks telltale ruts or tracks. Maple and black cherry interweave the hemlock; the open midstory allows eyes to search far into the forest. The understory ferns, viburnum, brambles, and club moss are especially pretty when bejeweled by rain.

From 0.75 to 1 mile the trail shows a mild ascent before returning to its meditation-inducing evenness. Striped maple and beech join the ranks, along with sarsaparilla, Mayflower, and clintonia.

At 1.5 miles a beaver-grown brook has swallowed the trail's footbridge. To cross the water now, top the dam of mud and sticks. Dark pools mirror the white pines, and scent mounds dot the shore. The trail resumes, edging the "pond."

Next pass through a meadow of tall weeds, wild berries, and shrubs. Where the trail returns to woods, it becomes more rolling, still traveling the grassy bed acquired back at the meadow. The forest becomes more open, dominated by deciduous trees.

At 2.1 miles the trail dips to cross several small drainages, any one of which is susceptible to a beaver's adoption. In the meantime, the crossings remain easy, with simple step-overs or log assists. At 2.3 miles bear right, still touring an open woods.

Where the trail descends toward the Independence River, look for the path to curve left and cross Second Brook via footbridge (2.9 miles). The trail now rolls up, over, and between rock outcrops, touring a pine-deciduous forest, coming to a primitive campsite and the first rocky access to the Independence River and lower Gleasmans Falls. Here the river pulses through a gorge shaped by outcrops, cliffs, and boulders—an exciting union of cascades, deep pools, dark water, and gneiss (metamorphic rock). Pockets of ferns adorn the gorge.

Continue along the north shore to top a cliff outcrop 50 feet above the rushing waters. Traverse the rim to find an open look at the uppermost falls at 3.1 miles before again losing the angle. The upper cascade shows the greatest drop, measuring some 12 feet. Overall, the falls drops some 50 to 60 feet over a 0.2-mile distance; long, flat stretches interrupt the half dozen stepped cascades.

Although most hikers halt at the 3.1-mile overlook, you may wade through the ferns clogging the upstream trail to reach a spur leading to a gravel bar

Independence River, Adirondack Park.

at the head of the falls (3.25 miles). The size of the bar will depend on the water's level. From here the more determined can push their way downstream through shrubs to emerge on the rocks directly above the upper cascade. At times of high water, the gigantic whoosh kicks out a skin-soaking spray; be careful when scrambling over the wet rocks. Downstream views of the river, gorge, and rock overhangs reward the investment. Return as you came.

22   Stony Pond Trail

General description:	This trail traverses varied terrain to visit Stony Pond along with its neighbors, Little and Big Sherman Ponds to the south and Center Pond to the north.
General location:	Adirondack Park, north of Minerva.
Special attractions:	Attractive blue ponds, hardwood and conifer forest, beaver sites, fall color.
Length:	8.8 miles round-trip.
Difficulty:	Moderate.
Maps:	Adirondack Mountain Club, Adirondack Central Region map.
Special concerns:	Trail may be affected by beaver activity.
Season and hours:	Spring through fall for hiking.
For information:	New York State Department of Environmental Conservation, Region 5.

Key points:
0.0	New York 28N trailhead; head east.
2.0	Stony Pond lean-to.
3.2	Big Sherman Pond outlet; backtrack to lean-to.
4.4	Cross Stony Pond outlet.
5.6	Center Pond; return to trailhead (8.8 miles).

Finding the trailhead: Find the trailhead east off New York 28N, 3.9 miles north of its intersection with Olmstedville Road in Minerva and 2.8 miles south of Hewitt Lake Club Road in Aiden Lair. Parking is roadside; a DEC sign indicates the trail.

The hike: The trail wears a single track down the middle of the woods road leading east away from NY 28N. Yellow snowmobile and red-disk markers help indicate this route, which slowly ascends. Fir, spruce, tamarack, birch, maple, beech, and hobblebush enclose the trail. At 0.2 mile the trail skirts

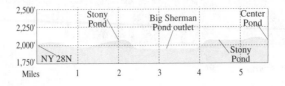

Stony Pond Trail

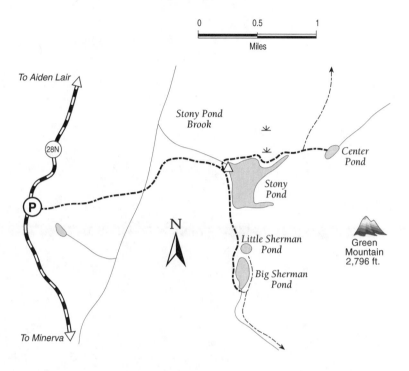

a slope that appears to have been quarried. Proceed forward, bypassing first a private trail to a small pond and then a closed woods road, both on the right.

At 0.5 mile the trail tops out and slowly descends, passing an area of domino-tumbled rocks. At 1.2 miles come to the Stony Brook crossing just below a beaver dam; sometimes the engineer can be spied. Here hikers have the uncommon experience of being at eye-level with the resulting pond. Cross via the dam or makeshift array of limbs, or simply give in and wade.

A slow ascent follows. Low spruce and hemlock grow roadside. Seasonally, runoff and wet pockets mar going. In half a mile follow the beaver bypass, heading right for drier footing. Where the bypass returns to the snowmobile trail, follow Stony Brook upstream to Stony Pond (2 miles). Stony Pond is a quiet enchantress with its wooded rim, Green Mountain to the east, a flat island, and nearshore rocks. As its lean-to looks out at the pond, you can enjoy this image until shut-eye.

Trails round the pond in either direction from the lean-to. Left, crossing Stony Brook via logs and rocks, leads to Center Pond, with Barnes and Hewitt Ponds beyond. Right leads to Sherman Ponds. Head right, following the orange or red disks, tracing a line where the hardwood slope and conifer

Stony Pond, Adirondack Park.

shore meet. At 1.7 miles pass below some distinguished 100-foot-tall vertical gray cliffs showing block fracturing, mossy ledges, and a whitewash of lichen.

At 2.5 miles the trail climbs away to the right to follow the snowmobile branch heading toward Sherman Ponds. Another snowmobile route heads left. Before long, the trail descends to Little Sherman Pond, enlarged by beaver-elevated waters. At 2.75 miles a spur left leads to the marshy shore; the primary trail bears right, rimming the lake through woods. Green Mountain adds to skyline views. Snowmobile and red-disk markers show the way.

Skirt the shallow neck joining Little and Big Sherman Ponds; snags rim the main lake body. Add views of a wooded peninsula as the trail progresses, and skirt a campsite before veering away from the pond. Although the trail continues along Big Sherman, the outlet at 3.25 miles signals the turnaround for this exploration. Return to Stony Pond lean-to (4.4 miles).

To visit Center Pond, cross Stony Brook at the pond outlet and follow the trail as it drifts away and above shore to round the wooded slope. At 4.7 miles overlook the gorgelike channel of an inlet brook before hopping across the inlet. Briefly the trail is wetter, with sphagnum moss beneath a fir-spruce complex, but the route climbs higher. The presence of trail markers is sporadic.

At the next small brook the trail jogs downstream to an easy crossing point. Stony Pond is but a 100-foot spur away. The trail returns upstream, contouring the slope above a beaver pond and later a larger pond with reflections of the nearshore snags and trees. At 5.3 miles, reach a junction. Straight via the red trail leads to Barnes and Hewitt Ponds; right via the yellow trail leads to Center Pond. Head right.

A steep climb and descent through a similar forest leads to Center Pond (5.6 miles). Hikers arrive at a narrow opening in the shrubby shoreline ring that otherwise limits access. This pond is about a quarter the size of Stony Pond but offers nice solitude. Mergansers may peel off the pond upon approach of the boot. Return as you came to Stony Pond lean-to (6.8 miles) and then backtrack to NY 28N (8.8 miles).

23 Middle Settlement Lake Loop

General description:	An all-day or overnight trek travels the forests and meadows of Ha-De-Ron-Dah Wilderness, visiting prized lakes.
General location:	6.5 miles southwest of Old Forge.
Special attractions:	Lakes and ponds, mixed forest, varied wildlife sightings, overnight lean-tos.
Length:	14.25 miles round-trip, including spurs to Middle Branch Lake and Grass Pond.
Difficulty:	Moderate.

Maps:	Adirondack Mountain Club, Adirondack West-Central Region map; Trails in the Old Forge–Big Moose Region brochure.
Special concerns:	Hikers should possess good trail and map skills. Be aware that in a few places the trail markers grow scarce or disappear altogether. Respect private property at trail's start.
Season and hours:	Spring through fall.
For information:	New York State Department of Environmental Conservation, Region 6.

Key points:

0.0	Trailhead; hike easement to trail.
1.2	Loop junction; head left.
3.2	Middle Settlement (Lake) lean-to.
5.7	Middle Branch Lake shelter; backtrack to loop.
9.2	Grass Pond.
13.0	Close loop; proceed forward to end at trailhead (14.2 miles).

Finding the trailhead: From Old Forge go 6.4 miles southwest on New York 28 and turn right at the signed easement for the trails to Ha-De-Ron-Dah Wilderness and Middle Settlement Lake. Go 0.5 mile north on the gravel road to find parking on the right; the arrow for the trail is just beyond it on the left.

The hike: This rolling, meandering tour gathers beauty and relaxation from Ha-De-Ron-Dah Wilderness, while using a relatively new access.

Round the metal gate to travel the conservation easement across paper company land. In 250 feet turn left to find the yellow-marked trail and register. This trail employs several time-healed logging roads and crisscrosses the faint grassy beds of others. A forest of maple, birch, beech, and viburnum enfolds travel. A wet passage poses a seasonal problem.

At 0.75 mile meet a narrow dirt road and follow it left for fast, easy travel. Periodic postings indicate the WILD FOREST PRESERVE. At 1.1 miles turn right, leaving the road and following an established footpath through similar woods. At times ferns overlace the trailbed.

Cross small, braided Stony Creek and ascend to the loop junction at 1.25 miles. Go left for a clockwise tour, now passing beneath some big black cherry. Mossy boulders accent the woods. The trail continues its rolling meander, crossing small brooks and soggy bottoms of sphagnum moss. Hikers must be attentive throughout, eyeing footing and spying markers.

At 2.4 miles descend to round the southwestern arm of Middle Settlement Lake, with cross-lake views featuring a large beaver lodge. Lily-pad clusters, evergreen points, and islands lend character to the large open-water lake; starflowers and a host of mushrooms spangle the woods floor. Ruffed grouse, owl, deer, beaver, mink, toad, frog, and red eft offer possible wildlife encounters.

Cross the inlet on either of two beaver dams within easy reach of the trail. Afterward stay low to the water before pulling away from shore and coming to a trail junction. To the left leads to Lost and Pine Lakes; bear right, staying with the yellow disks, to reach Middle Settlement lean-to.

Middle Settlement Lake Loop

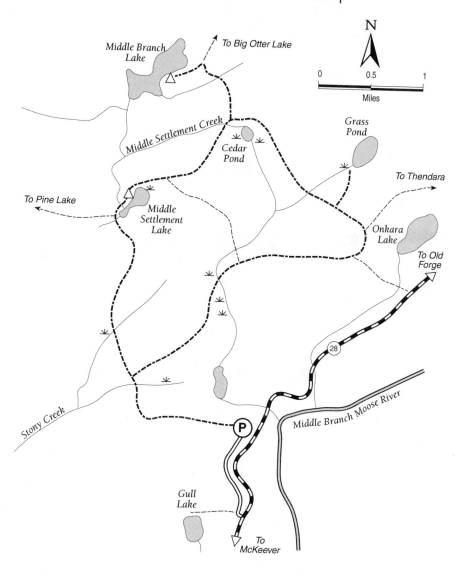

Middle Branch Lake

To Big Otter Lake

N

0   0.5   1
Miles

Grass Pond

Middle Settlement Creek

Cedar Pond

To Thendara

To Pine Lake

Middle Settlement Lake

Onkara Lake

To Old Forge

28

Stony Creek

P

Middle Branch Moose River

Gull Lake

To McKeever

2,250'
2,000'
1,750'
1,500'

Loop junction
Middle Settlement Lake
Middle Branch Lake
Grass Pond
Close loop

Trailhead

Miles   2   4   6   8   10   12

After crossing the outlet via rocks and boot-polished logs, find the prized shelter at 3.2 miles, atop a 10-foot-high outcrop overlooking the main body of Middle Settlement Lake; its shimmery depths suggest a swim. For the privy, follow the red-marked trail past the huge boulders and into the woods.

The loop resumes north, rounding the wooded shore on a well-traveled path; here the forest floor appears hummocky. Among the gargantuan boulders at the end of the lake, find the junction at 3.5 miles. Uphill to the right lies the blue trail to NY 28 (a more-established access); bear left, staying along the drainage for the loop.

At 4 miles the yellow trail passes through a soggy meadow, coming to a stone-stepping crossing (or high-water wading) of picturesque Cedar Pond outlet with its fern-flowing banks. At 4.25 miles glimpse Cedar Pond, a mosaic of open water and soggy shrub islands and shores. Spruce, maple, and birch compose the forest.

At the 4.5-mile junction, the red trail straight ahead continues the loop, but detour left on the yellow trail to add a visit to Middle Branch Lake. The detour shows more-marked climbs and pitches. At the junction in 1 mile, turn left to reach the shelter, which occupies a small point overlooking the long water body of Middle Branch Lake. During rainstorms one can pass the time reading the hiker sagas penned in the lean-to journal.

At 7 miles resume the clockwise loop back at the 4.5-mile junction, now following red markers. The trail rolls through an open woods, sometimes marshy or rocky. Pretty pockets of bunchberry and club moss seduce photographers.

At 8.25 miles cross stones over the dark-ale water of Grass Pond outlet. In another 0.5 mile look for the yellow trail angling left to the pond. On the detour to Grass Pond, young beech, striped maple, and viburnum frisk hikers as they pass. At 9.2 miles find a camp flat between the spruce woods and meadow shore. The main pond sweeps away to the right but requires a bushwhacking approach.

Resume the clockwise tour of Middle Settlement Lake Loop with a tranquil woods stroll. At 10 miles continue forward, again on a yellow-marked trail, crossing a boardwalk through a wet bottomland near the state lands boundary. At the junction ahead again stay straight on the yellow trail, which is now wide, flat, and easy. To the left lies NY 28 and the popular Scusa Access. Hardwoods claim the forest.

At 11 miles, where a blue trail heads right to Middle Settlement Lake, stay on the yellow trail to bring the loop to a close; the route grows less broad and refined. Nearing a beaver pond, turn left, cross atop the earthen dam, and again turn left to travel along the wooded edge of the expansive floodplain meadow. Markers become scarce.

At 11.7 miles turn right following an overgrown woods road; the tracked trail remains visible beneath the masking ferns. Although pleasantly removed from grand central station, this section of the hike requires greater attention to avoid straying off trail. Bottom areas can be soggy, even in August.

Continue to follow the overgrown roadbed as it curves away from the flood-plain of Middle Settlement Creek. Where deciduous trees gain a stronghold, rocks and leaves replace the fern wadings. At 12.95 miles veer right off the woods road to close the loop at 13 miles. Continue straight for Copper Lake Road, retracing the initial 1.25 miles to the trailhead.

24 Peaked Mountain Trail

General description:	This split-character trail joins an easy hike to Peaked Mountain Pond with a rugged summit ascent.
General location:	Siamese Ponds Wilderness, 16 miles southeast of Indian Lake, off New York 28.
Special attractions:	Lake, brook, pond, forest, and meadow habitats; summit vistas; loons, beavers, frogs, and toads.
Length:	6 miles round-trip.
Difficulty:	Easy to pond; strenuous to summit.
Maps:	Adirondack Mountain Club, Adirondack Central Region map.
Special concerns:	Expect difficult footing on summit ascent; wear boots.
Season and hours:	Best in summer and fall; rain compounds the difficulty of attaining summit.
For information:	New York State Department of Environmental Conservation, Region 5.

Key points:
0.0   Thirteenth Lake trailhead.
2.4   Peaked Mountain Pond.
3.0   Peaked Mountain summit; return by same route.

Finding the trailhead: At the hamlet of North River on NY 28 (12 miles east of Indian Lake), turn south on Thirteenth Lake Road for Siamese Ponds Wilderness/Thirteenth Lake. Go 3.3 miles and turn right on improved-dirt Beach Road to reach the wilderness entry and trailhead parking in another 0.5 mile.

The hike: This trail holds great variety and offers a fine wilderness stroll for its first 2.7 miles. The final 0.3 mile laughs at gravity, uniting boot-skidding, steep dirt surfaces and severe bare-rock inclines. For anyone uninitiated with the rugged nature of the Adirondacks, this summit approach shouts a loud, clear "howdy!"

The hike begins on a barrier-closed road shaded by birch, beech, and fir. Pass campsites and a privy, coming to a trail register at a primitive boat launch on Thirteenth Lake (0.1 mile). At low water a thin rocky beach greets

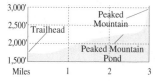

Peaked Mountain Trail

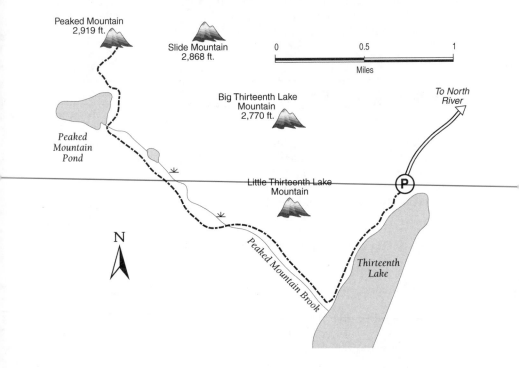

hikers; high water presents an alder-shrub shore. From the launch, a foot trail rounds the west shore of Thirteenth Lake, with red paint dots and disks showing the way.

For the next 0.5 mile enjoy a mildly rolling shoreline tour, seldom straying more than 25 feet from the lake's edge. Thirteenth Lake is a big, elongated water body at the base of Balm of Gilead Mountain; this saddle-shaped peak dominates cross-lake views. Canoes ply the water, while loons or mergansers suggest the raising of binoculars.

Picture-pretty birch, beech, aspen, and some towering white pines frame both trail and shore. Despite some rock studding and roots, the path remains highly passable. Lake overlooks occur at regular intervals.

At 0.6 mile turn away from the lake, following the rocky outlet of Peaked Mountain Pond upstream. Depending on flow, the upper brook may show exciting chutes, cascades, and bedrock water slides. Massive boulders loom trailside, while hemlock and birch shade the brook-hugging tour.

At 1.2 miles the trail levels prior to a stone-stepping crossing of the brook. Ahead, small muddy drainages spot the way. At 1.4 miles glimpse Peaked and Big Thirteenth Lake Mountains. The trail then crosses over a rise, rounding an expansive grassy meadow—a classic mountain beauty edged by low alders and snuggled below Little Thirteenth Lake Mountain.

A conifer stand with a rich understory of oxalis, bunchberry, whorled aster, trillium, and clintonia gives pause before the next meadow rounding, this one below Hour Pond Mountain. Silver snags and logs, boulders, and an abandoned beaver lodge accent this grassy opening. Next, find another treed passage, coming out at an active beaver pond.

A brief, steep ascent presents Peaked Mountain Pond at 2.45 miles. At the pond look for the main trail as it curves right for the summit ascent. A detour straight ahead finds a shoreline outcrop overlooking a thin cove severed from the main pond by a slender shrub-mantled peninsula. Continue rounding the shore to the left to attain cross-pond views of rock-crested Peaked Mountain.

The summit route takes hikers across the outlet just below the pond, passing over an old beaver dam. As the trail again turns toward shore, stay right. Here trail markers are briefly absent, but a few ribbons may cue the way. Before long, the trailbed regains definition and markers return.

At 2.6 miles ascend and round the slope of Peaked Mountain, passing through a picturesque stand of paper birch. Above a meadowy pond extension, look for the trail to enter its mad summit ascent. Even while being careful, hikers can find themselves up-ended by the skidding dirt, pitched slopes, and grip-defying canted outcrops. Some of the worst areas have been bypassed by wiser hikers, who have gone off trail, shaping switchbacks. Consider following their lead.

At the top (3 miles), easily mounted outcrops among the low-growing spruce unfold a 270-degree view; looks north require more effort. Best views sweep

Peaked Mountain summit, Adirondack Park.

the immediate neighborhood with Peaked Mountain Pond; the meadows; and Big and Little Thirteenth Lake, Slide, and Hour Pond Mountains. Distant looks round up the Adirondack High Peaks and Vermont's Green Mountains. Ravens offer noisy commentary, as vultures drift on the thermals.

On return, watch your footing. As you near Peaked Mountain Pond, keep an eye out for a 2-inch-diameter garnet that studs a rock in the trail. Prior to wilderness protection, garnet mining occurred near Peaked Mountain, but collecting is now forbidden.

25 West Canada Lakes Wilderness

Overview

Within Moose River Recreation Area in the west-central Adirondacks, this designated wilderness represents one of the last regional wilds to be opened to foot travel and human visitorship. It sports picturesque spruce-hardwood forests, charming meadows, and large wilderness lakes. From this excursion wilderness hikers may access the trans-Adirondack Northville-Placid Trail or visit such other celebrated features as Spruce Lake and Cedar Lakes.

General description:	An overnight outing or demanding all-day hike travels to the core of West Canada Lakes Wilderness, passing through conifer-deciduous forest and meadow breaks to visit three pristine lakes: Falls Pond, Brooktrout, and West.
General location:	20 miles southeast of Old Forge.
Special attractions:	Wilderness forest and lakes, beaver ponds, gentian meadows, solitude, loons, fall foliage.
Length:	18.2 miles round-trip, including Falls Pond detour.
Difficulty:	Moderate to strenuous.
Maps:	Moose River Recreation Area brochure; Adirondack Mountain Club, Adirondack West-Central Region map.
Special concerns:	Drivers entering Moose River Recreation Area must register upon entering. Beware; several backcountry privies exist in disrepair.
Season and hours:	Memorial Day weekend through fall.
For information:	New York State Department of Environmental Conservation, Region 5.

Key points:

0.0	Trailhead; round barrier.
2.0	Falls Pond.
6.5	Brooktrout Lake lean-to.
8.9	First West Lake lean-to.
9.4	Meet Northville-Placid Trail; head right.
9.6	Second West Lake lean-to; return to trailhead (18.2 miles).

West Canada Lakes Wilderness

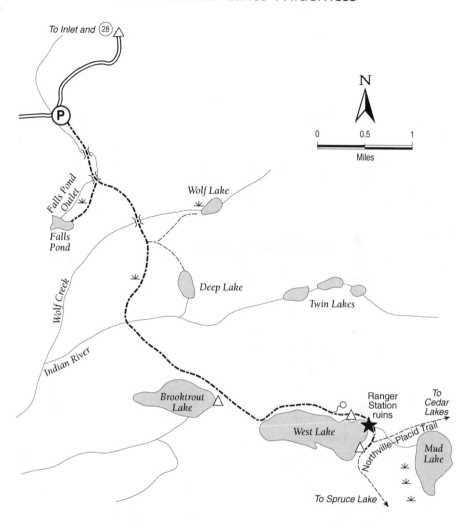

Finding the trailhead: From central Inlet, go east on New York 28 for 0.8 mile and turn south on Limekiln Road for Moose River Recreation Area. Go 1.8 miles, turn left, and register for the recreation area. Continue east on the wide improved dirt road (15 miles per hour), following the signs to Otter Brook. In 11.4 miles cross the Otter Brook bridge and follow signs to Brooktrout Lake (right). Find the trailhead on the left in 0.9 mile and parking for a dozen vehicles.

The hike: Go around the barrier, following a retired logging road for a steady ascent, overlooking a series of beaver ponds. Young maples, small spruce,

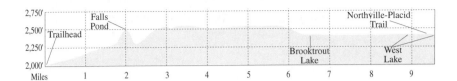

2,750'
2,500' Trailhead
2,250'
2,000'
Miles   1   2   3   4   5   6   7   8   9

Falls Pond   Brooktrout Lake   West Lake   Northville-Placid Trail

birch, and beech overlace the route. At the sides of the trail grow sarsaparilla, ferns, whorled aster, grasses, and brambles. The trail has a good walking surface, with only a few rocky or cobbled areas.

Cross a small logging bridge at 1.2 miles, and in another 0.25 mile look for the marked Falls Pond Trail on the right. Some yellow markers point the way as the trail tours a scenic fir-spruce woods, skirts the edge of the outlet meadow, and crosses the outcrop at the head of the meadow to return to forest. The trail tags the lake outlet, a campsite, and an outcrop view before drawing to an end.

A mountain beauty with an irregular shoreline, Falls Pond enchants with outcrop points and islands, a fir-spruce rim, and enfolding deciduous hillsides. The morning mist and the distressful cry of an unseen loon can conjure a haunting image.

Resume the wilderness hike at 2.5 miles, turning right on the main trail. Outcrops open up the trail corridor, while dense stands of low-growing spruce and fir squeeze it. By August's last days, the leaves show the onset of change, with orange, yellow, red, and maroon hues.

The trail tops out and slowly descends, crossing the bridge over the Wolf Lake outlet at 3.2 miles. Go 200 yards past the bridge to find the access trail to Deep and Wolf Lakes, heading left. Deep Lake lies 0.9 mile off trail; Wolf Lake, a mile. Wetlands and beaver flooding create a soggy trek to the latter.

For this description, forgo these side excursions, keeping to the main trail as it passes over exposed bedrock (slippery when wet) and among young deciduous trees. The cairn at 3.4 miles points hikers to the lower edge of the outcrop, which leads to the foot trail's continuation. Paired planks cross wet spots and meadow habitats. At 3.6 miles skirt a meadow swath adorned in late summer by blue gentian and sunlit nodding cotton grass.

The trail again skirts a scenic beaver pond and meadow at 4.1 miles. Wildlife watching likewise reflects the changing of the seasons. Beavers may tug leafy branches across the pond to anchor them below the surface in preparation for winter.

After 4.4 miles lose all trace of the old road, as well as such niceties as the wetland foot planks, although more yellow disks guide the way. The trail rolls, descending to and then ascending from the stone crossing of Deep Lake outlet.

At 5.5 miles pass a scenic cluster of mossy boulders and logs, keeping left and traversing a spruce bog. The trail becomes muddied both literally and figuratively; beware of impostor paths. Ahead, cross over a rise where hobblebush and young beech frisk passersby to contour the wooded slope above

Falls Pond, Adirondack Park.

Brooktrout Lake—a gleam in the basin. Because the wilderness trail is removed from the lakes, take advantage of all side trails to camp flats and lean-tos to admire the waters.

Find Brooktrout Lake lean-to at 6.5 miles. Side trails venture to the lake, reaching a boulder-and-marsh shore that prohibits travel. Although the legacy of acid rain still silences these remote lakes, their beauty is uncompromised. Pass the lean-to and bear left, rounding away from the lake, following red and yellow disks. Again the trail crosses over a rise at 7.3 miles, touring above a meadow basin at the upper extent of West Lake. At a trail sign near a split boulder, find a spur to a lakeside camp. From this lake corner views span West Lake to Pillsbury Peak.

The rolling trail now contours the forested slope above West Lake. In places, brushy growth and spruce intrude. At 8.8 miles find piped spring water. In another 0.1 mile reach the first of two lean-tos along West Lake. Spurs branch to the bouldery lake shore, with a pretty treed island offshore.

Continue rounding the lake to the southeast, crossing rotting footboards in the wet meadow. Where the trail returns to woods, beautiful carpets of oxalis complement the curvature of the trail. After crossing the outlet bridge and bypassing an old dump from the former rangers cabin, find a junction post in the meadow.

Here hikers meet the blue Northville–Placid Trail. To the left leads to Cedar Lakes; go right for the second West Lake lean-to, the ending for this hike. To your right at the junction, find a cross and an old rock foundation. The cross commemorates the rangers cabin that stood here; the ruin is what's left of the fireplace from French Louie's cabin, which preceded the rangers cabin. The cross inscription reads RIP WEST CANADA LAKES RANGERS CABIN JAN. 29, 1987 AGE ABOUT 50 YRS. "YOU DID NOT CONFORM."

Continuing to the second West Lake lean-to, bear right at the next junction. Reach the prized lean-to at 9.6 miles. It looks out at West Lake, its bouldery shore, a string of rocks concluding at a small rock island, and an attractive rolling wooded terrain. Return as you came, or investigate some of the other wilderness lakes.

26 Siamese Ponds Hike

General description:	This easy all-day or backpack hike travels a scenic low-elevation Central Adirondack forest, parallels the East Branch Sacandaga River, and visits a large wilderness pond.
General location:	9.5 miles south of Wevertown off New York 8.
Special attractions:	Historic 1800s Bakers Mills–North River Stagecoach Route; colorful fall foliage; bear, beaver, mink, otter, grouse, and other woodland creatures.
Length:	11.8 miles round-trip.
Difficulty:	Easy.
Maps:	Adirondack Mountain Club; Adirondack Central Region map.
Special concerns:	None.
Season and hours:	Spring through fall.
For information:	New York State Department of Environmental Conservation (DEC), Region 5.

Key points:
- 0.0 New York 8 trailhead; head west.
- 0.4 Cross shoulder of Eleventh Mountain.
- 1.5 Cross Diamond Brook bridge.
- 3.9 Cross East Branch Sacandaga River suspension bridge.
- 5.9 Siamese Ponds; return to trailhead.

Finding the trailhead: From Bakers Mills (south of Wevertown), go 3.8 miles south on NY 8; a small DEC sign marks the trail's large gravel parking lot on the west side of highway.

The hike: Ideal for a family backpack or a first backpack outing, this trail journeys west into Siamese Ponds Wilderness, initially ascending via a former roadbed through an arbor of young birch, aspen, and maples. The blue-disk trail markers are few in number, but little needed. In places

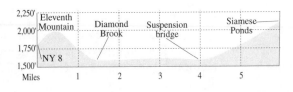

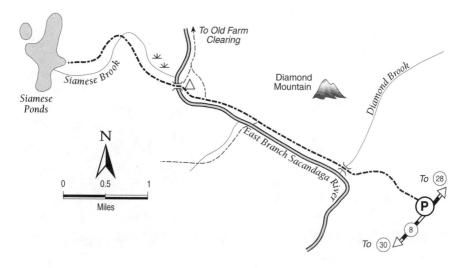

rocks riddle the bed. Ferns, hobblebush, and sarsaparilla contribute to the woodland understory; jewelweed, the moist drainages.

The grade eases as the trail parallels a small drainage upstream, crossing over the low shoulder of Eleventh Mountain (0.4 mile). From here the historic stagecoach route hosts the descent. The forest's spatial order and changing mix create visual diversity. By 1.1 mile firs and spruce fill out the complex, and black cherry trees enter the mix. In the meadow clearings discover joe-pye weed, asters, and dogwood.

As the stage route levels off, enjoy carefree strolling above the riparian corridor of the East Branch Sacandaga River. At 1.5 miles comes the Diamond Brook bridge crossing. Budding biologists often detour to the bank in search of tiny fry, crayfish, and mud puppies.

Goldenrod, brambles, and low alders contribute to the riparian meadow bordering the trail. At a plank bridge at 1.6 miles, look for Diamond Mountain to the right. Woodland travel resumes within 100 feet of the river.

At 2 miles the trail briefly tags the herb-and-forb riverbank for an open look at the shallow 50-foot-wide river marked by occasional riffles, rocks, and bedrock. Its mood varies widely from times of high water to times of low water. The mild-grade earthen trail frees eyes to enjoy the setting, perhaps even to spy a bear slogging across the river.

By 2.6 miles the trail draws farther from the river, again somewhat rolling. Abandoned apple trees and a younger, more open woods hint at a former farm. Afterward, the trail drifts back toward the river.

At the 3.5-mile fork the old stagecoach route continues to the right toward Old Farm Trailhead. To reach Siamese Ponds bear left, following a former road grade as it dips to a drainage crossing. The hike then resumes along the wooded riverbench for occasional views.

East Branch Sacandaga River, Adirondack Park.

At 3.9 miles a suspension bridge spans the East Branch Sacandaga, continuing the trail to Siamese Ponds. On the east bank at the crossing site, a lopsided lean-to overlooks the water. This rain-tight lodging comes complete with table, fireplace, and functional privy. A connecting spur to the Old Farm Trail passes in front of the lean-to; avoid it.

From the suspension bridge find fine up and downstream views of the East Branch Sacandaga River. Upon leaving the bridge, continue straight ahead because side spurs branch to camp flats and shore. The trail rolls and at 4.2 miles dips to a small runoff meadow, with a pair of hewn logs for crossing.

A rock-riddled ascent follows, but easy travel resumes with an earthen bed and nothing more strenuous than a moderate grade. Fir, spruce, birch, hemlock, and striped and sugar maples shade the way, with a fickle showing of ground cover.

At 4.8 miles cross Siamese Brook atop rocks. Another rocky ascent and brief muddy stretch follow, marking the start of a more continuous ascent. By 5.4 miles a few boulders dot the slope, trees exceed 18 inches in diameter, and the trail gently rolls. A woodpecker, grouse, or red eft may divert eyes. The trail then passes campsites, descending to the main Siamese Pond (5.9 miles).

Shaped like an amoeba, Siamese Pond presents a bouldery-sandy beach at its point of access. Humped-back conifer-deciduous hills, including Hayden Mountain to the north, overlook the pond; aquatic vegetation spots its shallow edge. Rounding the shore for new perspectives or reaching Upper Siamese Pond requires bushwhacking. When ready, return as you came.

27 Tongue Mountain Range Loop

General description: This demanding loop tags five summits of the peninsular Tongue Mountain Range for unsurpassed looks at the Lake George countryside. It then dips to lake level and visits Point of Tongue before returning along Northwest Bay.

General location: 6.5 miles northeast of Bolton Landing.

Special attractions: Spectacular lake, island, and ridge views; diverse woods; colorful autumn foliage; marsh, cliffs, and vernal pools; wildlife sightings.

Length: 14 miles round-trip.

Difficulty: Strenuous; steep pitches may require hand assists.

Maps: Adirondack Mountain Club, Adirondack Eastern Region map.

Special concerns: Carry adequate drinking water; beware— rattlesnakes live in this rugged terrain.

Season and hours: Spring through fall.

For information: New York State Department of Environmental Conservation, Region 5.

Tongue Mountain Range Loop

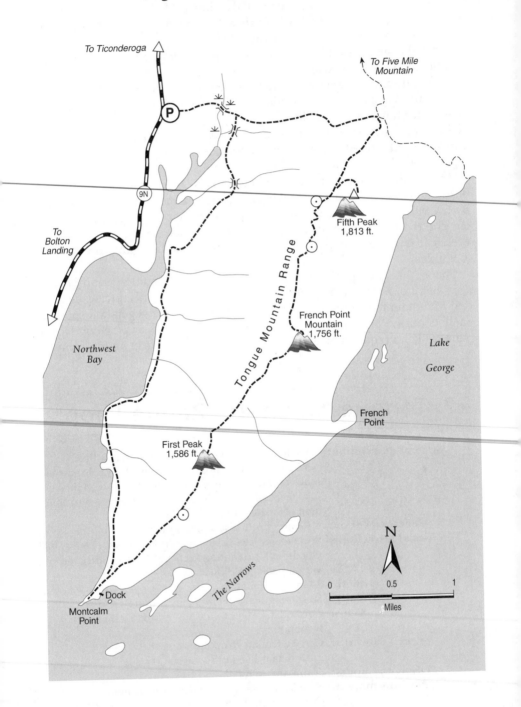

To Ticonderoga

To Five Mile Mountain

P

9N

To Bolton Landing

Fifth Peak 1,813 ft.

Tongue Mountain Range

French Point Mountain 1,756 ft.

Northwest Bay

Lake George

French Point

First Peak 1,586 ft.

The Narrows

Dock

Montcalm Point

N

0   0.5   1

Miles

Key points:

- 0.0   Clay Meadow trailhead.
- 0.4   Loop junction; bear left (straight).
- 2.6   Fifth Peak lean-to and vantage; return to loop.
- 3.9   Third Peak.
- 4.9   French Point Mountain.
- 6.0   First Peak.
- 8.4   Montcalm Point (Point of Tongue); return to loop.
- 13.6   Close loop; backtrack left to trailhead.

Finding the trailhead: From Interstate 87 take exit 24 and head east toward Bolton Landing. In 5 miles turn north on New York 9N and go 4.4 miles to find head-in parking on the east side of the highway at the old quarry pond. Find Clay Meadow trailhead just south of the parking lot; the trail heads east.

The hike: Blue disks initially guide the way along a woods road passing through a conifer plantation. Where the trail crosses a wetland boardwalk, common sightings include white-tailed deer, frogs, and herons. At 0.4 mile is the loop junction; for a clockwise tour bear left (straight) toward Fifth Peak lean-to.

Red disks now mark the steadily ascending woods road, sometimes rocky and rootbound. In 1995 a severe windstorm gleaned some of the framing hemlock, beech, and maple, opening up the passage. Where the trail grows steeper at 1.3 miles, look for it to switch back left. The trail now rounds below mossy outcrop cliffs, traversing a scenic hemlock–birch plateau. At 1.6 miles the ascent resumes.

At the saddle junction (1.9 miles), turn right for the loop, continuing toward Fifth Peak lean-to, and stay right for a pleasant rolling tour to the shelter junction at 2.4 miles. A 0.5-mile round-trip detour follows the yellow markers left to Fifth Peak lean-to, where hikers find a dry overnight wayside, privy, and open outcrop for a southern Lake George vantage.

At 2.9 miles the primary loop journeys south along a narrow, less-used foot trail, descending a hemlock-pine slope to reach a moist deciduous bottom. On Fourth Peak top outcrops within an old fire zone, opened up with silvered snags, sumac, aspen, and young oak; views stretch south and west.

At the base of an outcrop at 3.5 miles, a trail marker on a snag points left. Briefly contour then sharply descend right, easing over rocks and coming

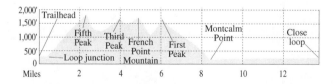

to a notch. Again climb from maple-hemlock woods to a piney crest, with overlooks of Lake George and the forested islands from South Sacrament to Floating Battery Island and with cross-lake views of Black and Erebus Mountains.

After topping Third Peak at 3.9 miles, find a steep pitch before climbing to another open view. The trail then pitches, rolls, and streaks up French Point Mountain for the best views of the hike. Looks encompass French Point (a peninsula extending into Lake George), the many treed islands of The Narrows, the chain of islands stretching north, and the ridges and mountains rolling east. Open outcrop vantages line up from 4.7 to 4.9 miles.

At 4.9 miles round a small cairn atop an outcrop and descend past a vernal pool and an outcrop presenting Northwest Bay and First Peak—the final summit conquest now separated by a 400-foot elevation drop and matching gain. The trail shows a similar pitch-and-climb character, passing through oak-grassland. Where the path again overlooks the steep eastern flank, views laud the narrow lake, the dark humped-back ridges, and jigsaw puzzle of islands.

Beech-oak woods claim the trail where it bottoms out at 5.4 miles. Atop First Peak at 6 miles, find a 180-degree Lake George vista. The trail now hugs the east side of the ridge, passing among oak, hickory, and ash. At 6.8 miles two small bumps add views toward Bolton Landing.

Ahead the trail opens up, descending among juniper, sumac, and small cedar; views include Montcalm Point. At 7.6 miles snare final low-angle looks at The Narrows, then curve away west, returning to hemlock-deciduous woods.

Lake George from Tongue Mountain, Adirondack Park.

In a half mile the loop bears right, while a detour left follows blue markers to Montcalm Point (Point of Tongue). It travels the forested peninsula, bypassing a state-owned boat dock (on the left) to reach the point. Find open views at both Lake George and Northwest Bay, as well as a large outcrop that calls to swimmers and sunbathers.

At 8.8 miles resume the loop north, passing through a moist woodland along Northwest Bay toward Clay Meadow. The trail rolls to and from shore, rounding shallow coves and cutting across points. It traverses muddy pockets, meadowy areas, and stands of birch. Wherever the steep bank meets an abrupt lake drop-off, the urge to take a plunge builds.

At 10.4 miles cross an ash swale (formerly a beaver pond). Beyond a tiny inlet flowing over a mossy boulder cliff, a canted outcrop offers lake access. At 11.25 miles the trail rolls away through mixed woods. Before long, a spur leads to a point overlooking the marshy head of Northwest Bay. Remain close to shore, obtaining passing looks at the marsh grass, lily pads, and stands of red maple and cedar.

At the 12-mile footbridge, drift inland for a steady 0.6-mile ascent. Warblers divert attention. The trail returns once more to the marsh's edge before crossing another footbridge to close the loop at 13.6 miles. Retrace the first 0.4 mile to the trailhead and vehicle parking.

28 Black Mountain Loop

General description:	This loop tops Black Mountain, the tallest mountain above Lake George, for a superb panorama of the lake region; eastern looks strain to Vermont. Ponds and beaver marshes put a stamp on the tour.
General location:	East ridge of Lake George.
Special attractions:	Lake, island, and ridge vistas; ponds and beaver marshes; overnight lean-tos; colorful fall foliage.
Length:	7 miles round-trip.
Difficulty:	Moderate.
Maps:	Adirondack Mountain Club, Adirondack Eastern Region map.
Special concerns:	Expect some soggy trail stretches.
Season and hours:	Spring through fall.
For information:	New York State Department of Environmental Conservation, Region 5.

Key points:
0.0 Trailhead; follow fire road.
1.0 Loop junction; head right.
2.4 Closed tower.
4.8 Lapland Pond lean-to.
6.0 Close loop; turn right, backtracking to trailhead.

Black Mountain Loop

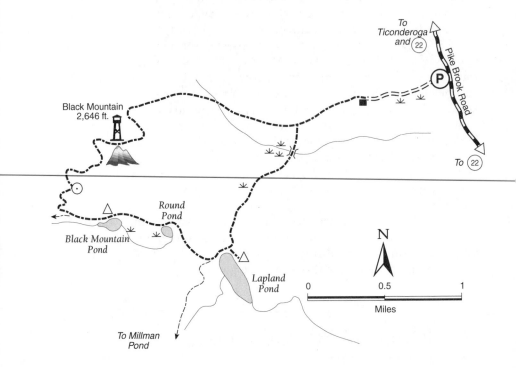

Finding the trailhead: From the junction of New York 74 and New York 22 at Ticonderoga, go 17 miles south on NY 22, turning west on Washington County 6 for Huletts Landing. In 2.5 miles turn south on Pike Brook Road, finding the gravel parking lot for the trailhead on the right in 0.8 mile.

The hike: This loop combines a fairly steep assault on the mountain with a tempered, switchbacking descent.

Red disks and snowmobile markers point the way along a fire road enclosed by maple, birch, beech, ash, viburnum, and wet-meadow vegetation. At 0.25 mile continue straight; remnants of an old corduroy and flat rock placements indicate that this stretch can turn to muck. At 0.6 mile turn right, following an arrow; the path ahead enters an old farmstead. Red efts and deer number among the sightings. Aspen join the mix. Skirting the farm area, the loop travels a time-narrowed woods road through a more mature hemlock-deciduous forest.

At 1 mile comes the loop junction; go right for a counterclockwise tour. Where the marked foot trail bears left at the fork in 1.3 miles, stay right, following the snowmobile trail to avoid areas of canted outcrop, loose rock, and mire and to avoid contributing to greater erosion. The two trails meet and part several times en route to the summit. Spruce join the mix; bunchberry, Mayflower, clintonia, and mosses adorn the sides of the route, and snags open up the canopy.

After the snowmobile trail briefly merges with the hiker trail at 2 miles, follow the shared trailbed for a couple hundred feet and turn right, returning to the red-marked hiker trail. Be careful on the ascent as runoff makes the outcrop slippery; stay to the right.

At 2.3 miles, where the trail tops Black Mountain at the site of a one-time ranger's cabin, a spur to the right leads to a picnic table and a view to the north and east, featuring the north end of Lake George, Elephant and Sugarloaf Mountains, and the nearby abandoned Black Mountain lookout tower.

As the trail reaches the tower (2.4 miles), the loop follows the path curving west into spruce–fir forest; a junction sign indicates that it leads to Black Mountain Point. Although the lookout tower itself is closed, the outcrop nose dishes up a grand view. Looks sweep northern Lake George with Main, Harbor, and Vicars Islands; Five Mile Mountain and the northern Tongue Mountain Range; and the ridges rolling east to Vermont. In fall the spired evergreens pierce a vibrant sea of deciduous color.

Bypassing a shaded picnic table, the loop begins a moderate descent off the summit. Multitrunked birch trees capture the imagination; pines replace the spruce and fir, and aspen join the mix. An early view finds Black Mountain Pond, with looks building to the south. Wild raspberry, striped maple, brambles, grasses, and ferns vegetate the clearings. From an open outcrop at 3 miles, the view sweeps Lake George, Bolton Landing, The Narrows, Point of Tongue, and Shelving Rock Mountain.

The trail now descends and rounds a striated boulder cliff, snaring additional Lake George–Black Mountain Pond views. At a second outcrop vantage, the trail turns right for a switchbacking descent, entering a fuller woods of hemlock, birch, maple, and big pines.

At the base of the mountain at 3.4 miles, bear left on the yellow-disk trail for the loop; the red trail to the right leads to Black Mountain Point on Lake George in 2 miles. Be alert; although this junction is marked, rangers report that several loop hikers have unintentionally found themselves at Lake George.

The loop now travels the north shore of Black Mountain Pond, an open water with a broad meadow shore of leatherleaf and other marsh shrubs. Fish tap the surface, leaving ever-widening rings. Dragonflies, kingfishers, garter snakes, and bullfrogs enliven the stage. Where the trail crosses an outcrop at 3.7 miles, uphill to the left sit a shelter, picnic table, and privy; the loop continues straight ahead.

At 4 miles the trail crosses the inlet drainage of Round Pond, which resembles the first pond but with a broader marsh shore, pockets of phragmites (tall, feathery-headed grasses), and small silvered snags. The trail stays in the rimming hemlocks. At 4.3 miles cross-pond views find Black Mountain.

At the 4.6-mile junction the path to the right leads to additional ponds. For the loop continue straight ahead, now following blue disks toward the Lapland Pond lean-to. After crossing a rocky drainage, the path ahead continues the loop. Detour right, following the Lapland Pond shoreline to visit the lean-to. Perched atop an outcrop, the lean-to looks out at the lily-sprinkled pond and across its rim to Black Mountain.

Back on the loop (5 miles), follow the drainage upstream away from Lapland Pond, traveling along a soggy meadow with ash, birch, beech, and hemlock. Crossing over the drainage, the trail skirts an old beaver pond of silvered snags, wetland, and dark standing water. From the pond the trail descends mostly through hemlock woods.

At 5.75 miles the trail approaches the shore of a larger snag-congested pond. From the footbridge over the outlet, views span the drowned woods to Black Mountain. The woods become more mixed as the loop draws to a close at 6 miles; retrace the first mile to the trailhead.

29 Jockeybush Lake Trail

General description:	An easy climb through rich mixed forest follows the outlet drainage to attractive Jockeybush Lake.
General location:	20 miles northwest of Gloversville.
Special attractions:	Fishing, rich forest, woods flora, colorful fall foliage.
Length:	2.2 miles round-trip.
Difficulty:	Easy.
Maps:	Adirondack Mountain Club, Adirondack Southern Region map.
Special concerns:	Expect some soggy reaches.
Season and hours:	Spring through fall.
For information:	New York State Department of Environmental Conservation, Region 5.

Key points:
0.0   Trailhead; ascend west.
0.4   Cross outlet brook.
1.1   Jockeybush Lake; return by same route.

Finding the trailhead: From the junction of New York 29A and New York 10 in the village of Caroga Lake, go north on NY 10 for 14.6 miles, passing through the village of Canada Lake and the small hamlet of Arietta. Find

Jockeybush Lake Trail, Adirondack Park.

the marked trailhead and paved parking area on the left side of NY 10, across from a lily pond. Find the register on the left at the hike's start.

The hike: Head west, ascending into the woods and following the orange snowmobile markers. The mixed-age, multistory forest of white pine, hemlock, birch, black cherry, maple, and beech, along with hobblebush and ferns, weaves an enchanting tour. Sunlight filters through the branches, and often a breeze lilts through the woods. At 0.15 mile a pair of grand hemlocks stand sentinel.

At 0.3 mile cross a mud hole atop the disorganized scatter of logs left over from an old corduroy. The trail now travels the north shore above the outlet brook. Early in the hiking season, side drainages may complicate travel. Most times, however, the foot trail presents a pleasant, meandering tour.

Next cross the 10-foot-wide clear-flowing outlet brook atop stones; high water may require wading. At 0.5 mile a mossy cascade accents the outlet as it washes over outcrop. Where the trail grows rockier with wet, muddy pockets, evasive paths may disguise the true trail. Keep the outlet brook to your right. Soon the trail and brook become more closely paired, and hemlocks wane from the south bank forest.

By 0.9 mile ascend the ridge to the lake basin, again finding a good earthen path. Arriving at the lake, cross the beaver dam at the outlet, now crowded with silver logs, to reach a shoreline outcrop. It presents an open view spanning the length

2,250'		
2,000'	Outlet brook	Jockeybush Lake
1,750'		
1,500'	Trailhead	
Miles	1	2

Jockeybush Lake Trail

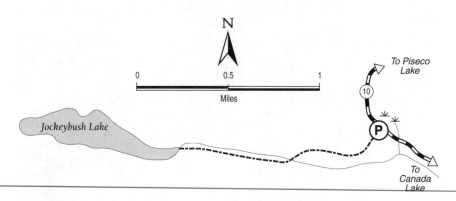

of this long, deep lake that takes in its shrub banks and enfolding conifer-deciduous rims.

Find a campsite above the outcrop. To round the shore to the main body of the lake requires some determination and bushwhacking through thick spruce and hobblebush.

Regularly stocked with fish, Jockeybush Lake offers anglers a challenge, if not always success. A fishing tube or small raft earns portage, freeing anglers from the shrubby entanglements of shore. Frogs and toads dwell lakeside, while insect hatches lift from the surface. Return as you came.

Niagara Frontier

At the northwestern extreme of New York State, the Niagara Frontier celebrates the migration west and the grand engineering feat of the Erie Canal. This land block boasts an inspired locale snuggled between Lake Erie to the west and Lake Ontario to the north. The Alleghenies nudge from the south, while the dramatic Finger Lakes Region shapes the frontier's east. Two famous rivers punctuated by raging falls grace the region, the Niagara and the Genesee.

Visitors to the area find lowland forest, plain, and swamp, with a comfortable rural backdrop beyond the frenzy of Buffalo and Rochester. The deep gouge of the Genesee River Gorge is the exception.

30 Erie Canal Heritage Trail

General description: The retired towpath of the Erie Canal provides a carefree avenue for hiking, cycling, jogging, and exercise walking, while tracing the past.

General location: Between Lockport and Rochester.

Special attractions: Historic canal, museum, lowland forest, rural setting, greenway parks, historic canal communities.

Length: 63 miles one-way from Lockport to Rochester. This hike description covers the 55 miles between Lockport and Henpeck Park because the trail grows more urban farther east.

Difficulty: Easy.

Maps: Recreational Map and Guide to New York State Canals, a New York State Canal Corporation brochure.

Special concerns: None.

Season and hours: Spring through fall, daylight hours.

For information: New York State Canal Corporation.

Key points:

0.0	Western trailhead (Lockport); follow northern towpath east.
6.0	Gasport.
10.0	Middleport.
15.0	Medina.
25.0	Albion.
35.0	Holley.
40.0	Brockport.
50.0	Spencerport.
55.0	End at Henpeck Park in town of Greece.

Erie Canal Heritage Trail

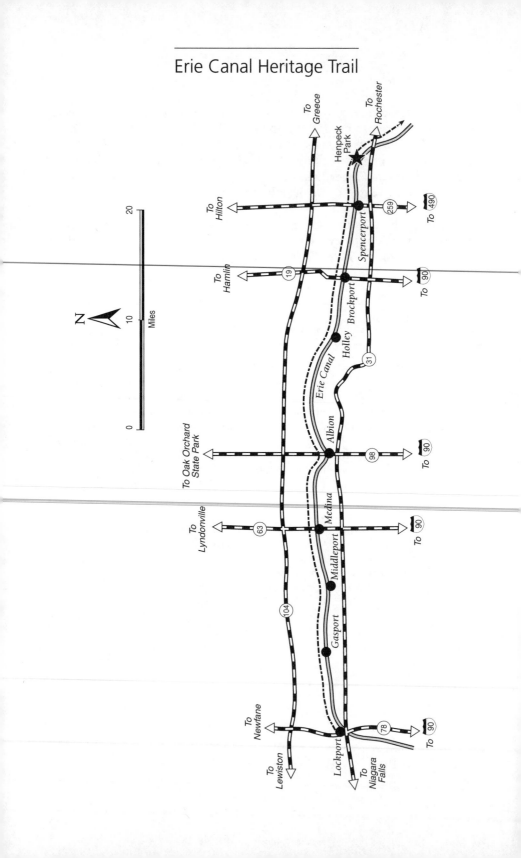

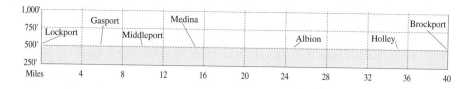

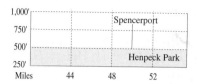

Finding the trailhead: Find the western terminus at Locks 34 and 35 in downtown Lockport at the corner of Cottage and Main Streets, opposite the Lockport Municipal Building and Visitor Center, where brochures are available. Multiple north-south roadways cross the canal trail, providing convenient access to or egress from the tour.

The hike: In the nineteenth century the Erie Canal linked the Hudson River to the Great Lakes, opening the remote western hinterlands to settlement and commerce. Today the historic canal serves recreationist, naturalist, and historian, offering a gentle escape from the settled, commercial world it fostered. The towpath variously shows a paved, fine cinder, gravel, or stone dust surface. The communities that sprang up along the canal continue to provide services and conveniences to canal travelers.

Making a west-to-east journey along the northern towpath, descend along Locks 34 and 35, where impressive gates of wood and steel close at an angle, sealed by the force of the water. Chambers fill and empty in fifteen minutes; boats rise to head west, drop to head east. Detour to the Canal Museum to find historic photos, artifacts, and accounts of this great engineering feat.

Where the trail crosses the grate of a thundering spillway, interpretive signs explain the operation and history of the canal. Dubbed the "Long Level," the canal tour from Lockport to Rochester is lock-free. At 0.25 mile the trail passes through tree-shaded Upson Park and travels a bypass route around the New York State Canal Corporation maintenance yard, one of a handful of breaks in the towpath tour.

Ensnared by wild grape and poison ivy, locust, mulberry (recalling an early venture into the silk industry), box elder, tall sumac, willow, cottonwood, walnut, and fruit trees shape an intermittent tree border. Queen Anne's lace, chicory, daisy, black-eyed Susan, mullein, tiger lily, and a dozen other wildflowers shower the trailside with color. As the sun can be harsh, carry plenty of drinking water. The canal typically funnels a cool breeze off the Great Lakes.

Orchards, cornfields, and cropland; farmhouses and silos; and historic homes compose much of the setting. The levee stands high enough above the flat terrain to provide a fine overview. Where marshes claim the levee base, cattails and loosestrife grow. Gulls, kingfishers, swallows, herons, and vultures may share the corridor.

At a few of the greenways, picnic tables and chemical toilets serve towpath travelers. A marina and a few primitive boat docks access the 60-foot-wide canal. Muggy summer days find local boys splashing about in the cool, murky green.

As the towpath passes through the small community of Gasport at about 6 miles, it crosses a site to release water. Here, as elsewhere along the tour, the primary community lies south of the canal. Single-lane bridges regularly span the canal and towpath; all date back to the 1910s.

Towns mark off the tour: Middleport (10 miles), Medina (15 miles), Albion (25 miles), Holley (35 miles), Brockport (40 miles), and Spencerport (50 miles). Attractive brick buildings with old-style business fronts add to their charm.

At about 17 miles the trail passes over Culvert Road, the only road that travels under the Erie Canal. Noted in *Ripley's Believe It or Not*, this 1823-built road shows a stone block construction and dripping archway. However, to appreciate the unusual feature, one must drive Culvert Road.

A few broad waters along the canal route break the trancelike spell of the continuous 60-foot band. Where the towpath approaches Albion (25 miles), ivy climbs an old brick chimney next to a weathered-board outbuilding and

Erie Canal and bikeway.

tower. Past Albion the riprap of the canal bank shows a reddish hue, giving the canal a new signature look.

At Fancher Bridge (about midway between Albion and Holley) the towpath surface changes to rock or coarse-grade gravel, making boots the preferred footwear. Here, too, the trail crosses over a watergate to an overflow pond.

A finer gravel surface leads to NY 260. East past Gallop Road Bridge, the towpath halts, putting hikers onto Canal Road for 0.2 mile. The tour then resumes on the northern towpath, where a canal breach feeds a lake on the south shore.

East past Brockport and Adams Basin the tree border fills out, casting shadows over the trail and closing out views. The landscape makes a transition from rural to rural-suburban. At Canal and Union in Spencerport, travelers may detour to Towpath Park on the south shore, a greenway with tables and benches—a likely stopping point.

Another potential end comes on the east side of the NY 386 bridge at the town of Greece's Henpeck Park (55 miles). In the 1800s Henpeck, the port of South Greece, boasted 8-Mile Grocery, a post office, school, apple dryhouse, two doctors, and a community of twenty-five homes. Briefly, the towpath is again paved.

To the east the towpath quickly changes to an urban route with some critical road crossings. At Long Pond Road cross over the road bridge, following Erie Canal Heritage Trail markers, to resume the eastbound tour along the south shore—now more an urban bike lane.

The route parallels NY 390 and requires a crossing of NY 31 (a feat of patience and good timing). More city road crossings and a railroad overpass advance the tour. At Lock 32 Canal Park (off NY 65), the trail arrives on the north shore, passing through the tree-shaded linear park and bringing home the tour at 63 miles. Painted blue and gold, Lock 32 and its gatehouse command the scene; an observation deck overlooks the lock.

31 Alabama Swamps Trails

Overview

Once the site of ancient Lake Tonawanda, the vast marshes north of Alabama represent a critical wildlife habitat and an exciting natural area. Together Iroquois National Wildlife Refuge and the adjoining New York State Wildlife Management Areas open the gate to some 20,000 acres of prime wetland, maintained in a fairly wild and protected state.

General description: Five easy walks scattered through this protected wetland introduce the habitat and its wildlife.
General location: 6 miles south of Medina.

Special attractions:	Bird-watching; nesting eagles; marshes, wet meadows, and wooded swamps; spring, summer, and fall wildflowers.
Length:	Selected trails range from 0.5 mile to 5 miles in length.
Difficulty:	Easy.
Maps:	Iroquois National Wildlife Refuge Trails and Overlooks brochure; Oak Orchard/Tonawanda Wildlife Management Areas brochure.
Special concerns:	Onondaga Nature Trail is off-limits to hiking during shotgun deer season, and hikers may want to avoid Feeder Road during its two months of hunting season. Contact the National Wildlife Refuge (NWR) for dates.
Season and hours:	Year-round, dawn to dusk. NWR Headquarters: 8:00 A.M. to 4:00 P.M. weekdays; also open weekends during the spring migration.
For information:	For Kanyoo, Feeder Road, Onondaga, and Swallow Hollow Trails, contact Iroquois National Wildlife Refuge. For the Oak Orchard Environmental Education Center trails contact the New York State Department of Environmental Conservation, Region 8.

Key points:

Kanyoo Trail:

    0.0   Kanyoo Trailhead.
    0.1   Loop junction; go right.
    0.9   Observation tower.
    1.1   Complete loop; return to trailhead.

Feeder Road:

    0.0   Feeder Road trailhead; follow gated road north.
    1.8   Fork (possible turnaround); continue straight.
    2.5   Dunlop Road gate; return by same route.

Onondaga Trail:

    0.0   Onondaga trailhead.
    0.3   End of marsh.
    1.5   Trail ends; return by same route.

Swallow Hollow Trail:

    0.0   Take boardwalk at south corner of Swallow Hollow parking.
    0.4   Cross side-water drainage.
    2.0   End loop at parking area.

Shoreline/Catwalk Hike:

    0.0   Oak Orchard Area; take leftmost trail at southeast corner of picnic area.
    0.5   End below pavilion.

Finding the trailhead: From the junction of New York 63 and New York 77 in Alabama, go north on NY 63 for 0.8 mile and turn left (west) on Casey Road to reach the refuge headquarters in 0.6 mile. Continue west on Casey Road another 0.8 mile and turn north on NY 77 (Lewiston Road) to reach the marked trailhead for Kanyoo Trail on the right in 0.9 mile. Gated Feeder Road lies east off NY 77, 300 feet farther north.

Alabama Swamps Trails

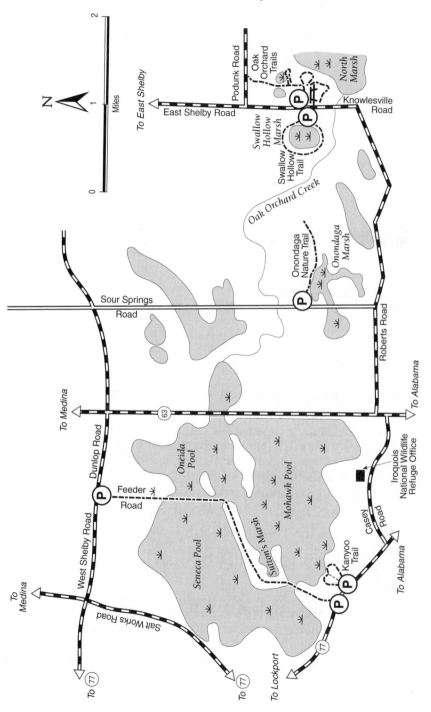

Kanyoo Trail

1,000' Trailhead
750'   Tower
500'   Loop   Close
250' junction loop
Miles   1

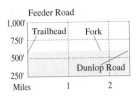

Feeder Road

1,000'
750'   Trailhead   Fork
500'
250'   Dunlop Road
Miles   1   2

Onondaga Trail

1,000'
750'   Trailhead
500'   Marsh
250'   edge
Miles   1

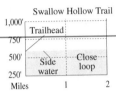

Swallow Hollow Trail

1,000' Trailhead
750'
500'   Side   Close
250'   water loop
Miles   1   2

Shoreline/Catwalk Hike

1,000' Trailhead
750'   Picnic
        area
500'
250'
Miles   1

For the other three trailheads, from the junction of Casey Road and NY 63 (east of the headquarters), go north on NY 63 for 0.1 mile and turn right (east) on Roberts Road. In 1.1 miles turn north on dirt Sour Springs Road to reach Onondaga Nature Trail on the right in 0.8 mile. For Swallow Hollow Trail and the Oak Orchard nature trails stay east on Roberts Road, go 1.5 miles past its intersection with Sour Springs Road, and turn north on Knowlesville Road. Find Swallow Hollow Trail on the left in 1.8 miles; Oak Orchard on the right, 0.1 mile farther north.

The hikes: The **Kanyoo Trail** doubles as a winter ski trail and has two interlocking, color-coded loops: blue and yellow. The external loop offers a 1.2-mile hike and includes the boardwalk section of the blue trail overlooking Mohawk Pool.

Begin to the right of the kiosk. Pass through a meadow of black-eyed Susan, chicory, and milkweed and cross over the wide swath of a ski trail to enter a woods of aspen, cherry, and silver and red maple. Go right on the blue trail for a counterclockwise tour. The route passes ski trails and benches, coming to the boardwalk at 0.5 mile. Shaggy-headed cattails, vegetated waters, snags, and bird boxes compose the view.

From the boardwalk the trail returns to a moist woodland. At 0.75 mile go right on the yellow trail to close the loop. An observation deck set back in the woods holds a tree-funneled look at Mohawk Pool. A few tulip trees join the mix as the tour draws to a close; stay right at the junctions.

At 2.5 miles long, gravel **Feeder Road** cuts south to north through a four-leaf clover of marsh pools, offering peripheral looks at the wetlands. To travel closer to the individual pools, hike along the dividing dikes, but remember that these side "trails" are closed during nesting season, March 1 to July 15; heed all posted notices.

The sun-exposed road tour passes between fields and a wetland mosaic of open water, cattail marsh, snags, and bulrushes. The far edge of the pools shows a broken tree line, but trees rarely grace the southern extent of the roadway. Where they do occur, cottonwood, sumac, maple, and elm compose the mix, with wild grape, honeysuckle, and brambles weaving a dense thicket. At times insects chew the leaves beyond recognition.

The road hugs the feeder canal except where the two bow apart at Sutton's Marsh. A cacophony fills the air. Heron, kingfisher, red-winged blackbird, geese, killdeer, and hawk prompt the raising of binoculars. Wildflowers spangle the roadside; black-eyed Susan and milkweed claim the field.

About midway find a house and gate. At the fork at 1.85 miles, follow the unkempt two-track straight ahead for Feeder Road. The now wooded corridor continues north to Dunlop Road in West Shelby. While the possibility for spying different birds exists, most hikers turn around at the fork. Be especially alert along this far end of the tour during hunting season.

At a separate location, **Onondaga Nature Trail** (3 miles round trip) visits Onondaga Marsh and the woodland to its east.

A gravel dike enters the refuge, dividing shallow Onondaga Marsh with its snags; cattail islands and mazes; aquatic mammal trails; and herons, ducks, geese, and muskrats. Vultures roost atop the snags. Milkweed, thistle, mullein, daisy, and other wildflowers color the tour. In the more extensive marsh, red maples win a foothold.

From the end of the marsh (0.3 mile), the trail passes from a fern meadow to a scenic woods of maple, ash, planted pine, aspen, and black cherry. Midway, the woods transition to hemlock, birch, and beech. The trail halts at a bench past a huge American beech. Seasonally, dogwoods and tulip trees sprinkle springtime through the canopy. Return as you came.

To the east, the 2-mile **Swallow Hollow Trail** lassos Swallow Hollow Marsh, traveling foot trail, boardwalk, and dike. Begin at the south corner of the parking area for a clockwise tour; the trail returns at the middle of the lot. Cottonwood, maple, ash, and hornbeam enclose the raised boardwalk, but hikers soon find the first marsh overlook.

Cattail, willow, buttonbush, and nightshade frame the scenic walkway as it alternates between cottonwood-maple woodland and willow-buttonbush habitat. At 0.4 mile the boardwalk ends after crossing a duckweed-painted side water. At the T-junction with a gravel dike, go right, traveling between the creek channel and a marsh woodland. Willow-buttonbush islands and bulrush bars add interest to the marshy terrain, as do the turtles sunning on logs. The trail concludes, touring hardwood forest, spruce plantation, and boardwalk.

Cattails, Oak Orchard Wildlife Management Area.

Across the way, at the Oak Orchard Wildlife Management Area Environmental Education Center, six unmarked interlocking trails radiate from the picnic pavilion to explore North Marsh. Mowed track, foot trail, and boardwalk explore the site's wetlands, ponds, fields, and woods.

The mowed path beneath the power pole to the north accesses the Orchard Trail, North Trail, and Old Field Trail, ending at Podunk Road. The three paths entering the woods at the southeast corner of the picnic area access the Shoreline and Catwalk Trails and eventually the link to Swallow Hollow.

For the chosen hike option, duck into the woods on the leftmost trail at the southeast corner of the picnic area for the 0.5-mile **Shoreline/Catwalk Hike.** The path passes through dense 10-foot-high shrubs, with aspen, honeysuckle, and herbaceous plants. Keep left to reach the rustic boardwalk of weathered wood overlooking the cattail marsh. Willow, maple, wild grape, and a bit of buttonbush frame the way. Tall cattails seal out the view from the bench at 0.3 mile, but the platform ahead applauds the vast open pond and textured mosaic of North Marsh. At 0.4 mile turn right to close the loop, coming out among the trees below the pavilion; the path straight ahead leads to Swallow Hollow, located across the road.

32 Tifft Nature Preserve

Overview

Near the Lake Erie shore, this 264-acre urban sanctuary marks a success story in land reclamation. Its low grassland hills (formerly a small landfill), wetland woods, thickets, ponds, and marsh support a thriving bird population while offering a peaceful retreat from Buffalo's city pace. Five miles of trail and three boardwalks tour the preserve.

General description:	Four easy nature walks examine most of the preserve's trails, ponds, and habitats.
General location:	In south Buffalo, 3 miles from downtown.
Special attractions:	Seventy-five-acre freshwater cattail marsh; bird and wildlife watching; flowering annuals, shrubs, and aquatic plants; viewing blinds; visitor center; Sunday guided walks.
Length:	Hikes range from a fraction of a mile to 1.3 miles.
Difficulty:	Easy.
Maps:	Preserve brochure.
Special concerns:	Entrance fee.
Season and hours:	Year-round, except holidays. Trails: dawn to dusk; center: 9:00 A.M. to 4:00 P.M., Tuesday through Sunday.
For information:	Tifft Nature Preserve.

Key points:

Mounds Trail:

    0.0   Mounds Trailhead; take left mowed path.

    0.1   First mound.

    0.2   Second mound; return to loop.

    0.6   Complete loop.

Mounds Bypass–Snakeroot Loop:

    0.0   Start at service road bridge; take Mounds Bypass Trail.

    0.4   Detour right for Warbler Walk.

    0.7   Mound vantage point; return to loop.

    1.3   End loop at service road bridge.

Berm Pond Hike:

    0.0   Start at service road bridge.

    0.3   Detour left to South Viewing Blind.

    0.7   End loop at service road bridge.

Heritage Boardwalk–North Viewing Blind Hike:

    0.0   Start at service road bridge; head northeast to Heritage Boardwalk.

    0.4   Turn right on Rabbit Run Trail.

    0.7   North Viewing Blind.

    1.0   Cross service road to Nettle Trail.

    1.2   Close loop; bear right to service road bridge.

Finding the trailhead: From New York 5 in south Buffalo, take the Tifft Street/Fuhrmann Boulevard exit. Westbound traffic, go 0.5 mile south from the exit, turn left under the freeway, and again turn left on a one-way road, merging with the traffic exiting from NY 5 East. Go 0.5 mile north on the one-way road to reach the preserve parking lot on the right (east). Locate the trailheads near the visitor center cabin or 0.1 east of the cabin, where the service road crosses a bridge over the southeast arm of Lake Kirsty.

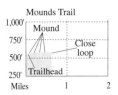

The hikes: The following four tours represent a few logical trail combinations for taking in the preserve highlights.

    The **Mounds Trail** is a 0.6-mile hike combining a loop and a spur to visit three of the nature preserve's four grassland mounds. On the opposite side of the road from the visitor center, three mowed tracks greet hikers. Take the left prong for a

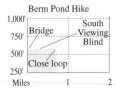

128

Tifft Nature Preserve

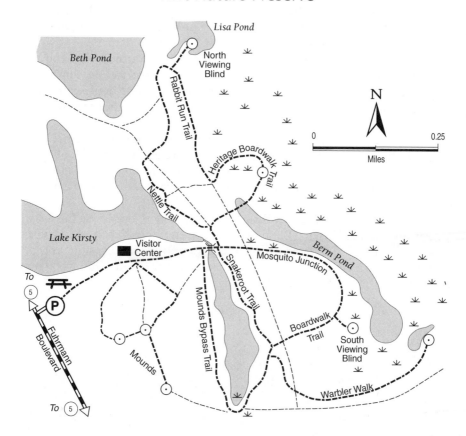

rolling clockwise tour. Grasses, bird's-foot trefoil, teasel, dandelion, butter-cup, vetch, chicory, and black-eyed Susan weave a wind-bowed carpet, while a few planted pines, fruit trees, and shrubs dot the slope.

The tops of the mounds present preserve overviews and views of the Lake Erie setting. Take in the close-by fields; lakes, ponds, and marshes; the Buf-falo city skyline; Lake Erie; and abandoned industrial buildings and grain elevators. At the first mound, a left adds the spur to the second mound; a right completes the loop, crossing over the third mound.

The 1.3-mile **Mounds Bypass–Snakeroot Loop** rounds the southeast arm of Lake Kirsty, with a Warbler Walk detour.

Begin a counterclockwise tour following the **Mounds Bypass Trail**, which starts near a pair of benches on the right just before the service road bridge. Bear left on the mowed track as it passes below the mounds, skirt-ing the lake rim of cottonwoods and shrubs. Blue and yellow wildflowers speckle the grasses, while dogwood, aspen, sumac, willow, mugwort, and viburnum fill out the lake buffer, screening out views. Songbirds enliven the area, and weathered beaver-cuttings may be discovered along shore.

Stay left, crossing the causeway; silvered snags rise up to the right. Just ahead, go left on the woodchip path of the **Snakeroot Trail** to continue the loop. Eight- to ten-foot high shrubs enclose the trail.

At 0.4 mile detour right on the wide, unmarked Warbler Walk and stay on it, passing a bench and crossing over a service road before coming out at an open marsh view. Snags claim this end of the marsh, dense cattails the far end. Tree swallows roost in the small snags; often a night heron hunches near shore.

As the Warbler Walk continues, views grow restricted until the trail ends atop a 10-foot-high mound (0.75 mile). From here enjoy a grand look at the cattail sea, with South Viewing Blind across the way. Highway noise, shipping traffic on Lake Erie, and a silent industrial plant confirm that this is indeed an urban wild.

Return to the **Snakeroot Trail** and resume the loop, bypassing the Boardwalk Trail to South Viewing Blind. A spur to the left offers an open lake vista, where on our visit a painted turtle had chosen to lay her eggs; yield right-of-way to nature. At a second spur to shore, a beaver-felled cottonwood may offer seating. Close the loop at the bridge.

Heritage Boardwalk, Tifft Nature Center.

Start the **Berm Pond Hike,** a 0.7-mile loop, by crossing the bridge and going right where the service road forks. At the junction in 0.1 mile, proceed straight ahead to travel the elevated boardwalk of Mosquito Junction, skirting Berm Pond.

At some 5 to 6 feet off the ground, the walk parts a dense stand of tall feathery-headed phragmites; midwalk is an observation deck. Aquatic plants coat the pond's surface, as does a dandruff of cottonwood seeds. Cattail, loosestrife, and bulrush contribute to the marsh tapestry. A foot trail continues the tour, passing within a scenic cottonwood wetland.

At 0.3 mile find a second boardwalk curving left to South Viewing Blind; the earthen trail ahead holds the loop's return. South Viewing Blind consists of a broad open-air deck masked by a 7-foot wall, overlooking the marsh and Berm Pond. Circular and oval cutouts allow visitors to manipulate their cameras, binoculars, and scopes for ideal viewing.

Return to the 0.3-mile junction (0.4 mile) and follow the earthen trail left. Turn right on either the service road or Snakeroot Trail to end the loop at the bridge.

Start the **Heritage Boardwalk–North Viewing Blind Hike,** a 1.2-mile loop, by crossing the bridge and going left at the service road fork. In 250 feet turn right to follow the wood-shavings path amid cottonwoods, nettles, shrubs, and mugwort to Heritage Boardwalk, which cuts the end of Berm Pond and extends overlooks of the aquatic vegetation. Cattail and phragmites shape a wetland border and form island clusters. Red-winged blackbirds, tree swallows, and frogs animate the scene. Benches invite study.

The boardwalk ends in a sea of cattails, replaced by an earthen trail through willow habitat. At 0.4 mile meet Rabbit Run Trail, a former railroad bed now favored by eastern cottontails, and turn right on the grassy lane.

Cottonwood, aspen, sumac, and white-berried shrubs shape the aisle. At the next junction, go right for North Viewing Blind; straight holds the return. Trail and boardwalk reach the blind in 0.1 mile. A 7-foot wall with viewing cutouts overlooks Lisa Pond, where duckweed, duck potato, and arrow arum coat and claim the shallows. Snags and nesting boxes pierce the pond, and a former grain elevator on the Buffalo River looms over the north end of the marsh.

Resume the counterclockwise tour on Rabbit Run, touring an open corridor of cottonwoods and shrubs. Bypass the right turn to Beth Pond and continue straight ahead. Where the trail crosses over a service road at 1 mile, follow the Nettle Trail along the thick shrub border of Lake Kirsty, but beware of the signature nettle. Where the Nettle Trail again meets the service road, turn right to close the loop in a few strides.

33 Letchworth State Park

Overview

Letchworth State Park encompasses the 17-mile-long Genesee River Gorge, featuring three major waterfalls as well as some elegant side-creek falls, the 400- to 600-foot sheer sandstone-shale cliffs, points of historical note, and second-growth forest. Numbered trails explore the developed park of the west rim; four of these provide a survey of the area.

General description:	The four walks of varying length hug the rim and overlook the falls on the Genesee River, tag the river shore, travel a spine between the river and Silver Lake Outlet, and visit a historic grave.
General location:	35 miles south of Rochester.
Special attractions:	Genesee River Gorge, falls, cliffs, vistas, museum, memorials, historic Glen Iris Inn.
Length:	Gorge Trail, 7.75 miles one-way; Saint Helena Trail, 1.6 miles round trip (exploring both river accesses); Kisil Point Trail, 2.8 miles round-trip; Mary Jemison Trail, 2.5-mile loop.
Difficulty:	Easy.
Maps:	State park map.
Special concerns:	Entrance fee.
Season and hours:	Spring through fall, 6:00 A.M. to dusk.
For information:	Letchworth State Park.

Key points:
Gorge Trail:
- 0.0 Upper trailhead; hike rim downstream.
- 0.2 Upper Falls view.
- 0.7 Middle Falls viewing deck.
- 1.4 Inspiration Point.
- 2.4 Spur right to Lower Falls area.
- 5.6 Great Bend Viewing Area.
- 6.6 Wolf Creek.
- 7.7 End at Saint Helena Trail.

Saint Helena Trail:
- 0.0 Saint Helena Picnic Area trailhead; descend.
- 0.1 Junction.
- 0.3 Genesee River shore via Trail 13; backtrack to junction.
- 0.8 Genesee River shore via two-track.
- 1.0 End of river bar; return to picnic area (1.6 miles).

Kisil Point Trail:
- 0.0 Campground trailhead; follow Trail 18.
- 0.4 Loop junction; head right.
- 0.9 Loop junction; proceed forward.
- 1.4 Kisil Point; backtrack to resume loop and return to trailhead (2.8 miles).

Letchworth State Park

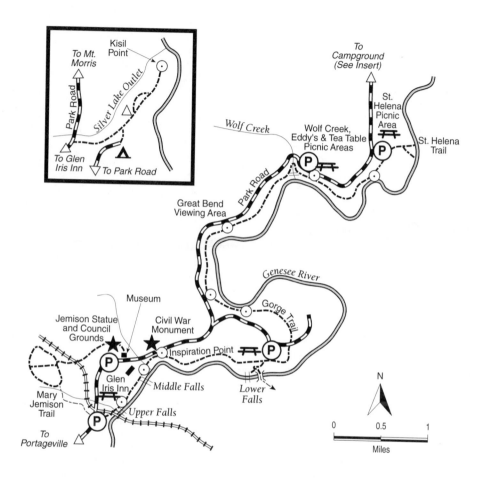

Mary Jemison Trail:

- 0.0 Museum Trailhead; head west.
- 0.1 Council Grounds.
- 0.2 Trail 2.
- 0.7 Loop junction; go left.
- 1.8 Complete loop; return to trailhead.

Finding the trailhead: From the New York 36–New York 408 junction in the village of Mount Morris, go north on NY 36 for 1.1 miles and turn left, reaching the Mount Morris entrance to the state park in 0.4 mile. From Mount Morris entrance, find the trailheads off the main park road. Locate Kisil Point Trail 4 miles south, Saint Helena Trail 10.8 miles south, Mary Jemison Trail/Council Grounds 14.9 miles south, and the Gorge Trail (upper trailhead) 15.8 miles south (0.4 mile north of the southern entrance).

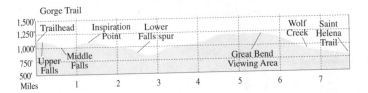

Gorge Trail

Miles							
1,500'	Trailhead	Inspiration	Lower			Wolf	Saint
1,250'		Point	Falls spur			Creek	Helena Trail
1,000'					Great Bend		
750'	Upper Falls	Middle Falls			Viewing Area		
500'	1	2	3	4	5	6	7

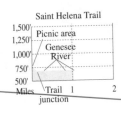

Saint Helena Trail

1,500' — Picnic area
1,250'
1,000' — Genesee River
750'
500'
Miles — Trail junction — 1 — 2

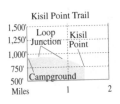

Kisil Point Trail

1,500' — Loop Junction — Kisil Point
1,250'
1,000'
750'
500' — Campground
Miles — 1 — 2

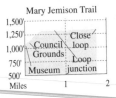

Mary Jemison Trail

1,500'
1,250' — Close loop
1,000' — Council Grounds — loop
750' — Loop junction
500' — Museum
Miles — 1 — 2

The hikes: The popular **Gorge Trail** (Trail 1) represents the premier hiking tour within the developed park. For a downstream tour, cross the park road from the upper trailhead parking lot, pass under the railroad bridge, and follow the rockwork steps that switchback downhill to the gorge rim. The first rim vista (0.25 mile) overlooks the 70-foot horseshoe drop of Upper Falls. A plume of mist shoots up and out from the white rushing fury, nurturing the green cloak of the east wall. Only the heavy railroad footings from High Bridge steal from the natural wonder and photographer's image.

As the well-groomed trail continues, it presents new perspectives. Basswood, maple, oak, and spruce overhang the route; poison ivy drapes the edging stone wall and abrupt slope to the river. As the trail skirts a landscaped day-use area, it offers downstream looks at the delicate streamers of side-creek falls and the bulging west cliff.

Next find a side perspective of a waterfall of Niagara proportion—Middle Falls. A viewing deck below Glen Iris Inn (0.75 mile) serves up a grand look at this 107-foot-high, 285-foot-wide waterfall, which thunders over an abrupt river ledge. The hike follows the yellow blazes up and away from the inn.

From this point on, the trail frequently travels the thin woods-and-grass buffer between the rim and the park road. After passing through a mixed evergreen stand planted in 1917, look for an obelisk dedicated to New York's First Dragoons of the Civil War. It occupies a roadway island green.

At Inspiration Point, a roadside vista at 1.4 miles, obtain an upstream view of Middle and Upper Falls and High Bridge. Interpretive signs now mark the tour; views come piecemeal.

Travel the rim, descending its tiers. In another mile come to the side trail with 127 steps descending to Lower Falls. A broad vista deck, a river bridge, and a 0.1-mile upstream spur present this 50- to 60-foot waterfall that shows a slight crescent along with an entourage of cascades. From the bridge, examine the platy shale and sandstone seams of the cliff.

Retrace your steps and resume the downstream hike at 3.25 miles, skirting below the Lower Falls day-use area. Hemlock and beech offer a rich shade. At the junction at 3.5 miles, bear right, bypassing a restaurant to again travel near the park road. At 4.25 and 4.75 miles, hikers again share roadside vistas with motorists, now overlooking Big Bend. Copper-gilded vultures soar on the thermals.

At 5.65 miles tag Great Bend Viewing Area to overlook the dizzying 550-foot cliffs, scoured bowl, and muddy green Genesee River. Afterward, descend fairly steeply, crossing a footbridge over a charming side water. Still the trail flip-flops from rim to road. At 6.6 miles the Gorge Trail explores

Genesee River Gorge, Letchworth State Park.

the beauty at Wolf Creek, with views of the eroded and fluted river cliffs, the broad Genesee River, and twisting Wolf Creek Falls within its own narrow canyon.

Now skirt the picnic areas of Wolf Creek, Tea Table, and Saint Helena, with their rustic stone-and-slab tables. The Gorge Trail ends at the lower Saint Helena Picnic Area, where it meets the Saint Helena Trail, Trail 13.

The **Saint Helena Trail** serves hiker, angler, and kayaker. It contours downhill through an open-canopied forest, reaching a three-way junction at 0.1 mile. Follow Trail 13 straight ahead or take the two-track to the right; both reach the river bar. Depending on river flow, a divided bar may greet hikers and require some wading to reach the main river channel. The trail extends a grand interior perspective on the gorge but a limited river acquaintance. Cottonwood, wild grape, grasses, and willow vegetate the bar. Return as you came.

Kisil Point Trail (Trail 18) offers a look at the Genesee River farther downstream and may be accessed from either Highbanks Campground (near Loop 100) or a roadside trailhead. The roadside trail merges near the campground trailhead. Travel the piney outskirts of camp past an old picnic shelter to arrive at a loop junction at 0.4 mile.

The right fork travels the Genesee River side of Kisil Point Ridge; the left fork overlooks Silver Lake Outlet. Go right for a counterclockwise tour. Pine plantation and a mixed deciduous woods cloak the thin, sharp ridge.

At 0.9 mile the spurs of the loop reunite. Continue forward to the end of the ridge and Kisil Point (1.4 miles). The view encompasses the tinsel stream of Silver Lake Outlet as it parts a thick swath of green and the Genesee River Canyon, with its steep gray cliffs, eroded silt skirts, and broad floodplain. Return to the junction at 0.9 mile and complete the loop, coming out at the picnic shelter. Retrace the initial hike distance.

The **Mary Jemison Trail** (Trail 2) honors a white-woman captive who came to revere the Seneca Indians with whom she lived. The trail begins at the museum and travels to Council Grounds, where a statue of Mary Jemison, an 1800s pioneer cabin, and a tribal Council House predating the American Revolution suggest a detour.

The trail then heads west and negotiates a series of confusing junctions; follow the number "2." The trail tours mixed woods of beech, maple, birch, and basswood; hemlock stands; and pine plantation to visit a couple of linear reservoirs. Evidence of beaver activity surrounds the ponds; in the woods deer commonly cross paths with hikers. Woods road and foot trail shape this rolling tour.

34 Letchworth Trail

General description:	This linear foot trail along the eastern rim of the Genesee River Gorge travels mixed woods and snares occasional river overlooks and grand waterfall views.
General location:	Letchworth State Park, 35 miles south of Rochester.
Special attractions:	Genesee River Gorge with its three major waterfalls and plummeting sandstone-shale cliffs, seasonal cascades and falls, historic canal and rail corridor, wildlife sightings, lush forest, colorful fall foliage.
Length:	26.5 miles one-way, including vista side spurs.
Difficulty:	Moderate.
Maps:	Letchworth State Park map; Finger Lakes Trail Conference (FLTC) maps, The Letchworth Trail L1 and L2.
Special concerns:	None.
Season and hours:	Spring through fall, 6:00 A.M. to dusk.
For information:	Letchworth State Park.

Key points:

0.0	Northern trailhead; hike south.
0.6	Overlook/picnic area.
5.5	Powerline corridor; spur to river vista.
10.0	Fiddler's Elbow Viewpoint.
12.5	Old Forks Ravine View.
17.2	Small log shelter.
18.4	Cross abandoned Saint Helena Road.
24.4	Pass below Parade Grounds Picnic Area.
25.0	Middle and Upper Falls view.
26.5	Southern trailhead, Portageville.

Finding the trailhead: For the northern trailhead, from the New York 36–New York 408 junction in Mount Morris, go south on NY 408 (Chapel Street) toward Nunda. In 1.8 miles turn right for Mount Morris Dam. In another 1.7 miles turn left to reach the dam overlook, parking area, and trailhead 0.1 mile ahead. Find the southern terminus in Portageville at the northeast corner of the NY 436 bridge, with off-road parking for a handful of vehicles.

The hike: A north-to-south tour between Mount Morris Dam and Portageville travels the undeveloped eastern rim of the Genesee River Gorge, rolling through mixed forest, pine plantation, and meadow scrub. Ravines punctuate the tour, prescribing the line of travel. While few in number, the river vistas are prized, especially along the trail's south end, where rim overlooks applaud two of the three river falls. Solitude abounds, and wildlife sightings vary, with turkey, raccoon, fox, grouse, deer, beaver, frog, and skunk.

Part of the greater Finger Lakes Trail (FLT), the Letchworth Trail is well marked with yellow paint blazes, FLT markers, and trail registers. The white

Letchworth Trail

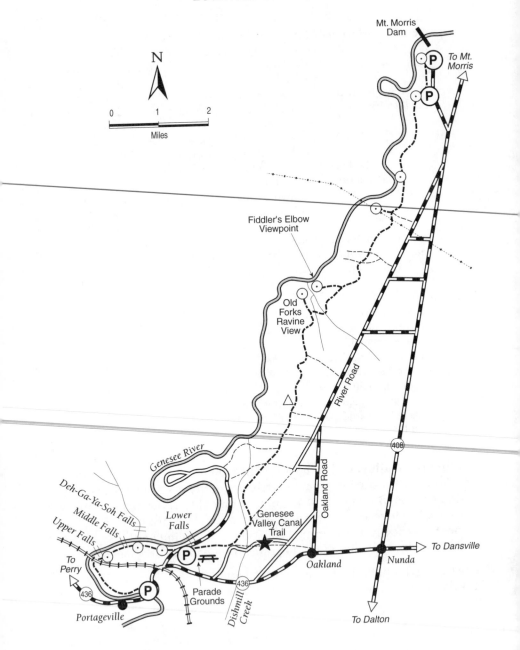

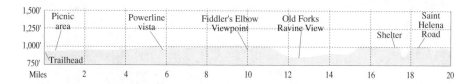

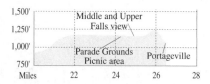

spurs to the left lead to access points off River Road and opportunities to shorten the tour. The spurs to the right lead to river overlooks. Numbers indicate the Letchworth State Park trails.

Take a moment to enjoy an overlook of the dam before hiking the FLT south (upstream) from the end of the parking lot. Vultures often roost atop the dam; cliffs and the broad green floodplain contribute to the view. The flat trail passes through a corridor of oak, aspen, maple, pine, and hickory, staying mostly within 10 feet of the rim's edge.

At 0.6 mile cross the groomed lawn of a picnic and overlook site maintained by Mount Morris Dam. The view brings together the peninsular ridge of Hogback, a pinched river bend, the developed west rim of Letchworth State Park, and the rural countryside beyond. Gravel and boardwalk ease wet-area travel. Poison ivy, Virginia creeper, waterleaf, witch hazel, birch, and basswood fill out the sides of the corridor.

Find the first of the ravines at 1.6 miles; many more follow. The trail becomes more rolling as it travels the rim plateau, distanced from the edge. Seasonally, the ravines carry water and show small cascades; a few ravines show the remains of old structures.

At 3.1 miles a 50-foot side trail leads to an open vista atop a loose mud-shale slope; stay well back of the dangerous eroding point. Fog sometimes claims the canyon, alternately masking and unmasking the cliff's ragged spires, ribs, and points. A half mile ahead, the bending river canyon again draws hikers aside. Where the trail edges a couple of fields with brushing shrubs, be careful of the trailing wire of old fences.

At 4.6 miles the FLT bears right as a side trail heads left to the road; a pine stand next claims the way. Where the trail crosses the width of a powerline corridor, an 0.8-mile round-trip detour west along the corridor finds a river view.

On the southbound tour, large oaks contrast with the tall thin trees composing much of the mixed forest. Where the FLT meets the northern segment of Trail 16 (a mowed track at 7.5 miles), continue south, passing

Middle Falls, Letchworth State Park.

through a tight moist corridor of mixed woods and shrubs to cross a second mowed track of Trail 16. Crows raise a noisy filibuster. Stay on the yellow trail, next entering a plantation of spiny-armed pines.

To the right at 9.6 miles, white blazes mark a detour to Fiddler's Elbow Viewpoint. Travel a deciduous flat and low ridge to the open vista. Hemlock and beech claim the ridge as it overlooks the gorge. Resume the rim hike south at 10.4 miles. Orange and red mushrooms and yellow fungi pepper the tour. The understory varies from the barren pine plantations to a crush of flora in the moist woods.

Where the trail exits from a deep, steep-forked ravine at 12.1 miles, look for another white-disk trail heading toward the river for a scenic view. It travels the spine of a thin wooded ridge between the forked ravine to the right and a bowled ravine to the left. At the tip, Old Forks Ravine View offers a fine canyon overlook. The river far below shows a split flow; cottonwood, willow, aspen, and meadow shrubs and flora weave a textured river tapestry.

Resume south on the FLT at 13 miles. Encounter some stately trees, including a gnarly old oak with eighteen major arm branchings (16.6 miles). At 17.2 miles a small log shelter is to the right of the trail. Another road access follows, and the ravines shape steeper climbs and descents. At 18.4 miles cross the overgrown road to the abandoned hamlet of Saint Helena.

Follow the woods road of Trail 9 to the left at 19.6 miles. Shortly the FLT splits away left, only to cross Trail 9 and tour a dark hemlock stand. Where the FLT crosses Trail 9 one last time, ascend the rim of Dishmill Creek, overlooking the many beaver enhancements. As the trail descends, cross a side drainage and bypass a big oak and big shagbark hickory.

At 21.3 miles the FLT comes out on a closed section of River Road (Trail 8) and follows it to the right, crossing the culvert of Dishmill Creek. Leave the road at 22.5 miles and round the gate to the right, as the Genesee Valley Greenway Trail (Trail 7) continues the tour.

A tracked earthen path paints a black stripe down the grassy lane of what once was the Pennsylvania Railroad; alongside it find the ditch of the 1862–1878 Genesee Valley Canal. A beaver pond and lodge mark the old canal, as do reeds, ferns, young woods, and the occasional cattail patch. Birch, basswood, beech, maple, and tulip trees lace over the trail, weaving a scenic green tunnel, but ravenous mosquitos can speed steps.

At 24.4 miles exit onto and cross the park road below Parade Grounds Picnic Area and follow the greenway to the river's rim. At 24.6 miles flat rocks at the rim's edge serve up a spectacular look at the 400-foot cliffs both upstream and directly across the river. Deep in the canyon, the broad Genesee River flows over outcrop. To the right at 25 miles a cross-canyon look finds the 200-foot waterfall on Deh-Ga-Ya-Soh Creek. Nearby, a short side trail serves up a view of the 107-foot Middle and 70-foot Upper Falls, with a look at High Bridge (a railroad bridge) spanning the canyon.

Between Middle and Upper Falls, a landslide currently breaches the rim trail, but the remaining trail fragments still provide vistas of each plummet. Hikers just need to take a few more strides to detour safely around the slide to round up the now-isolated vistas. (Although park authorities are investigating whether the hillside can be stabilized and reopened, in the meantime take the indicated detour.)

Upper Falls is a powerful, surging horseshoe falls that seemingly courses right at the spectator. The upstream cascades dazzle in their own right. From Upper Falls the rolling FLT continues upstream to emerge at the NY 436 bridge in Portageville at 26.5 miles.

Chautauqua-Allegheny Region

This region occupies the southern corner of western New York, shaped by Lake Erie and the Pennsylvania border. The region includes the long flat summits and V-shaped valleys of the Allegheny Mountains, the Upper Genesee River, and Chautauqua Lake and Creek Gorge. The region puts forth a soothing landscape of hardwood-evergreen forests, boulder realms, wildflower meadows, and relaxing waters—the ideal escape for the frazzled and harried.

35 Deer Lick Nature Sanctuary

Overview

This hike presents the tranquil beauty of a 400-acre National Natural Landmark that wins over visitors with familiarity versus drama. Quiet hardwood forests, dark hemlock stands, lush meadows, and gentle creeks are the hallmarks of this sanctuary owned by The Nature Conservancy (TNC). Bordered to the north by the South Branch Cattaraugus Creek and New York State's Zoar Valley Multiple Use Area, the sanctuary completes the puzzle of unbroken open space that forms a vital natural wildlife corridor.

General description: A relaxed day hike strings together the four color-coded trails of this sanctuary.

General location: 4 miles southeast of Gowanda.

Special attractions: Mixed hardwood-hemlock forests, abandoned pasture, meadows, spring wildflowers, fall foliage, quiet.

Length: 5 miles round-trip; shorter tours possible.

Difficulty: Easy.

Maps: Sanctuary map; locator maps posted along the white trail.

Special concerns: No pets, smoking, or picnicking; obey all posted TNC rules.

Season and hours: Spring through fall, daylight hours.

For information: The Nature Conservancy, Central and Western New York Office.

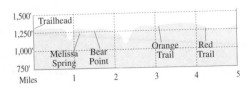

Deer Lick Nature Sanctuary

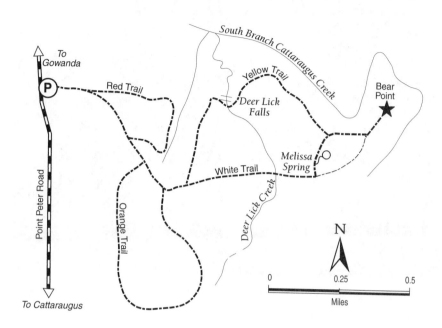

Key points:

0.0	Trailhead; follow white trail east into sanctuary.
1.0	Melissa Spring Loop junction; head left.
1.1	Melissa Spring.
1.4	Bear Point; backtrack to take yellow trail (1.6 miles).
3.1	Follow 1.1-mile orange trail left.
4.3	Follow 0.6-mile red trail to right.
5.0	Conclude at parking area.

Finding the trailhead: From central Gowanda, go south on New York 62 for 0.5 mile and turn left (east) on Hill Street. In 0.4 mile turn right on Broadway Road, and in another 0.6 mile turn left on Point Peter Road. Stay on Point Peter Road for 2.3 miles and turn left to enter the sanctuary (0.5 mile past the Point Peter Road–Forty Road fork). Find a small parking area, trail register, and pit toilets near the trail's start.

The hike: The white trail, which traverses the sanctuary from west to east, serves as the main artery; the side-branching colored loops, the capillaries. As forest duff can mask the footpaths, keep a keen eye for paint blazes, some of which are faded. For this tour stay to the white trail entering the sanctuary; pick up the colored trails on the return.

Step over the cable, following a mowed swath east through a transition zone where wild raspberry, milkweed, and daisy grow in the field; sumac, apple, and black locust frame the route. To the right lies a small cattail marsh.

Forest canopy, Deer Lick Nature Sanctuary.

Keep an eye out for a good-sized American chestnut to the left. This nearly lost species of the plant world has beaten the odds, achieving bloom in 1995. Most of these trees fall victim to a pervasive blight before reaching the size and maturity of this tree. The chestnut was a food staple of native peoples and early settlers.

Past the first junction, a mixed woodland draped by woody vines claims the earthen trail as it traverses a low ridge. At 0.3 mile a gap in the tree cover offers an open look at the ridges rolling away to the northeast. Where the trail mildly descends, eastern hemlock, beech, and big-toothed aspen compose the canopy. Bird notes fill the air. At 0.75 mile a spring muddies the trail and, despite rustic corduroys, proves a nemesis to members of the white-sneaker set.

The white trail crosses Deer Lick Creek, ascends, coming to the 1-mile junction with the yellow trail and Melissa Spring Trail. For this hike turn left for Melissa Spring. The white trail dead-ends in 0.2 mile on a small ridge and wooded plateau characterized by huge beech trees. The treed rim denies views, save for seasonal glimpses. Do not try to better your view; the cliffs are dangerous and subject to erosion.

Follow the dual yellow-and-white blazes through hemlock-hardwood forest to Melissa Spring in 0.1 mile. Mud again precedes the spring. At 1.2 miles reach the next junction. Here turn right to add the spur to Bear Point before taking the yellow loop.

In a couple hundred feet, the trail curves right to top the rim edge of a steep slope dropping to a U-bend on the South Branch Cattaraugus Creek, but trees again restrict view. Ahead, at the T-junction go left to spur onto the actual nose of the rim (Bear Point) at 1.4 miles, which still denies views but is attractive with sounds of the creek; to the right is the southern half of the Melissa Loop.

From Bear Point backtrack the northern half of Melissa Loop, picking up the 1.4-mile yellow loop for a counterclockwise tour at 1.6 miles. This rolling tour traverses a scenic mature hemlock-hardwood plateau and low ridge before dipping sharply to Deer Lick Creek. Hike upstream a few steps to find the crossing; high water may dictate wading. A waterfall sounds downstream, but the trail provides no views.

The yellow trail next ascends through hardwood forest, passes through a disturbed area of windfalls and snags, and then travels a young maple woodlot ensnared by vines. Ferns dress the floor. Beautiful beech trees claim the rise above the path as it rejoins the white trail (3 miles); head right.

In 0.1 mile follow the 1.1-mile orange loop left for a clockwise tour and rolling descent. An old orchard and meadow lie beyond the hemlock-hardwood forest of the trail. The orange loop next follows a small ribbony drainage upstream, touring a moist bottomland of woods and meadow, finding muddy pockets and downfalls to cross.

The trail then ascends steeply near the headwater forks, touring stands of hemlock and hardwood or young maple and mature tulip trees to return to the white trail. Turn left to continue toward the parking lot and to reach the red trail.

At 4.3 miles find the 0.6-mile red loop heading right. The trail tours a tight stand of small maples and a hemlock rim, overlooking first an abandoned pasture and then a small drainage before entering the pasture meadow at a gas well. Go right on the overgrown two-track as it swings into the meadow. At the junction in 250 feet, turn left, wading through the tall grasses of yet another doubletrack.

A few abandoned apple trees, popular with area deer, and maple dot the meadow. Black-eyed Susan, milkweed, daisy, clover, and spotted knapweed spangle the tall grasses. The doubletrack gives way to a woods road before meeting the white trail; bear right to return to the parking area at 5 miles.

36 The Fred J. Cusimano Westside Overland Trail

General description: This long-distance linear trail strings through a series of state forests in Chautauqua County. The multiple trailheads allow hikers to vary the hike's length; established shelters allow overnight stays and stargazing.

General location: Chautauqua County, east of Sherman and west of Panama.

Special attractions: Changing forest, meadow and pond habitats, agricultural easements, rural and forest views, wildlife, solitude, overnight shelters.

Length: 24 miles one-way; this hike focuses on the northern 19 miles between trailheads A and Q (see brochure).

Difficulty: Easy to strenuous, depending on length of hike and amount of gear carried.

Maps: *The Fred J. Cusimano Westside Overland Trail* brochure (necessary to locate trailheads; has incremental mileages for shortening hike into segments).

Special concerns: Some sections overgrown or subject to mud. Respect easements through and along private lands, which are open to hikers only. No camping within 150 feet of road, trail, or water and none on private land. Overnight forest stays for more than three nights at a single site require a New York Department of Environmental Conservation (DEC) permit. All DEC rules apply for fire building and wood collecting. Trailheads are well signed, with the trail generally well blazed.

Season and hours: Year-round; spring through fall for hiking.

For information: Chautauqua County Visitors Bureau.

Key points:

0.0	Northern trailhead; hike south.
3.0	Cross New York 430.
6.5	Shelters.
9.3	Cross under Southern Tier Expressway (Interstate 86).
12.6	Enter Edward J. Whalen Memorial State Forest.
14.8	Follow Eggleston Hill Road left.
15.5	Enter North Harmony State Forest.
16.4	Panama Campsite shelters.
19.2	Hike ends at New York 474 Trailhead (west of Panama).

Finding the trailhead: For the northern terminus, from Interstate 86 take exit 6 at Sherman, go north 0.4 mile on New York 476, turning right (east) on NY 430. Proceed 7.3 miles and turn left on Hannum Road. Follow Hannum Road for 3.1 miles to find the trailhead at road's end (last 0.8 mile on dirt). For the hike's southern terminus, from the junction of NY 474 and County Road 33 in the village of Panama (5.6 miles south of I–86), go 1.8 miles west on NY 474. Trailhead parking is north off NY 474.

The hike: On a north to south trek, from the southwest corner of the Hannum Road trail parking, round the boulder barricade to ascend the blue-blazed

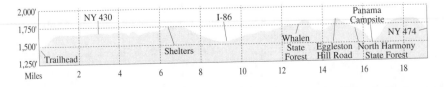

The Fred J. Cusimano Westside Overland Trail

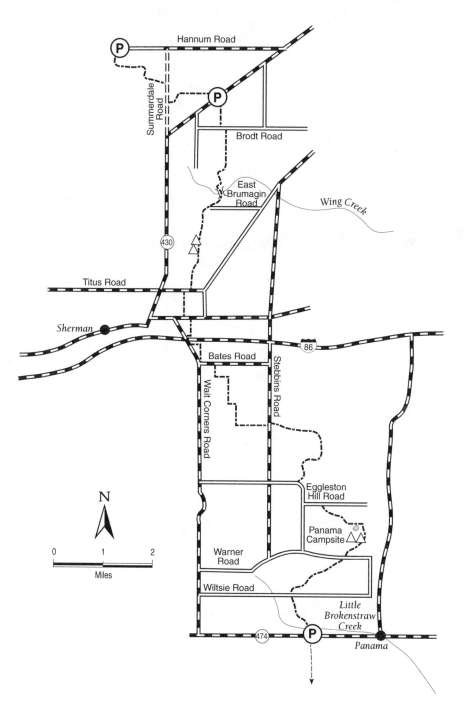

trail south into Chautauqua State Forest. North is Chautauqua Gorge. Pass through second-growth woods of maple, black locust, ash, and hop hornbeam. A meadowy shrub ground cover spills beneath the trees. After traversing the lower end of a field, the trail returns to woods. A closed road and drainage crossings mark off distance before the trail emerges at Summerdale Road (1 mile).

Follow the roadway right (south) 0.5 mile to resume the trail, heading left (east). Private land abuts the trail to its left. Pass through a similar woods, later finding stands of hemlock and beech. At the small drainages fish or frogs may be spied. At a field at 2.5 miles, the trail briefly follows an overgrown vegetated path to return to forest.

At 3 miles the trail crosses NY 430 to arrive at a large trailhead parking lot and enter Mt. Pleasant State Forest at the lot's east side. Beyond a meadow break, a tree-shaded mowed track leads the way. Oaks appear in the upper canopy. Ferns, wild raspberry, horsetail reed, and poison ivy appear in the vegetation tangle. As the trail climbs and levels, find a return of the earthen bed. Where the trail traverses a bog, planted spiny-armed spruce and hardwoods face off. Forest changes vary travel.

At 3.8 miles cross Brodt Road, a single-lane dirt country road with tiger lilies adorning its sides. A deep, dark, dense spruce grove next swallows or is edged by the trail. Where a log walk spans a bog, aspens and pines appear. A few muddy strides exceed the reach of the logs. Eventually maples become the dominant tree, and the trail shows modest uphill grade.

Bear right where a grassy track merges on the left to journey through a more-mixed woods and begin a gentle descent. Again, a log walk spans a bog. An occasional big, old maple or beech may attract note. The trail then drops down to a footbridge crossing of a creek. Watch for arrows and blazes showing the changes in direction. After crossing a gravel road and a couple more creek bridges, arrive at East Brumagin Road at 5.75 miles.

Follow East Brumagin Road to the right for 0.3 mile to resume the forest trek south on an old woods road. A richly mixed forest leads to a pair of three-sided log shelters at 6.5 miles. Shelters are available first come, first serve and have tables, trash cans, fire rings or barbecues, a working well, and pit toilet. Beyond the shelters follow the dirt road right for 0.1 mile to resume southbound, all well blazed. A younger, less abundant woods hosts travel.

The trail rolls, passing from red pine plantation to field. To the left is a man-made pond visited by geese and ringed by grass and shrubs. The trail resumes in the young transition woods reclaiming the meadow's edge. Cross a gas well track and pass abandoned apple trees to leave the state forest, and meet and follow dirt Titus Road to the right for 0.2 mile.

At 7.6 miles turn south off Titus Road to travel along private land, following a section of fence and plank boardwalk and skirting a wetland meadow and transition-shrub corridor. A woods of tall young maples next houses travel as the route follows straight lines at fences. Again, watch for the blazes indicating turns, especially because the route can be overgrown in places. Interstate 86 becomes a part of the terrain.

The trail exits onto a county road at 8.4 miles. Briefly walk it left to pick up the southbound trail next to another fenceline at the edge of a field. At the base of the field, look for the trail to turn right (west), crossing a hiker step stile over a fence to reach Wait Corners Road, and follow it south under the I–86 Expressway (9.3 miles).

The trail resumes on the east side of Wait Corners Road. Although it remains on private land, such field segments offer different wildlife viewing. Turkey, owl, and hawk may capture attention. Keep to the trail and be respectful of the landowners and their property. The rolling fields afford the vistas of the trip.

At 10 miles the trail follows Bates Road (used by area Amish) east to resume its way south at the top of the hill in 0.5 mile. The hilltop trail then draws a seam between rolling fields. Views are rural, with hay bales, fields, silos, barns, and huddles of black-and-white dairy cows. Blue-capped fence posts serve as guides; step stiles ease fence crossings. Field and woods edge much of the hike.

The trail angles left across Stebbins Road at 12.6 miles to return to forestland at Edward J. Whalen Memorial State Forest. Here hikers rediscover shade in a red pine plantation sprinkled through with maple and other hardwoods. The mowed path offers easy strolling, showing but a mild incline. Deer and squirrels favor the woods coverage.

Cross a cable corridor, beginning a gentle descent between spruce plantation and maple hardwood forest. Rain can make for muddy going. Footbridges span the deeper hollows, and rustic benches invite pause. Afterward, the woods tour is mainly in hardwood forest with hemlocks introducing a richer shade. Upon meeting a forest truck road, turn right (west) to pick up the southbound trail in another 0.8 mile. Be alert for blazes.

A deep hardwood forest with some huge ash trees in its ranks welcomes hikers upon the return to the trail. Ahead, an attractive ramped footbridge spans a trickling flow shadowed by hemlocks. Mature beech also add to viewing. A climb then leads to the next road stretch, Eggleston Hill Road (14.8 miles).

Follow this sun-drenched dirt road left for 0.3 mile to a road junction and again turn left, following the arrows. A long view stretches east. Continue 0.4 mile to resume south in the towering forest of North Harmony State Forest. An enjoyable woods meander follows, but the trail's wetter areas show damage from mountain bike tires. Arrows point out direction changes. In a shrubby clearing the quaking of aspen leaves can enchant. Stay on forestland, avoiding routes left.

A meadow opening and cattail-edged bass pond announce the Panama Campsite shelters, located on the forested south slope above the pond (16.4 miles). The trail follows the east shore to the shelters. The pond area is often noisy with crows and geese, and the shelters are well used. The Adirondack-style shelters look out on the pond, meadow, and reflected forest. Tamaracks rise above camp. Tables (if not lost to vandalism), fire rings, garbage cans, a pit toilet, and a water pump complete the camp offering.

The trail continues away from Panama Campsite, passing east of the shelters. A sharp climb then leads to the crossing of a two-track. Afterward the trail parallels Warner Road to the right before crossing over it to resume its course south at 17 miles.

Now travel the southern half of North Harmony Forest to Snake Forest Road (a truck trail). Trace it briefly left before resuming on a foot trail to the right. Tranquil forest travel leads to the direct crossing of Wiltsie Road, the last interruption until the trail emerges at NY 474, the chosen ending for this hike (19.2 miles). On this final leg, travel a meadow swath, pass a spiny hemlock, and view big birch trees near the footbridge crossing of a headwaters to Little Brokenstraw Creek. Because mountain bikers favor the NY 474 access, be alert hiking out.

The Westside Overland Trail continues its southern odyssey across the highway, edging private land. Carry the brochure and watch for blazings to end at Town Line Road (24 miles).

37 Allegany State Park, Red House Lake Area

Overview

This growing "wilderness" state park in southwestern New York (already the biggest in the state) brings together even-height peaks and ridges, V-shaped valleys, man-made lakes, second-growth forests, and block-fractured boulder realms. The park's two recreation areas, Red House Lake and Quaker Lake, make logical breaks for discussing the park trails. Four trails of varying length represent the Red House Lake Area.

General description:	The four trails explore the area ridges and peaks, touring woods and meadows but offering limited views.
General location:	6 miles south of Salamanca.
Special attractions:	Mixed hardwood-evergreen forests, ferns, wildflowers, springs, rocky realms, wildlife sightings.
Length:	Red Jacket Trail, 0.7-mile loop; Osgood Trail, 2.7-mile loop; Beehunter Trail, 6.5-mile loop; Eastwood Meadows–North Country–Conservation Trail tour, 7.2 miles one-way.
Difficulty:	Red Jacket and Osgood, easy; Beehunter, moderate; Eastwood Meadows–North Country, easy to moderate.
Maps:	Allegany State Park Guide Map.
Special concerns:	Fee area. Beware of a few bogus trail markings; blue disks mark the official state park trails.
Season and hours:	Spring through fall.
For information:	Allegany State Park.

Key points:

Red Jacket Trail:
- 0.0 Administration Building trailhead.
- 0.7 Complete loop at Administration Building.

Osgood Trail:
- 0.0 Osgood trailhead.
- 0.2 Loop junction; proceed uphill.
- 1.4 Hill's meadow crown.
- 2.5 Close loop; bear left to trailhead.

Beehunter Trail:
- 0.0 Beehunter trailhead (opposite Red House Lake bathhouse).
- 2.2 Cross Beehunter Creek.
- 3.5 Ridge high point.
- 6.5 Close loop at Beehunter Picnic Area.

Eastwood Meadows–North Country–Conservation Trail tour:
- 0.0 ASP 1 trailhead; hike north.
- 0.5 Junction; go left for Eastwood Meadows Loop.
- 1.9 Vista.
- 3.2 Resume North Country Trail left.
- 4.8 Conservation Trail junction; follow east arm.
- 7.2 End at Administration Building.

Finding the trailhead: From the Southern Tier Expressway, Interstate 86 (formerly New York 17) west of Salamanca, take exit 19 for the Red House Lake Area, reaching the entrance station in 0.7 mile. The trails radiate from the lake area, off Allegany State Park (ASP) routes 1, 2, and 2A.

Indian Pipe, Allegany State Park.

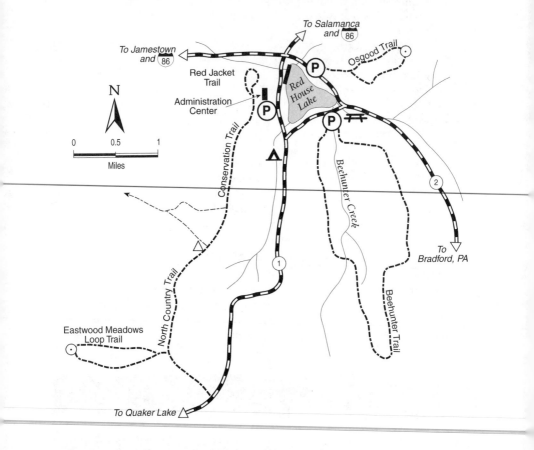

Allegany State Park, Red House Lake Area

To Salamanca and 86
To Jamestown and 86
Red Jacket Trail
Administration Center
Red House Lake
Osgood Trail
Conservation Trail
Beehunter Creek
North Country Trail
Beehunter Trail
Eastwood Meadows Loop Trail
To Bradford, PA
To Quaker Lake

N

0   0.5   1
Miles

The hikes: The **Red Jacket Trail** presents a good area synopsis and begins on the west side of the Administration Building, so pick up your maps and take a look.

Stairs, bridge, and path—all of rustic stone—lead uphill to the marked trail junction beneath a power line. Go right, coming to the loop junction in 250 feet. This split-level loop contours the maple, black cherry, and hemlock cloaked slope above Red House Lake. The green understory displays half a dozen fern varieties; pines claim the lower slope. At the edges of day, deer browse near the trail.

Views from rustic benches offer open looks at the forest and leaf-filtered glimpses at Red House Lake, its outlet, the park bikeway, and a round-topped hill. Midway, a recessed stone wall and a rusted steel tower masked by trees hint at the ski jump that once stood here.

The **Osgood Trail** travels the round-topped hill off the northeast end of Red House Lake. East of the ASP 1–ASP 2 junction, turn north off ASP 2 onto McIntosh Trail to find the trailhead just ahead on the right.

Red Jacket Trail

Osgood Trail

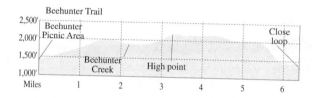

Beehunter Trail

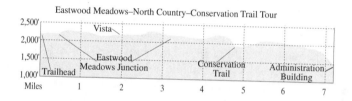

Eastwood Meadows–North Country–Conservation Trail Tour

Pass through the fruit tree corridor to the left of the sign, entering the hemlock-pine woods, barren of greenery except along the springs. Here and elsewhere in the park, the trail is notably rock-free. What is now Allegany State Park alone escaped the advance of the Wisconsin Glacier at the end of the Ice Age that scoured New York State, broadening valleys and depositing rocks across the terrain.

The trail ascends, crossing the springs at their origins and bypassing a side trail to the left before reaching the loop junction at 0.2 mile. Continue uphill; the unmarked trail to the right closes the loop. Chipmunks, songbirds, woodpeckers, and deer play cards of surprise. Maple, beech, oak, ash, and black cherry join the evergreens. As the trail contours left above the McIntosh drainage, flat rock slabs punctuate the forest.

At 1.4 miles find the hill's meadow crown and a funneled look west out a break in the tree rim. Go left, passing between the trees to descend the ridge. At 1.8 miles the trail passes through an attractive meadow plateau drained by springs; logs ease soggier crossings.

Where the trail enters an area of moss-and-fern-decorated rock slabs, be watchful. A well-worn false trail heads straight downhill, while the loop curves right. Continue contouring and descending to the right to close the loop at 2.5 miles and to reach the trailhead at 2.7 miles.

South of Red House Lake, the **Beehunter Trail** travels the ridges drained by Beehunter Creek. Look for the trailhead on the west side of the field opposite the bathhouse and west of Beehunter Picnic Area (both off ASP 2A).

The trail ascends steadily and steeply for 0.2 mile, attaining the spine of the ridge for a more comfortable tour. Thick grasses spread beneath an open forest of oak, maple, ash, and hemlock. Filtered views east span the Beehunter Creek drainage to a sunbathed ridge. After 0.9 mile a pinched trail rounds the east side of the upper ridge, touring amid brambles, nettles, and ferns. Mossy, slick rocks compose the trailbed; the blue disks wane. Big black cherry and young beech offer shade as the trail descends.

At 2.2 miles find and cross 15-foot-wide Beehunter Creek with its clear water and rock-and-gravel bed; it requires wading at times of high water. Disk markers return as the trail again climbs, following a side drainage and crossing the small headwater forks. The rich even-aged forest of 18-inch-diameter hardwoods, the flowing green carpet, and open midstory call to mind a city park atmosphere.

As the trail tops a broad saddle, turn left and ascend the ridge; oak and beech trees return to the mix. At 3.5 miles the trail tops out, now descending via the forested ridge. Red-berried elder gains a stronghold, displaying bright sprays of red berries in August. By 4.5 miles the trail leaves the ridge and levels. Look below the trail at 5.1 miles for a scenic fern-draped split rock with equisized 10- by-10-foot rock halves.

Passing through a hemlock grove, the trail comes to a T-junction at a nature-softened woods road; descend left. Stay on the woods road, crossing over a service road to enter a field. In the field find a dirt road with a trailhead sign. Turn right following the dirt road downhill and bear left past the rest rooms to reach the bike trail (6.25 miles). Now go left, crossing over Beehunter Creek to close the loop at Beehunter Picnic Area, 6.5 miles.

Hikers may customize the **Eastwood Meadows–North Country–Conservation Trail Tour** to their desired length. The described trek passes south to north from the trailhead on ASP 1 (4 miles south of Red House Lake Campground) to the Administration Building.

From ASP 1 a rolling northbound journey alternately tours stands of beech, maple, and hemlock and the shrub-fern meadow clearings from the former ski runs. The white blazes of the North Country Trail join the blue disks of the state park trails.

At 0.5 mile the North Country Trail turns right; go left to add the **Eastwood Meadows Loop.** For the meadow tour, where the trail meets a grassy woods road (0.75 mile), turn right to find the ends of the loop on the left in 500 feet. Go left for a clockwise tour. The forest sameness relaxes eye and soul; big-toothed aspen whisper in the canopy. The trail remains flat until 1.4 miles, where it again rolls, generally ascending.

At 1.9 miles find the loop's return to the right; a limited vista lies 100 feet ahead. The view stretches west across a meadow clearing and the Bay State Brook drainage to feature another Allegany ridge. The loop resumes, descending through a similar forest but with a shrubby understory of nettles and brambles. While not exactly a gauntlet, hikers must evade the prickly overhanging branches. Black cherry remains the giant of the woods. By 2.4 miles ferns replace the nettles. Close the loop at 2.9 miles and return to the 0.5-mile junction (3.2 miles).

Northbound, the North Country Trail offers an idyllic stroll, showing a modest gradient and trouble-free path. A hemlock-hardwood forest enfolds the route, ferns embroider the sides, and snags open up the cathedral. Ahead, a midstory of red-berried elder alternates with the spatially open forest.

As the trail descends after 4.3 miles, mountain elder becomes more prevalent. Upon crossing a drainage, look for the next trail junction (4.8 miles). Here the North Country Trail and the west arm of the **Conservation Trail** (CT) both head left. This hike proceeds forward, following the blue-blazed route of the east arm of the CT to the Administration Building.

The east arm passes an earthen-floor lean-to that actually does lean. Next to it, a decrepit, mossy road-width bridge spans a drainage; look for the trail's crossing just upstream. The trail starts out level, touring among midaged hardwoods, hemlock groves, and pockets of young beech and shrubs. As the trail descends past large upturned roots (5.6 miles), the west arm of the CT returns on the left; bear right, descending to the Administration Building.

Briefly, mossy rock slabs alter the forest appearance. At 6.5 miles the descent accelerates with uneven steep spurts. Where the trail edges meadow clearings, noise from the campground carries up slope. Beneath a power line at 7.1 miles, find the trailhead sign for the CT and turn right, descending past an old foundation to reach the Administration Building.

38 Allegany State Park, Quaker Lake Area

Overview

Conceived to bring a "wilderness playground" to western New York, this 64,000-acre state park succeeds. Hikers find solitude, challenge, and natural beauty in the terrain of even-height peaks and ridges and V-shaped valleys. Four trails represent the offerings of the Quaker Lake Area.

General description: These trails travel ridges, tag peaks, explore a boulder realm, and visit a natural spring.

General location: 6 miles south of Salamanca.

Special attractions: Mixed hardwood–evergreen forests, springs, wildflowers, block-fractured boulder caves.

Length: Mount Tuscarora Trail, 5 miles round-trip; Three Sisters Trail, 2.5-mile loop; Bear Caves–Mount Seneca Trail, 3 miles round-trip; Bear Springs Trail, 0.5 mile round-trip.

Difficulty: Bear Springs, easy; the others, moderate.

Maps: Allegany State Park Guide Map.

Special concerns: Fee area. Bring flashlight for looking at boulder caves; be prepared for stooping and squeezing. Expect small rooms and passages less than 200 feet long. Consider taking the naturalist's tour to locate the openings.

Season and hours: Spring through fall.

For information: Allegany State Park.

Key points:

Mount Tuscarora Trail:

  0.0 Mount Tuscarora trailhead; head west.

  2.5 Summit/abandoned fire tower; return by same route.

Three Sisters Trail:

  0.0 Three Sisters trailhead (west of rental office).

  1.4 West Sister.

  2.2 Reach Ranger Trail (a road) at cabins.

  2.5 Close loop; turn right.

Bear Caves–Mount Seneca Trail:

  0.0 ASP 3 trailhead; hike north.

  0.2 Bear Caves.

  0.7 Slide Hollow crossing.

  1.5 Mount Seneca summit; return by same route.

Bear Springs Trail:

  0.0 Bear Springs trailhead.

  0.2 Springs grotto; return as came.

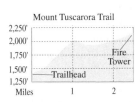

Finding the trailhead: From the Southern Tier Expressway, Interstate 86 (formerly New York 17) west of Salamanca, take exit 18 for the Quaker Lake Area and go 4 miles south on NY 280 to the entrance station. Find trails off Allegany State Park (ASP) Routes 3 and 1.

The hikes: The **Mount Tuscarora Trail** starts 0.2 mile south of the Quaker Lake entrance station; road-shoulder parking only.

The foot trail heads west off ASP 3, traveling a dark hemlock-hardwood forest, ascending parallel to a drainage. At 0.5 mile the trail curves right and, with another burst of climb, tops the ridge (0.7 mile). Although the park map shows a view, time has stolen it.

The ascent calms as the trail traces the ridgeline. Indian pipe, baneberry, huckleberry, witch hazel, striped maple, beech, and small oaks contribute to discovery. The trail claims the first summit (elevation 2,064 feet)

Allegany State Park, Quaker Lake Area

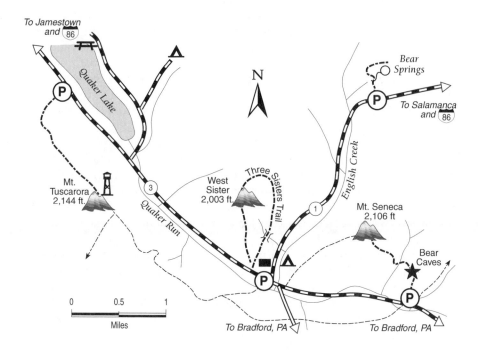

at 2.25 miles. It then ascends to traverse the next ridge tier to the abandoned fire tower (elevation 2,144 feet) at 2.5 miles. An out-of-place tulip tree or an occasional hickory rises among the oaks and maples.

Missing its lower flight of stairs and several of its landings, the fire tower now serves only as a landmark and destination. Trees completely enfold the site. Although the trail continues along the ridge to Coon Run Road, turn around and return as you came.

The **Three Sisters Trail** travels to only one sister—West Sister—and begins west of the rental office; find the rental office west of the ASP 1–ASP 3 junction.

Pass into a pine-hardwood forest with a shrubby understory, bypassing a pine-hemlock stand and crossing under a power line. The midstory ferns, nettles, and brambles sometimes swipe at hikers. Crossing a footbridge at 0.4 mile, the trail traverses both grassy meadow and open forest—a virtual sauna on sunny, humid days. Pockets of bee balm, a red member of the mint family, adorn the drainage.

The steadily ascending trail can be rocky, with rustic corduroys aiding passage over soggy reaches. Gradually, the forest fills out. At 1 mile the trail tops and follows the ridge to the left. Red-berried elder interweaves the ridge forest, as the hiker passage grows squeezed. The matted-grass trail ascends and rounds through a beech grove, tagging the top of West Sister (1.4 miles), but it delivers no view.

As the trail drops away from the summit, be aware that the grassy footpath can be slippery when wet. At 1.8 miles a large rock slab offers a natural crossing to a spring. After passing under the power line, the foot trail meets Ranger Trail (a road) near cabins 1, 2, and 4. Follow the markers, descending Ranger Trail. Prior to reaching ASP 3, take the footpath heading left into the woods to return to the pine-hemlock stand near the start. Turn right to end the hike.

The preferred access to the **Bear Caves–Mount Seneca Trail** is the eastern one; go 1.4 miles east on ASP 3 from the ASP 1–ASP 3 junction. Find parking on the south side of ASP 3; the trailhead, on the north.

This trail offers a different look at the park; it ascends a broad, worn trail up a steep bouldery slope, reaching an entire community of the massive boxy boulders and outcrops. Crossbedding, balanced rocks, eroded nooks, fissures, and overhangs plus the adorning moss, lichen, and fern contribute to the discovery. At the base of the rocky realm, the primary trail heads right; a secondary trail rounds to the left.

Go right, rounding and ascending to traverse the wooded top of the rocks. At 0.2 mile the trail overlooks the first cave opening, an inconspicuous natural spacing in the sandstone conglomerate. The small rooms and thin passages (enlarged joints) intrigue the curious. As the trail traverses the top of the rocks, look over the edge to spy a deep, narrow fissure. Similar features shape the caves; only overlaying rocks conceal them.

Forest, Allegany State Park.

At 0.3 mile a second cave opening calls the intrepid hiker to literally drop in. By 0.4 mile the trail is again at the base of the rocks, touring the familiar Allegany forest intermixed with bramble, fern, and red-berried elder. The trail descends and then crosses Slide Hollow; high water may dictate wading. Follow the blue-marked trail uphill to the right; a side path descends along the drainage. Bee balm puts its red signature to the scene.

The trail contours then turns sharply right for a steep assault on Mount Seneca. Clintonia, trillium, and Mayflower decorate the floor. At 1.3 miles push through the congestion of red-berried elder, wild raspberry, and gooseberry to emerge at the summit (1.5 miles). The top holds a look at the wooded ridge of Mount Onondaga to the northeast and the immediate peak to the east. While the trail continues, return as you came.

Bear Springs Trail begins on the west side of ASP 1, 2.2 miles north of the ASP 1–ASP 3 junction.

Enter a woods of maple, black cherry, and hemlock to the left of the sign. The trail slowly descends. The spatially open forest shows a lush fern floor and a profusion of woods flora not seen elsewhere in the park. Oxalis, Mayflower, trillium, and whorled pogonia and other orchids contribute to the array. Soon after crossing a drainage, the trail reaches the 6-foot-high stonework grotto protecting the springs. Although the trail continues, traveling field and hardwood forest and meeting old woods roads, return as you came.

Finger Lakes Region

In central New York, the vast Finger Lakes Region enjoys a signature landscape. The long, thin glacier-gouged lakes look as though Mother Nature raked her fingers down the state's middle. Dramatic east-west river gorges, with spirited falls, tumbling cascades, and imposing cliffs likewise contribute to the region's singular image. Rolling woods and grasslands, low steep-flanked ridges and hills, vital wetlands, and diked ponds complete the discovery.

The long-distance Finger Lakes Trail unites the splendors of the region. Discover the history of early New York at the site of a Sapony Indian village or while strolling lands awarded the soldiers of the Revolutionary War.

39 Howland Island Unit, Northern Montezuma Wildlife Management Area

Overview

The Barge Canal and Seneca River isolate this 3,100-acre interior island, where eighteen dikes create an extensive network of ponds that draw waterfowl to the area. Low, rolling hills (drumlins deposited by glacial action 10,000 years ago), planted floodplain, unkempt fields, and hardwood stands complete the island mosaic. The vital habitat supports some 200 bird species, as well as woodchuck, rabbit, deer, fox, turtle, frog, fish, and newt. Management roads and dikes suggest the tours, while offering easy strolling.

General description:	This relaxing wildlife area hike strings together views of a dozen ponds as it travels untamed and cultivated fields, wetlands, and woods.
General location:	In north-central Cayuga County, about 25 miles west of Syracuse.
Special attractions:	Bird-watching, impoundment ponds, fields, marsh, low-elevation hardwoods, spring and summer wildflowers.
Length:	6.4-mile round-trip, including primary wetland loop and Pump Pond spur.
Difficulty:	Easy.
Maps:	Howland Island Unit, Northern Montezuma Wildlife Management Area brochure.
Special concerns:	Bring insect repellent and mosquito netting for a more enjoyable visit. Hikers may choose to avoid the area during hunting season; contact the Department

Howland Island Unit, Northern Montezuma Wildlife Management Area

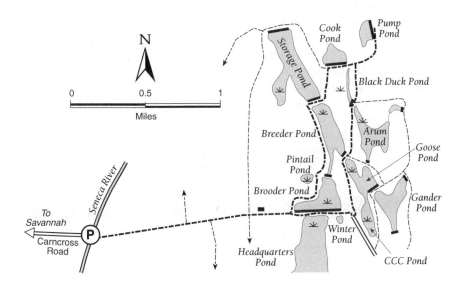

of Environmental Conservation (DEC) for dates. At times of high water, the entire unit may be inaccessible (Seneca River fording required to enter wildlife complex).

Season and hours: Spring through fall, daylight hours. Closures occur April 1 to May 31 for waterfowl nesting.

For information: New York State Department of Environmental Conservation, Region 7.

Key points:

0.0	Carncross Road trailhead; cross Seneca River at culvert.
1.5	Loop junction; turn left (north).
2.9	Cook Pond.
3.2	Pump Pond.
4.9	Close loop; continue west to trailhead.

Finding the trailhead: From Interstate 90 take exit 40 at Weedsport. From the toll booth go south on New York 34; in 0.2 mile turn west on NY 31. Passing through the village of Port Byron, reach Savannah in 13.5 miles and there turn north on NY 89. Go 0.3 mile and at the north edge of town, turn east on County Route 274 (Savannah–Spring Lake Road). Proceed 2.3 miles and turn right on Carncross Road to reach trail parking where the road dead-ends at the Seneca River culvert in 0.6 mile. There is parking for a handful of vehicles.

The hike: Round the gate and cross the culvert. The culvert generally allows a dry crossing or simple wading, but high waters can turn back hikers. This spot on the river is popular with

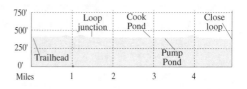

local fishermen, who share the access. Follow the main service road east into the Howland Island Unit. The route offers a fine, fast walking surface, rolling through pleasing habitats. Hike past marsh, field, and mixed woods, and discover huge sugar maples and willows near the site Quonset hut.

Keep to the eastbound service road, topping the first hill at 0.9 mile and crossing over the second hill at 1.3 miles. Both afford wildlife area overlooks. Descend past the Quonset hut (now a maintenance building in disrepair; no services) to locate the loop junction (1.5 miles) at the southwest corner of Brooder Pond. Brooder Pond is the big water body north of the service road. Headquarters Pond is to its south.

Turn left to hike the west shore of Brooder Pond, beginning a clockwise loop. Brooder Pond is an enormous, mostly vegetated water, with croaking bullfrogs and perhaps the startling plop of a namesake "brooder." Queen Anne's lace, daisy, chicory, loosestrife, clover, milkweed, and a host of other wildflowers bring splendor to the tallgrass field. Monarch butterflies alight on the milkweed.

Past a spruce stand, Pintail Pond catches the eye with its roundish shrub islands, nesting boxes, and lily-pad mosaic rimmed by tall wetland and meadow. Yellow warblers, kingfishers, and ducks add to a growing list of sightings. On a channel to the left, look for turtles slipping off logs.

As the left side of the trail changes from meadow to cornfield, Breeder Pond replaces Brooder Pond on the right. The presence of hikers sometimes offends the feeding geese, causing them to march out of the field in comical haughtiness.

At 2.4 miles the trail tours a corridor with cottonwood and basswood, coming out on a dike between Breeder and Storage Ponds. A heron lifting off the water, raining drops from its wings, or an osprey atop the large snag on the east shore of Breeder Pond can cause hikers to pause. Under a cottonwood at the end of the dike, find a junction; go left for the loop. Black walnut trees and a mild meadow slope now frame travel.

At arrowhead-shaped Cook Pond (2.9 miles) turn right, bypassing a small extension of Black Duck Pond where a birdhouse holds center stage. At the upcoming T-junction a detour left finds Pump Pond in 0.2 mile; the loop continues right, traveling a straightaway often enclosed by elm, locust, and walnut. Black Duck Pond may be glimpsed beyond the shrub tangle. A better view of this long, thin duckweed pond comes at the junction at 3.7 miles; go right for the loop.

The trail passes between Black Duck and Arum Ponds to round above the latter. Trees keep Arum Pond a puzzle, pieced together by stolen glances. Ahead,

Breeder Pond, Howland Island Unit, Northern Montezuma Wildlife Management Area.

an open meadow shore spans to Arum and Goose Ponds. Overgrown jeep tracks arrive on the right and left, as hikers near the dike between Breeder and Goose Ponds.

The vegetated ponds hold a lesson in succession. Purple loosestrife, an exotic, overwhelms the CCC Pond at 4.4 miles; although pretty in its July bloom, loosestrife displaces native vegetation. With a mild ascent, the trail bypasses an overgrown track on the right to return to the original service road at 4.5 miles near Winter Pond, a small, lily-capped square at the foot of a slope.

Follow the service road right (west) passing between Winter and Brooder Ponds to complete the loop. Locust, maple, hickory, oak, willow, and apple shape a border congested with vines and shrubs. Beware of poison ivy along the grassy edge. As the Quonset hut appears on the hill to the west, Headquarters Pond replaces Winter Pond on the left. Trees and shrubs rim half this large, lily-ringed open water; a planted field extends up the western slope. Reflections of trees and passing clouds call to photographers.

Near the end of Headquarters Pond, cattail, loosestrife, alder, and milkweed overtake the shore. Swallows perch on the line overhead, while red-winged blackbirds animate the marsh. At 4.9 miles complete the loop between Brooder and Headquarters Ponds, and proceed west on the service road 1.5 miles to return to the trailhead.

40 Beaver Lake Nature Center

Overview

At this 550-acre Onondaga County Park, 9 miles of superbly groomed nature trails and boardwalks explore lake, marsh, meadow, and woods habitats for outstanding wildlife sightings and nature study. The trails welcome all abilities, and repeat tours bring new appreciation; ask the park's "one-hundred milers" who regularly tour the eight trails. The three hikes described below sample five of the trails. The site's interpretive panels, benches, observation platforms, a blind, and high-powered binoculars enhance a visit.

General description: The selected trails are all easy, ranging from a fragment of a mile to 3 miles in length; Lakeview Trail has the most convenient lake access.

General location: 15 miles northwest of Syracuse.

Special attractions: Thirty thousand spring-migrating Canada geese and ten thousand fall migrants; songbirds, osprey, heron, deer, fox, beaver, frog, turtle, and toad; pitcher plants; spring wildflowers; massive beech trees and hemlock hollows.

Length: Lake Loop, 3-mile loop; interlocked Hemlock Hollow and Bog Trails, 1 mile round-trip; Lakeview Trail, 0.3-mile loop.

Difficulty: All easy.

Maps: Beaver Lake Nature Center flier.

Special concerns: Token vehicle fee. Carry repellent.

Season and hours: Year-round, dawn to dusk; building opens 8:00 A.M. In winter, the trails are popular for cross-country skiing and snowshoeing; snowshoes are provided free of charge.

For information: Beaver Lake Nature Center.

Key points:
Lake Loop:
- 0.0 Trailhead at visitor center; head right.
- 0.5 Lake outlet.
- 1.2 Shelters and canoe landing.
- 2.5 Go left on Three Meadows Trail.
- 3.0 Visitor Center.

Hemlock Hollow and Bog Trails Hike:
- 0.0 Hemlock Hollow trailhead; go counterclockwise.
- 0.2 Hike Bog Trail west.
- 0.5 Lake platform; return to Hemlock Hollow Loop.
- 1.0 Hemlock Hollow trailhead.

Lakeview Loop:
- 0.0 Trailhead at visitor center.
- 0.2 Lake vistas.
- 0.4 End at visitor center.

Beaver Lake Nature Center

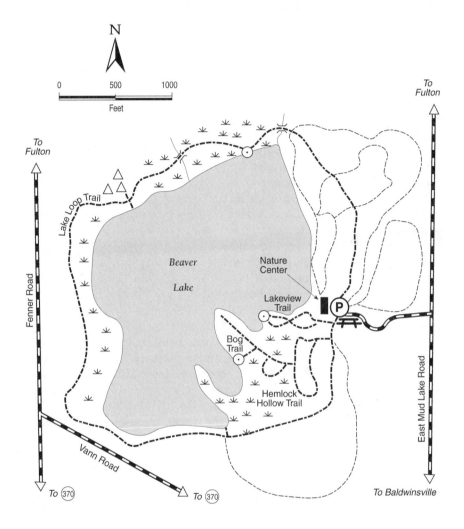

Finding the trailhead: From New York State Thruway Interstate 90, take exit 39, go north on Interstate 690/New York 690 for 5.8 miles, and take the second Baldwinsville exit as indicated for the nature center. Go west on New York 370 for 2 miles, then turn right on East Mud Lake Road, following the signs. The nature center is on the left in 0.7 mile. The Lake Loop starts to the right of the visitor center; the other named trails start to the center's left. Scenic carved signs identify each trail.

The hikes: A woods walk characterizes the early distance of the **Lake Loop,** which seldom hints at centrally located, 206-acre Beaver Lake. The wide woodchip path travels among spruce-pine woodland, towering tulip and beech trees, and a congestion of young, spindly maples. Virginia creeper, poison ivy, and fern contribute to the understory. Where Lake Loop crosses the other park trails, signs indicate the junctions.

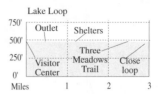

At 0.5 mile the loop follows a boardwalk over the lake outlet, where white water lilies decorate the flow in summer, and turtles sometimes sun on logs. Highbush blueberry, alder, nettles, dodder, ferns, and cattails pierce the wetland tangle. At 0.7 mile an elevated bench overlooks Beaver Lake.

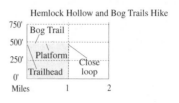

Duckweed coats a small inlet drainage where cardinal flowers decorate a log. At 1 mile a wide foot trail replaces the boardwalk, and at 1.25 miles side trails branch right to three lean-tos and left to a canoe landing site. Periodically, the county offers guided canoe trips. In the wet ash–maple woodland, poison ivy abounds.

At 1.7 miles the loop again travels a boardwalk, passing a small catfish water with rimming cattail, loosestrife, and arrowhead. The trail then passes through pine plantation and meadow, skirting below the Vann Road lake overlook. At 2.25 miles cross a service road.

Where Lake Loop meets the Three Meadows Trail (2.5 miles), follow the Three Meadows Trail left to complete the circuit. A quick spur left leads to a water-lily cove. Hemlock hollows and transition woods alternately claim the route, as it passes a small wetland pond and picnic shelter, reaching the walkway to the visitor center (3 miles).

En route to the visitor center, bypass the Hemlock Hollow, Bog, and Lakeview trailheads. With **Hemlock Hollow Trail** being the lone access to the **Bog Trail,** these two hikes naturally combine. The Hemlock Hollow Trail swings a 0.4-mile loop through a dark hemlock woods with oak, birch, beech, and interspersing witch hazel. Midway, the ladle-shaped Bog Trail branches west, traveling boardwalk and trail along a former island, now a marshy Beaver Lake peninsula.

By keeping right at the two initial Bog Trail junctions (the ladle loop), hikers explore the length of the peninsula. Spurs lead to a bog-pond overlook, a one-story lake observation platform, and a couple of lakeshore accesses. At the lake platform, high-powered binoculars pull cross-lake herons into close scrutiny. On the return take the boardwalk loop, capping the tour with a marsh study. Sweet gale, arrowhead, cranberry, loosestrife, and pitcher plant number among the discoveries.

166

Trailhead sign, Beaver Lake Nature Center.

The wheelchair-accessible **Lakeview Loop** draws a figure-eight through similar deep woods, with plaques explaining the intricate habitat interactions. A beautiful big oak marks the second loop junction. Off the second loop, spurs lead to two lake vistas. At the larger viewing stop, find benches and telescopes, including one telescope low enough for comfortable use from a wheelchair.

An osprey snatching a fish from the lake, the growing wake of a beaver, or some thirty thousand migrant geese awaiting the spring thaw in Canada can dazzle onlookers. Late March to early May marks the peak time for viewing Canada geese; in fall a smaller contingent stops over on the lake.

41 High Tor Wildlife Management Area

Overview

Three separate land parcels compose High Tor Wildlife Management Area (WMA); this trail explores the southernmost and largest of the three. Hikes in this 3,400-acre parcel follow service road, jeep track, and foot trail, exploring wetland, gully, woods, and field. An occasional interpretive sign introduces the natural history.

General description: With side spurs to a wildlife pond and an overlook of Conklin Gully, this barbell-shaped tour showcases the WMA's varied habitats and hill-and-gully terrain.

General location: 6 miles south of Canandaigua Lake, 3 miles east of Naples.

Special attractions: Striking 400-foot-deep chasm, isolated waterfall, wildlife ponds, wildlife sightings, wildflowers.

Length: 7.5 miles round-trip with side tours to pond, oak, and gully.

Difficulty: Easy.

Maps: Wildlife management area brochure.

Special concerns: Sun-drenched tour; bring water. There is no individual camping, but organized-group camping can be prearranged.

Season and hours: Spring through fall; daylight hours.

For information: New York State Department of Environmental Conservation (DEC), Region 8.

Key points:
- 0.0   Trailhead; hike north.
- 0.1   Lower loop junction; go left.
- 1.4   Four-way junction; detour left to pond.
- 2.1   Turn left on FLT foot trail (upper loop).
- 2.5   Pass historic oak.
- 3.2   Conklin Falls/Gully vantage point.
- 4.7   Back at 1.4-mile junction; head left for lower loop.
- 5.1   Skirt wildlife pond.
- 7.4   Close lower loop; return to trailhead.

Finding the trailhead: From the junction of New York 53 and New York 21 in Naples, go south on NY 53 for 0.8 mile and turn left (east) toward Italy Valley on Ontario County 21. In 1.9 miles turn left on Bassett Road. Find trailhead parking 0.3 mile ahead on the left.

The hike: Hike the tree-edged service road north, rounding the gate and passing between two wildlife ponds. Cattails and marsh grasses shape the rims; a scummy mat coats the left pond. Clover, daisy, chicory, buttercup, and morning glory sprinkle the grassy shoulder. Swallowtail, monarch, and admiral butterflies flutter about ankles and flowers.

At 0.1 mile go left on the primary service road for a steady moderate ascent; the secondary road to the right marks the close for the lower and larger loop of this lopsided-barbell tour. Maple, oak, and hickory now compose the tree border, distanced from the trail by a 10- to 30-foot-wide shoulder. Sightings of yellow warbler, muskrat, hawk, ruffed grouse, and white-tailed deer bounding through the tall grasses can enrich a tour.

At 1.2 miles a spur to the left leads to Campsite One. These DEC camps are made available only to educational groups and only by written permission; phone Region 8 at (607) 522–3323 for details and camp information. A 0.1-mile detour to the camp finds a picture-pretty circular pond rimmed by cattails and noisy with bullfrogs.

High Tor Wildlife Management Area

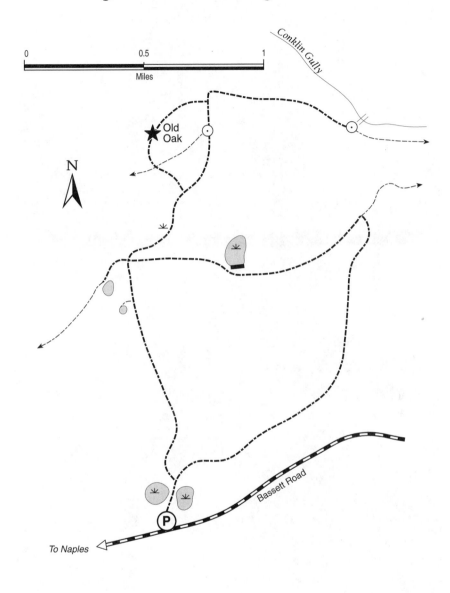

Majestic oak, High Tor Wildlife Management Area.

At the four-way junction at 1.4 miles, the service road continues north to the upper loop and Conklin Gully; the overgrown doubletrack to the right advances the lower loop. A detour left (west) on the orange Bristol Hills Branch of the Finger Lakes Trail (FLT) leads to another, larger wildlife pond (1.6 miles). A deciduous border rims two-thirds of this pond. Snakes, frogs, and birds number among the sightings.

Upon return to the 1.4-mile junction, continue north toward Conklin Gully, following the eastbound Bristol Hills Branch of the FLT. Past a cattail wetland, look for a roadside post with double orange blazings just as the road curves right (2.1 miles). Take a couple of steps north past the post, turn left, and follow the FLT (now a foot trail) into woods.

The trail descends sharply through full cool woods, crossing over a blue-blazed doubletrack. Before long, pass beneath the broken arm of a granddaddy oak, boasting a 6-foot diameter and twelve major branchings; paying homage to this tree alone justifies the trip. At 2.75 miles reach a grassy woods road. Turn right, staying with the FLT to close the upper loop. To add a side trip to Conklin Gully, turn left and follow the blue blazes.

The side tour quickly curves right for a serious descent on a broad, exposed road corridor offering looks north. Cross a small, steep ravine at 3 miles and ascend to round the nose of a ridge for a grand overlook of the "gully"—a rather unassuming characterization for such an awesome chasm (3.25 miles). Keep well back from the edge; it has a dangerous, unstable overhang.

At Conklin Gully, sun-beaten 400-foot-tall grayish-brown cliffs open to the sky, with a crystalline waterfall slipping through a green wooded seam halfway down the north wall. Elsewhere, pine and aspen dot the shale mudstones. Free from protective barriers, this site extends perhaps the most heart-thumping gorge vista in the entire state.

Retrace your steps uphill to the 2.75-mile junction (3.75 miles), and resume the upper loop, ascending and keeping to the grassy doubletrack straight ahead. Orange FLT and blue blazes initially point the way. Do not follow the FLT, which quickly turns left. At Campsite Two (4 miles) a rim view to the north overlooks the nearby wooded ridges and farms and Canandaigua Lake. Pass through the parking area to the service road and head left (south).

Continue south on the service road to complete the upper loop. Past a cattail pond, reach the 1.4/1.8-mile junction at 4.7 miles, and turn left (east) on the overgrown doubletrack to finish walking the lower loop. The parallel tracks remain clear for easy walking. Again, the set-back woods grant but spotty shade.

At 4.8 miles an interpretive sign explains the snapped treetops and missing branches; they are the legacy of a 1991 ice storm. The trail next rounds a wildlife pond at least ten times the size of the previous ones. Snags, open water, marsh islands, and dragonflies contribute to its persona. Detour onto the levee for an unobstructed view.

An ascent through a long narrow meadow of elbow-high grasses interwoven with white, pink, and yellow wildflowers leads to a T-junction at 5.8 miles.

Here the loop turns right; the path downhill to the left leads to more wildlife ponds, beginning in 0.5 mile. Stay on the loop, ascending a daisy-clad road.

The trail tops out at 6.25 mile and descends via a similar long meadow corridor. By 7 miles, spruce plantations alternate with the meadow openings. Where the lower loop closes (7.4 miles), turn left to return to the trailhead.

42 Interloken National Recreation Trail

General description: This linear multiuse route strings north to south through New York State's lone national forest, exploring natural and planted forests, meadow, transitioning shrub lands, and pond habitats.

General location: 10 miles northeast of Watkins Glen, between Seneca and Cayuga Lakes.

Special attractions: Habitat diversity, bird-watching, fishing, wildlife sightings, cultural history, wildflowers.

Length: 12 miles one-way.

Difficulty: Moderate.

Maps: Finger Lakes National Forest brochure; U.S. Department of Agriculture (USDA) Finger Lakes National Forest map.

Special concerns: Despite trail improvements such as boardwalks and gravel, muddy patches can be encountered. Because the trail is shared-use, hikers need to be alert for horseback riders and yield the right of way to them. The use of horses is prohibited during the spring wet season, when the potential for trail damage is greatest.

Season and hours: Spring through fall.

For information: Finger Lakes National Forest, Hector Ranger District.

Key points:
- 0.0   Northern trailhead; hike south.
- 1.2   Cross Townsend Road.
- 2.5   Teeter Pond; pass along west shore.
- 3.2   Cross Searsburg Road.
- 5.6   Foster Pond.
- 6.9   Picnic Area Road; hike west (right) to foot trail.
- 7.7   Cross Mathews Road.
- 10.2   Travel levee of wildlife pond.
- 11.0   Meet Finger Lakes Trail (FLT).
- 12.0   End at Southern trailhead.

Interloken National Recreation Trail

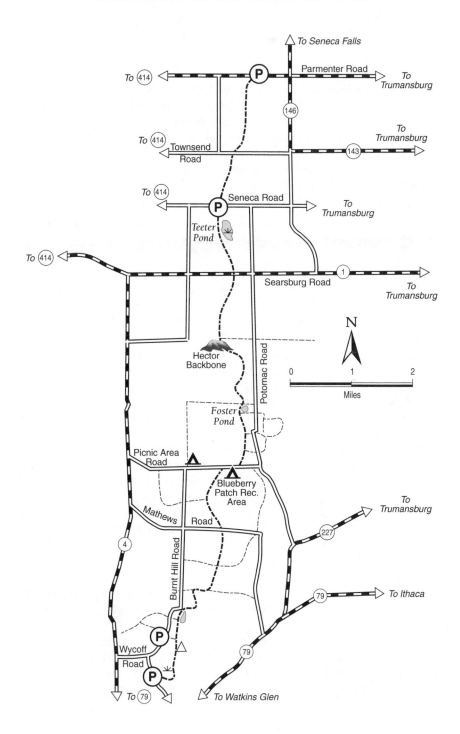

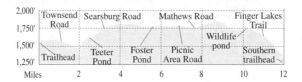

Finding the trailhead: From the New York 227–New York 96 junction in Trumansburg, go north on NY 96 for 1.5 miles and turn left onto Seneca County 143 for 4.8 miles. Turn right on County 146 for 1 mile, then go left on Parmenter/Butcher Hill Road for 0.6 mile; the northern trailhead is on the left.

For the southern trailhead, at the Schuyler County 5–New York 79 intersection in Burdett, go 0.9 mile east on NY 79 and turn left on Logan Road/County 4 for 1.1 miles; turn right on Wycoff. In 0.5 mile go right on Burnt Hill Road for 0.4 mile; the trailhead is on the left.

The hike: Once inhabited by Iroquois Indians and later partitioned into military parcels and given to veterans of the Revolutionary War, the gentle ridges and open flats of this national forest eventually returned to government hands through a farmer's relief act during the Great Depression. Stabilized through reforestation, the land once again thrives, serving interests of naturalist and recreationist.

On a north-south tour, the orange-marked trail enters a mature mixed woods with a lush understory. An aspen-shrub complex, a woodlot of young maple and seedling pine, and an open meadow variously claim the route. At 1.25 miles cross Townsend Road, and at 1.5 miles cross a 10-foot-wide drainage that may require wading during high water. Veer left for a mild ascent leading to a gate; pass through, leaving all gates as you found them.

Stay with the orange blazes, wading knee-high grasses, descending to and crossing Seneca Road; bypass the No-Tan-Takto Horse Trail. Next the national recreation trail (NRT) passes through an aspen-shrub complex, reaching Teeter Pond (2.5 miles). This expansive marsh and open water attracts warmwater anglers and wildlife. Snags, shrub islands, and reflections of the cloud-filled sky add to its welcome. Pass to the right of the pond.

Leaving the pond at 2.8 miles, tour a full mixed forest, coming to a gate at the corner of a large pasture. Follow the diagonal-staked course of the NRT, touring knee- to waist-high grasses sprinkled with clover, daisy, and buttercup to cross Searsburg Road at 3.2 miles.

A mowed swath enters the woods for a gentle climb, but muddy passages can weigh down boots. Green leaves stretch from the lower story to the canopy, with a bright azalea patch at 3.8 miles. Sightings of red eft, deer, and warbler spice the journey.

At a signed junction with the Backbone Trail, continue straight for the NRT, touring a pine plantation with accents of fairy slipper. Back amid an oak-maple woodland, bypass private property on the right. As the trail curves left and slowly rises, reroutes evade some of the more impassable

174

muddy reaches. A thinned forest of big trees and boardwalks precede the shrubby outskirts of Foster Pond.

At the pond outskirts follow the tracked path straight ahead. The Backbone Trail (northbound) heads left; in 200 feet its southbound counterpart journeys right. Afterward, the Interloken Trail rounds the south shore of Foster Pond, passing amid grass and shrubs.

Look for it to turn right at the marked junction at 5.75 miles. This is the first of three junctions where side trails branch east (or left) to Potomac Road. Ski markers and ribbons help mark the route, which still travels aisles of thick grasses and shrubs; orange blazes resume in the woods, where boardwalks ease passage.

At Picnic Area Road (6.9 miles) hike west (right) along the road for 0.2 mile, passing Blueberry Patch Recreation Area to pick up the NRT as it resumes south among pines. At 7.4 miles a side trail heads left, and at 7.5 miles the Ravine Trail heads right; continue straight ahead.

Pass from a younger woods of maple and big-toothed aspen to a more mature, mixed complex, coming to a gate and another pasture stretch. The footpath now angles uphill to the left, with a microwave tower visible to the east; ridges and farmland sweep west. Although tall grasses overhang the path, it is more passable than it first appears.

From Mathews Road return to woods, soon passing amid snags and 8-foot-tall shrubs. At 9.1 miles cross the overgrown corridor of a forlorn Burnt Hill Trail. Planted and natural woods alternately claim the rolling meander. Upon meeting the Gorge Trail, follow it right for 0.1 mile, and then go straight

Interloken Trail, Finger Lakes National Forest.

where the Gorge Trail turns right. Mature oaks and flavorful early-summer strawberries slow strides, but beware of poison ivy when reaching for berries.

Pine, spruce, and larch plantations now interrupt the deciduous stands. At 10.2 miles travel the levee of a small wildlife pond at a corner on Burnt Hill Road; the scummy crescent percolates with frogs. Because poison ivy abounds, keep to the thin hiker track. Continue straight past South Slope Trail.

At 11 miles meet the Finger Lakes Trail (FLT) and bear left. A 0.2-mile detour right leads to the FLT trailhead on Burnt Hill Road. At the trailhead an interesting historical display features an 1864 handwritten letter from an area farmer to his wife that recounts the taking of Atlanta.

A lean-to presides in the grassy clearing to the left of the NRT at 11.1 miles; continue straight, following the FLT/Interloken Trail marked by white and orange blazes. With a rolling descent, travel a woodland-shrub bog, skirting a frog pond, crossing through a gap in a stonewall, and traveling along a boardwalk to reach the southern terminus (12 miles).

43 Taughannock Falls State Park

Overview

While the Finger Lakes Region boasts several prized east-west gorge features with similarly named trails, each has its unique signature. Taughannock Falls autographs this park with a flourish. Cradled in a cliff amphitheater and spilling 215 feet from a hanging canyon, the waterfall conjures images of Yosemite National Park in California and ranks as one of the tallest falls east of the Mississippi River.

General description:	A pair of trails explore the belly of the gorge and its canyon rim for exciting views.
General location:	West side of Cayuga Lake.
Special attractions:	Rich geologic, natural, and cultural history; waterfalls; Taughannock Creek; 400-foot cliffs.
Length:	Gorge Trail, 1.5 miles round-trip; Rim Loop, 3.5-mile loop.
Difficulty:	Easy.
Maps:	State park brochure.
Special concerns:	No swimming in Taughannock Creek. Leashed pets are allowed, but mountain bikes are prohibited.
Season and hours:	Spring through fall, daylight hours. The Gorge Trail remains open year-round.
For information:	Taughannock Falls State Park.

Taughannock Falls State Park

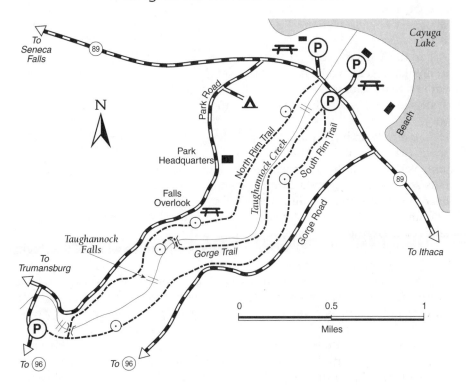

Key points:

Gorge Trail:

    0.0   Trailhead; hike west into gorge.

    0.7   Taughannock Falls; return by same route.

Rim Loop:

    0.0   Trailhead; follow South Rim Trail left.

    1.8   Cross Taughannock Creek bridge to North Rim Trail.

    2.5   Falls Overlook.

    3.2   New York 89; turn right crossing bridge.

    3.5   End at trailhead parking.

Finding the trailhead: From the junction of New York 13/34 and New York 89/96/79 (the corner of State and Meadow Streets) in Ithaca, go north on NY 89 and travel for 9.1 miles. Turn left (west) to enter the trailhead parking lot; trails leave the southwest corner of the parking area.

The hikes: The Gorge Trail and Falls Overlook on the north rim tender the best Taughannock canyon–falls vantages, but hiking the Rim Loop grants perspectives otherwise denied. The trails start from a site once occupied by Taughannock Indian camps and a cabin that sheltered a soldier in the Revolutionary War.

Gorge Trail

For the **Gorge Trail** (an interpretive trail) hike west along the paved walk. Next to the trail information hut, the South Rim Trail veers left; continue west into the gorge.

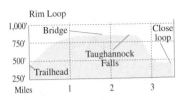

Rim Loop

At 0.1 mile an impressive 15-foot ledge spans the 75- to 100-foot width of Taughannock Creek. At the northern corner the falls spills at an angle, its chutes carving deep channels into the sedimentary ledge. The uniformly flat bedrock was planed long ago by torrents of melting ice and rock. Hemlock, basswood, maple, and oak overhang the improved-surface trail. In another 0.1 mile a second ledge spans the width of the creek; this one measures 2 feet high.

Steep wooded slopes yield to skyward-stretching cliffs. Where a woods buffer isolates the trail from the creek, side paths branch to shore. Swallows, hawks, and cardinals dwell in the canyon as do great-horned owls, whose appetites spelled an end to a peregrine release program in the 1970s.

By 0.5 mile the sandstone-shale cliffs become more prominent, steep, eroding, and jointed, with boxy overhangs and tenuously held trees. Sycamores join the ranks. Across the bridge the waterfall amphitheater humbles onlookers. With multiple streamers and wisping spray the 215-foot vertical falls plunges to an awaiting pool 30 feet deep. Spray-nurtured greenery adorns the canted base of the 400-foot cliffs. Who could ask for a more lovely or authoritative stop sign? Return as you came.

For a clockwise tour of the **Rim Loop,** start on the South Rim Trail near the trail information hut. Ascend stairs and trail to top the rim at 0.25 mile, turning right (upstream) for a mild ascent alongside a mesh fence. A mixed deciduous–hemlock forest shades the trail; deer encounters are possible. By 0.5 mile replace the teasing glimpses of the gorge with open up-canyon views spotlighting the upper reaches of Taughannock Falls.

At 0.8 mile the rim terrain pushes the hiker trail onto Gorge Road to round a steep side drainage. Afterward the buffer between trail and road remains thin. At a U-shaped scouring of the rim, a dizzying look down applauds the canyon bottom. The trail next travels a broad wooded plateau and rounds a deep gash in the gorge rim, passing through a setting of cedar, birch, willow, berried shrub, tiger lily, daisy, and harebell.

At 1.75 miles cross the hiker bridge over Taughannock Creek before reaching a road bridge and the park boundary. Upstream a 100-foot falls spills at a hairpin turn of the now-pinched gorge; downstream a strong tree-capped rim, jutting points, vertical cliffs, and an ancient plunge pool washed by the slow-moving stream compose the scene.

Taughannock Falls, Taughannock Falls State Park.

Resume the loop, following the North Rim Trail through a small field, bearing right to follow the mowed shoulder of the park road for 0.4 mile. Back on the rim the trail travels a narrow hemlock-hardwood corridor, once more alongside a wire-mesh fence.

At 2.5 miles find Falls Overlook for a bird's-eye view of the rock amphitheater and starring falls. This vantage presents the upstream water flowing up to and over the abrupt ledge of the hanging valley and the full length of the 215-foot drop. Taughannock House, a luxury hotel that operated from the 1860s until the turn of the twentieth century, formerly claimed this view.

The trail now descends, skirting a picnic area and later the campground. Views span downstream, taking in the broad creek bottom, wooded canyon, Cayuga Lake, and its east ridge. With the descent, the tour grows sunnier. At 3.25 miles stone stairs lead to NY 89, reaching the north side of Taughannock Creek bridge. Turn right, cross the bridge, and return to the parking area.

44 Onondaga Trail

General description:	Part of the greater Finger Lakes Trail (FLT), this trail rolls from rim to drainage, touring hemlock glen and hardwood forest between Spruce Pond and Cuyler.
General location:	25 miles southeast of Syracuse.
Special attractions:	Hang-gliding site and vista, waterfalls, deep hollows, a lean-to, wildlife sightings, fall foliage.
Length:	12 miles one-way.
Difficulty:	Strenuous.
Maps:	Morgan Hill State Forest brochure; Finger Lakes Trail Conference map, The Onondaga Trail, Section 01.
Special concerns:	This trail travels both public and private lands, so keep to the trail and obey posted notices.
Season and hours:	Spring through fall.
For information:	New York State Department of Environmental Conservation (DEC), Region 7.

Key points:

0.0	Northern (Spruce Pond) trailhead.
1.3	Jones Hill–Labrador Hollow State Unique Area.
2.5	Gulf rim of Tinker Falls Creek.
4.0	Cross Shackham Road.
6.0	Cross Morgan Hill Road.
10.3	Cross Cardinal Brook.
11.7	Spicer Falls.
12.0	End at West Keeney Road trailhead.

Onondaga Trail

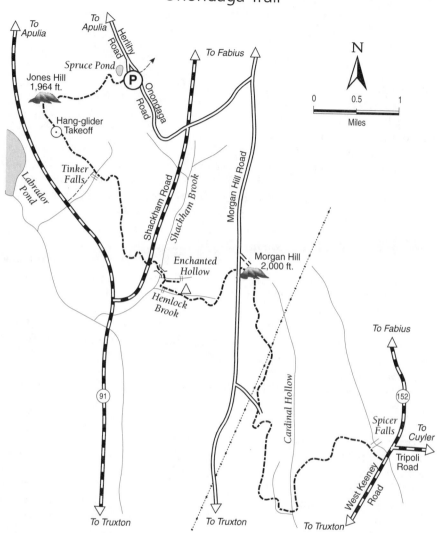

Finding the trailhead: From Interstate 81 take exit 14 for Tully and go east on New York 80 for 4.5 miles, passing through Tully and merging with New York 91 North. At 4.5 miles turn south on gravel Herlihy Road, go 1.9 miles, and continue straight at the junction to reach the Spruce Pond Fishing Access in another 0.1 mile; there is parking for ten vehicles.

For the southern terminus, in Cuyler follow Lincklaen Road west for 0.7 mile; where it crosses New York 13, the road name changes to Tripoli. At the intersection with West Keeney and Eaton Hill Roads, turn left on West Keeney Road. Look for the stepladder stile crossing the fence on the right. Limited road shoulder parking exists for shuttle vehicles.

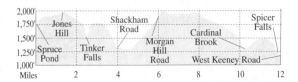

		Shackham				Spicer
2,000'						
1,750'	Jones	Road				Falls
1,500'	Hill			Cardinal		
1,250'	Spruce	Tinker	Morgan	Brook		
1,000'	Pond	Falls	Hill	West Keeney	Road	
Miles	2	4	Road 6	8	10	12

The hike: This orange-blazed route travels foot trail and woods roads, touring Labrador Hollow State Nature Preserve, Morgan Hill State Forest, and private land. When following woods roads, keep a sharp eye out for where the foot-trail segments resume. A long lapse between markers may indicate a need to backtrack and find the trail.

For a north-south tour, cross the earthen levee of square Spruce Pond and then strike up the beech-and-maple wooded slope. Where the climb levels off, ferns and brambles find habitat. A dark spruce plantation, aspen-ash woods, and an aisle of fragrant azalea in turn claim the way.

Atop Jones Hill enter Labrador Hollow—a unique area (no camping; no fires). As the trail passes above the steep western slope, faint side paths branch to the rim for obscure, seasonal views; keep to the orange trail to traverse the meadow gap of the hang-glider takeoff (1.5 miles). Open views present the steep-sided north-south valley of oval Labrador Pond. Would-be hang gliders must secure a special permit from the DEC.

Follow the doubletrack south, descending the rim. On this poorly marked segment, keep an eye out for the foot trail heading left into the deciduous forest at 1.7 miles. The tour again flip-flops between road and trail; keep left, continuing to descend.

The route contours and changes direction for a sharp descent to the gulf rim of Tinker Falls Creek (2.5 miles). The severity of the slope restricts views of the 50-foot falls, where droplet streams weep from an overhang. Do not approach the dangerous, sloughing edge or attempt any cross-country travel to gain a better falls perspective. A few steps to the right, though, afford a look into the cliff bowl and gorge; the trail continues left.

Cross Tinker Falls Creek just upstream from the overhang for a steep angular ascent to a woods road; follow it left a few steps to pick up the foot trail on the right. The tour again alternates between foot trail and woods road as it ascends, curving away from the Tinker Falls Creek drainage. Cross the nose of a ridge and descend through plantations of spruce and tamarack to cross Shackham Road at 4 miles.

In a conifer-hardwood forest, follow Shackham Brook upstream, crossing its footbridge. Just ahead, white side trails travel either side of Enchanted Hollow. Cross over the hollow to follow the second one, a woods road, upstream for unobstructed views and easier walking. This 0.2-mile round-trip detour finds a stepped cascade spilling over bedrock ledges.

Return downstream and resume the Onondaga Trail as it contours the hemlock-spruce slope, following Shackham Brook upstream. Pass a blue trail on the left. Before long the Onondaga Trail hooks left to parallel upstream along aptly named Hemlock Brook. Past an 8-foot waterfall and camp flat, reach a lean-to overlooking the steep-sided drainage (5 miles). Descend to and cross Hemlock Brook atop flat stones. The foot trail now angles sharply uphill.

Back on woods road be alert for where the foot trail descends to the left; do not be confused by the orange snowmobile markers along the road. The trail now dips through a steep side drainage and ascends to cross Morgan Hill Road at 6 miles.

Angle across the road, picking up the trail as it ascends. Stay to the orange-blazed route as white trails branch left to the Morgan Hill bivouac area. Spruce wanes from the mix. Continue to watch for the Onondaga trail markers because truck trail and snowmobile routes interweave the area. The hike passes through plantation and mixed woods, with some big-diameter trees. At 7.3 miles traverse the breadth of an open utility corridor.

After crossing a lightly used truck trail (8 miles), the trail rolls and contours, crossing two more woods roads. Maple, beech, black cherry, and tamarack cloak the slope. The intervals between blazes grow longer but occur frequently enough to reassure. Woodpecker, grouse, and deer may surprise.

At 8.8 miles the trail enters private property for the remainder of the tour. Uneven foot trail and overgrown jeep track lead the way. Watch for blazes as the trail descends through woods and bramble–fern patches, frequently changing direction. At 10 miles cross a hollow where the brook pours over slate and shows a steep gorge downstream.

Next ascend for a rolling tour along the hemlock-treed rim of the downstream gorge—and watch your footing. The brook flows 80 to 100 feet below. Despite a few markers being down, the trail is followable. Ahead the trail

Curved snag.

and drainage both bend left to reach Cardinal Hollow. Descend to cross this larger brook, where wading may be required.

Turn upstream, cross a rocky side drainage, and ascend the slope to parallel Cardinal Hollow upstream. On woods road ascend away from the hollow, then veer left, descending via woods path to Spicer Falls at 11.7 miles. Best views of this two-stage, 60-foot waterfall come when autumn denudes the trees. Follow the drainage rim downstream to cross a step-stile over a fence. Descend and pass through a cow pasture, ending at West Keeney Road (12 miles).

45 Watkins Glen State Park

Overview

This park presents one of the premier gorge and waterfall settings in the Finger Lakes Region and in the country. Charged with excitement, the hike brings together majestic 200-foot cliffs, nineteen waterfalls that punctuate a 545-foot drop on Glen Creek, turbulent chutes, deep plunge pools, and scenic bridges, tunnels, and twisting staircases.

General description:	The north shore loop examines the gorge from within and above; the south rim hike travels the wooded rim to an upstream man-made lake.
General location:	In the village of Watkins Glen.
Special attractions:	Waterfalls, cascades, chutes, and still-water calms; brooding cliffs; diverse woods.
Length:	Gorge Trail–Indian Trail Loop, 2.8-mile loop; South Rim Hike, 3.5 miles round-trip.
Difficulty:	Easy to moderate for both.
Maps:	State park brochure.
Special concerns:	Fee parking; lot may fill at peak times. Beware: Springs and waterfalls can dampen the steps and walks, making them slippery and dangerous.
Season and hours:	Mid-May through November 10; daylight hours.
For information:	Watkins Glen State Park.

Key points:
Gorge Trail–Indian Trail Loop:
0.0   Lower (concession area) trailhead; hike upstream.
0.3   Spiral Tunnel/loop junction; remain on Gorge Trail.
0.7   Rainbow Falls.
1.5   Ascend Jacob's Ladder to Indian Trail.
2.4   Point Lookout.
2.5   Close loop at Spiral Tunnel; backtrack to lower trailhead.

Watkins Glen State Park

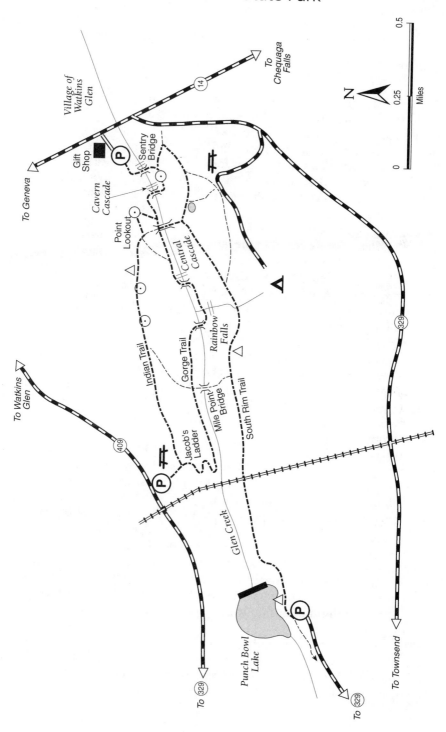

Village of Watkins Glen

To Geneva

To Chequaga Falls

14

Gift Shop

Sentry Bridge

Cavern Cascade

Point Lookout

Central Cascade

Indian Trail

Gorge Trail

Rainbow Falls

Mile Point Bridge

South Rim Trail

Jacob's Ladder

To Watkins Glen

409

Glen Creek

Punch Bowl Lake

To 329

To 329

To Townsend

329

N

0   0.25   0.5

Miles

South Rim Hike:

0.0   Lower (concession area) trailhead; hike upstream.
0.1   Cross Sentry Bridge to Finger Lakes Trail (FLT).
1.2   Pass under railroad bridge.
1.7   Punch Bowl Lake; return by same route.

Finding the trailhead: In Watkins Glen, find the park entrance west off Franklin Avenue/New York 14, south of Fourth Street.

Gorge Trail–Indian Trail Loop

The hikes: If a trail choice must be made, make it the **Gorge Trail.** A shuttle bus runs between the lower concession and upper entrance for those who have time for just a one-way tour or for those who prefer to descend rather than ascend the trail's 832 steps. Purchase tickets at the gift shop.

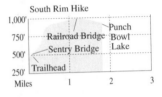

South Rim Hike

The bustle at the park entry echoes the site's roots as a private resort in the late 1800s. Off-hour, off-season, and rainy-day visits allow for a quieter, unhurried communion with the gorge grandeur. An upstream tour starts at the west end of the parking lot; bring plenty of film.

Early looks feature the stone arch of Sentry Bridge and bulging canyon walls that together shape a keyhole view of a waterfall recessed in the shadows. Ascend the first of three tunnels bored into the rock, emerging at Sentry Bridge, which presents an up-canyon view of the pinched gorge, long-distance views of Watkins Glen, and close looks at the jointed, layered rock. The Gorge Trail crisscrosses Glen Creek four times but bypasses High and Mile Point Bridges.

At 0.1 mile the Finger Lakes Trail (South Rim Hike) heads left; remain in the gorge, skirting the Timespell laser show setup. As the trail ascends the stairs to Cavern Cascade, look down to see a heart-shaped plunge pool. Now pass behind the droplet curtain for a unique perspective; ahead lies the Spiral Tunnel staircase, which opens to a view of the suspension bridge (High Bridge). Keep to the gorge, passing under the bridge.

As the canyon walls cup and divide, each bend holds an aura of mystery. A leafy bower claims the Narrows; a dry, concave bowing of the gorge characterizes the Cathedral. A tiered upstream cascade feeds the 60-foot plunge of Central Cascade, the highest in the park. At 0.7 mile Rainbow Falls showers over the south rim. Beyond find a bridge and Spiral Gorge, a dark, more brooding passage.

The trail returns to the glaring light at Mile Point Bridge. Continue west along the north wall, bypassing both the bridge and a trail to the right. In the calm above the lower-canyon storm, ascend the stairs of Jacob's Ladder to Indian Trail (the loop's return) and upper entrance (1.5 miles).

Sentry Bridge, Watkins Glen State Park.

Look for the **Indian Trail** to head right just beyond a midway bench on Jacob's Ladder. A low rock wall or mesh fence edges the broad trail as it travels the north rim and slope. Evergreens, dogwood, oak, maple, beech, sassafras, and black cherry contribute to a forest roster concealing Glen Creek.

At 1.8 miles the spur from Mile Point Bridge arrives on the right; at 2 miles the trail overlooks Rainbow Falls. Staying along the rim, find a Central Cascade overlook for a totally new perspective. The trail then skirts a cemetery and descends sharply, bypassing a lean-to, to reach the suspension bridge. Lovers Lane arrives on the right; continue straight ahead (east) to Point Lookout and the park entrance.

A detour onto the bridge provides a grand look 85 feet down to the creek and out the canyon; Point Lookout offers a fine cross-gorge view. Descend the stairs, meeting the Gorge Trail at Spiral Tunnel, and retrace the first 0.25 mile.

The **South Rim Hike** shares the first 0.1 mile with the Gorge Trail. After crossing Sentry Bridge, veer left on the Finger Lakes Trail (FLT), ascending some one hundred steps to the south rim. Turn right on the service road, following the white blazes of the FLT. At 0.25 mile discover a tiny lily pond, topped by just a few blooms. Ahead, stone pedestal and disk-slab tables mark a forlorn recreation site.

Bear right, ascending the chestnut oak and hemlock rim, passing spurs to the south entrance and, much later, the campground. At 0.75 mile a lean-to presides next to the trail; upstream from the lean-to, a stairway descends to the gorge. Much of the way, the appreciation of the gorge is audio rather than visual.

Follow the wide trail ahead at 1.2 miles, passing under a scenic railroad bridge where robust deciduous vegetation interweaves the rusting trestle. Pine, cherry, hickory, and ash briefly frame the tour. As the trail veers toward the rim, a ragged vertical outcrop attracts attention.

The trail next rounds the nose of a hemlock-shaded point for filtered looks at Glen Creek. Stay with the white blazes, descending in spurts to Punch Bowl Lake (1.75 miles). Overlook the dam and its vertical falls and then dip to where beaver gnawings dot the lakeshore. Bullfrogs, cedar waxwings, and red-winged blackbirds animate the site. Marsh grasses claim the upper lake; cattail peninsulas extend into the open water. Much of the pond shows aquatic plants. Site picnic tables remain usable, but a rest room facility has collapsed.

Return as you came, or follow the FLT upstream.

46 Buttermilk Falls State Park

Overview

Buttermilk Falls caps a dramatic 500-foot free fall of Buttermilk Creek that occurs over a distance of 0.75 mile. Cascades, rapids, bedrock slides, emerald pools, platy cliffs, and a 40-foot rock spire compose the prized setting.

General description:	Easy interlocking trails explore the Buttermilk Creek gorge, its upstream glen, and Treman Lake. A first-rate interpretive loop examines a unique marsh.
General location:	Southern outskirts of Ithaca.
Special attractions:	Buttermilk Falls and Creek, upland forest, marsh, scenic rockwork dam, wildlife sightings.
Length:	Gorge-Rim Loop, 1.7-mile loop; Bear Trail–Treman Lake Loop, 3.5 miles round-trip; Larch Meadows Trail, 1-mile loop.
Difficulty:	Easy for all.
Maps:	State park brochure; Larch Meadows Trail brochure.
Special concerns:	Fee area. Wear insect repellent in meadows.
Season and hours:	Spring through fall (gorge trails close November 10); daylight hours.
For information:	Buttermilk Falls State Park.

Key points:
Gorge-Rim Loop:
- 0.0   Start below falls swimming hole; cross dam to south wall.
- 0.6   Pinnacle Rock.
- 0.8   Cross West King Road bridge to Rim Trail.
- 1.4   Buttermilk Falls Overlook.
- 1.7   End loop near refreshment stand.

Bear Trail–Treman Lake Loop:
- 0.0   West King Road trailhead; follow Bear Trail upstream.
- 0.7   Picnic area.
- 0.9   Treman Lake Loop; proceed upstream.
- 2.6   Close loop; backtrack downstream.

Larch Meadows Trail:
- 0.0   Ballfield trailhead.
- 1.0   End loop at ballfield.

Finding the trailhead: From the junction of New York 79 and New York 13/34 (the corner of Seneca and Meadow Streets) in southwest Ithaca, go south on NY 13/34 for 1.8 miles and turn left to enter the main area of Buttermilk Falls State Park. For the upper area, continue 0.1 mile farther south on NY 13/34 and turn left (east) on Sandbank Road. Go 2.2 miles and turn left on West King Road. In 1.2 miles turn right on the park road to reach the upper day-use area in 0.8 mile.

Buttermilk Falls State Park

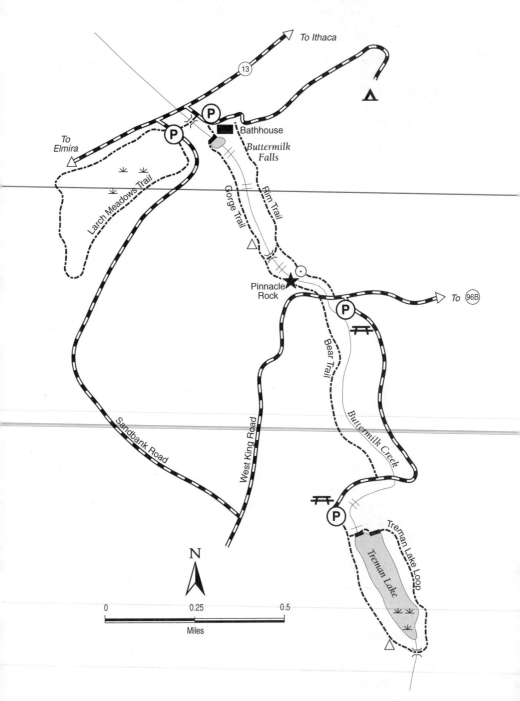

To Ithaca

13

To Elmira

P

P

Bathhouse

Buttermilk Falls

Larch Meadows Trail

Gorge Trail

Rim Trail

Pinnacle Rock

To 96B

P

Bear Trail

Buttermilk Creek

Sandbank Road

West King Road

P

Treman Lake Loop

Treman Lake

N

0   0.25   0.5

Miles

The hikes: In the main area, find the popular **Gorge–Rim Loop** near the swimming hole at the base of Buttermilk Falls. Cross the dam and ascend along the south wall. Broad Buttermilk Falls sheets over a magnificent canted cliff sloping to the man-made pool. Crossbeds accent the light-colored rock, and small ledges fold the waters into cascades.

A steep stairway ascends alongside the falls, isolating aspects of the watery spectacle. Beech, hemlock, and a burst of understory greenery contribute to the hike's visual component. Prior to reaching the upper level of the falls, the stairs turn away. At 0.2 mile a three-tier, three-dimensional falls graces the creek. One level spills through a grotto where the gorge walls pinch together; some ten falls accent this canyon tour.

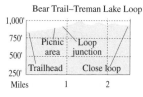

Cascades, historic plunge pools, eroded cliff scallops, and hemlock coves build on the fascination. The trail affords perspectives from below, alongside, and atop the cascades. A lean-to is uphill to the right just before a crescent footbridge (0.5 mile) that spans Buttermilk Creek to the north wall and Rim Trail. Stay along the south wall for the full 1.7-mile loop.

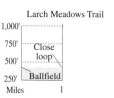

A ribbony side falls washes over the cliff as a split-level hourglass falls punctuates Buttermilk Creek. Next find Pinnacle Rock, a 40-foot chiseled gray spire isolated from the cliff. Delicate ferns decorate the erosion-resistant ledges. Maple, ash, and basswood shade the trail as it nears West King Road (0.8 mile).

From here Bear Trail continues upstream on the south shore. For the Gorge–Rim Loop, cross the road bridge and turn left on the Rim Trail, a wide dirt lane isolated from the edge by a wire-mesh fence. Past an overlook of Pinnacle Rock, the trail gently descends. At 1.1 miles the side trail arrives from the creek; views are few and short-lived.

As the descent steepens, the trail shows a paved surface, and the corridor becomes more open. Beyond Buttermilk Falls Overlook (a filtered view), the trail descends and contours the slope above the campground road to exit at the refreshment stand.

For a longer creek hike, delay taking the rim return at 0.8 mile and instead follow the **Bear Trail** upstream to **Treman Lake Loop.** Bear Trail travels the broad wooded glen upstream, passing some 40-feet away from the stream. Hemlock, basswood, maple, oak, and beech shade a plush, green understory. Side trails descend to the bank, while skunk cabbage claims the moist slopes. In 0.75 mile (1.55 miles), the trail comes out at a picnic area. Continue upstream along the creek or follow the road to the site's comfort station, where the Treman Lake Loop starts.

191

A counterclockwise tour stays along the south shore, bypassing the dam and spillway feeding the picnic area falls. As the hike continues through the mixed deciduous–hemlock forest, cross-lake views find an attractive cliff scallop and cove. The trail ascends, drawing 100 feet above the water. Geese occupy a small island.

Cross a side-drainage footbridge to round the upper marshy head of Treman Lake, bypassing an orange-blazed trail near a second lean-to. Afterward, cross the scenic stone bridge over Buttermilk Creek to travel the north shore, closing the loop. Stay low along the rock wall upon leaving the bridge.

Stairsteps ascend a knoll for an overlook of the lake's cattail waters before the trail returns to shore. Sunfish guarding their gravel-cleared nests or a snapping turtle may delay hikers' strides. Beware of poison ivy along shore.

Another set of stairs leads to a second vista featuring the attractive stonework and natural cliff outcrop that form the dam's curvature. Continue rounding the lake, staying left to cross the stone dam and outcrop to close the loop. The trail returns to the comfort station at 2.6 miles (3.4 miles), to West King Road at 3.5 miles (4.3 miles), and to the lower park via the Rim Trail (5.2 miles).

Start the **Larch Meadows Trail** next to the ballfield rest room, 0.1 mile south of the main entrance off Sandbank Road. A fine brochure (available at the entrance station or trailhead) explains this unique habitat, part of ancient Cayuga Lake.

Falls on Buttermilk Creek, Buttermilk Falls State Park.

Until 1779 this site held a Sapony Indian village of log cabins. In that Revolutionary War year, word of the advance of the Sullivan Campaign forced the tribe to flee. When the troops arrived they torched all cabins, ending an era.

For the hike, follow the southern edge of the ballfield, bearing left prior to the end of the field on a wide mowed swath. The trail tours habitats of mixed woods; skunk cabbage wetland; stands of willow and spreading black walnut; and waist-high ferns, grasses, and wildflowers. Passing a 4-foot-diameter sycamore, the trail meets and briefly follows a service road to the right. The trail then resumes to the right, returning to the ballfield to close the loop.

Central-Leatherstocking Region

Squeezed by the Adirondacks, the Catskills, and the Finger Lakes Region, this region occupies the belt buckle of the state and celebrates the countryside made famous by James Fenimore Cooper. The region boasts shining lakes, forested ridges, swamps, fields, caverns, and caves. A section of the original Erie Canal channels hikers throught the past. A tranquil pastoral setting claims the outlying territory.

47 Old Erie Canal Heritage Trail

General description:	This multiuse national recreation trail travels the towpath of the Erie Canal between DeWitt and Rome, passing museums, parks, and historic structures.
General location:	East of Syracuse.
Special attractions:	Historic canal, towpath, aqueducts, culverts, and cannery ruins; trailside museums; Green Lakes State Park; wildflowers; wildlife sightings.
Length:	36 miles one-way, with a 2.2-mile interruption between Durhamville and State Bridge (New York 46 and New York 31); the tour thrice requires road travel to bridge towpath units.
Difficulty:	Easy.
Maps:	State park flier.
Special concerns:	Pick up a flier for both the map of the Old Erie Canal and the mileage log. Wash after any contact with canal waters. Find rest rooms and drinking water at Cedar Bay and Poolsbrook picnic areas and at Green Lakes State Park. Tour fees are collected at museums and at Erie Canal Village.
Season and hours:	Year-round, dawn to dusk.
For information:	Old Erie Canal State Historic Park.

Key points:

0.0	Western (Ryder Park) trailhead.
3.0	Manlius Center.
8.6	White Bridge Road trailhead.
11.0	Chittenango Landing Canal Boat Museum.
16.4	Canastota; follow Canal Street.
22.4	Interstate 90 overpass to Durhamville (road stretch).
31.0	Lock 21.
35.0	Fort Bull Road, hike's end (May through September).
36.0	Erie Canal Village, hike's end (October through April).

Old Erie Canal Heritage Trail

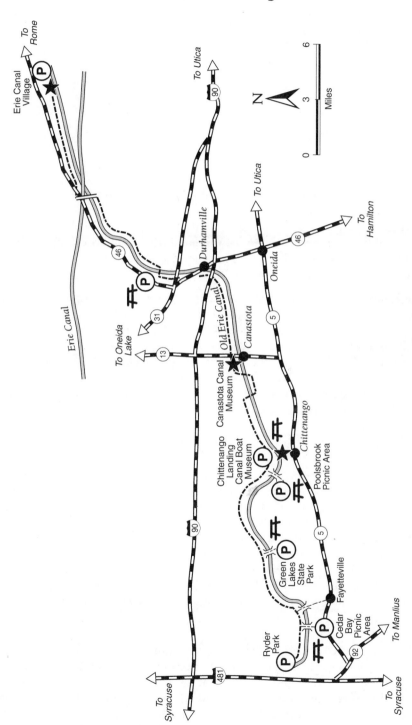

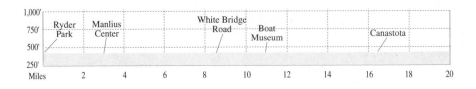

Finding the trailhead: From Interstate 481 in East Syracuse, take exit 3E for New York 5/New York 92 and go east toward Fayetteville. In 0.8 mile, where NY 5 and NY 92 split, go north (left) on Lyndon Road for 0.8 mile, bearing left on Kinne Road. Go 0.4 mile and turn right on Butternut Drive to find Ryder Park and the western trail terminus on the right in 0.1 mile. Find the eastern terminus west of Rome, off NY 46.

The hike: This linear New York State Park salutes a 36-mile vestige of the historic 363-mile Erie Canal, which linked the Atlantic Ocean and Great Lakes. One of the great engineering feats of its day, the canal opened the West to transportation and commerce—a great boon to nineteenth-century New York State. The trail traces the towpath that was plodded by barge-towing mules from 1825 to 1918.

The multiuse trail variously shows cinders or a natural surface. Footbridges at Cedar Bay and Poolsbrook Picnic Areas, at Green Lakes State Park, and opposite the Fayetteville side canal allow for passage between the north and south shore along the western end of the tour. Road bridges serve the eastern end.

Virginia creeper, poison ivy, and wild grape entangle the diverse tree border of maple, locust, box elder, elm, ash, sumac, black willow, and dogwood. Queen Anne's lace, chicory, purple loosestrife, dandelion, and spotted knapweed color the towpath sides.

For the most part, the canal corridor remains undeveloped, with a few encroaching houses as the trail nears towns. Parallel roadways sometimes add noise, but mostly the hike brings relaxation, following the straightaways and gentle bends of the canal. Woodchucks, painted and snapping turtles, kingfishers, yellow warblers, rough-winged swallows (which nest in the unmortared stonework), bluegills, and carp are among the canal corridor inhabitants.

On a west-to-east tour from Ryder Park Nature Area in DeWitt to the outskirts of Rome, initially find mileage markers and crossroad labels regularly marked, but such travel aids wane by later miles. The hike's 6-foot-wide cinder trail crosses Butternut Creek for overlooks of the cut stones and concrete of a lateral aqueduct. Frogs and turtles hide in the algae, while carps

196

Stonework arches, Old Erie Canal Heritage State Park.

part the murky water. A cattail marsh lies beyond the trees to the left, as the route rounds the bald hill of a former landfill to reach the northern towpath.

Cross under the rustic steel footbridge that leads to Cedar Bay Picnic Area on the south shore, bypassing the Canal Center. Despite the center having been closed now for several years, the grounds still hold an old tow hoist and watering basin from the canal days, as well as a memorial honoring Moses DeWitt (1766 to 1794).

The tour now slips into character with areas of intermittent and full shade and uninterrupted overlooks of the canal. Where the Erie Canal widens into a pond beyond Burdick Street, a side canal paired with its own towpath trail arrives from Fayetteville; a footbridge ties this spur to the national recreation trail. Notice the big, cut stones of the side canal.

From Manlius Center at 3 miles, a sparsity of trees makes for a hot passage, while an old barn alongside the trail hints at the rural canal setting. From the footbridge to Green Lakes State Park (4.6 miles), a 0.2-mile service road ascends to a New York 290 crossing. With the park facilities located well south of the highway, plan on a mile detour for drinking water and rest rooms, but the park invites with two deep lakes.

At Kirkville Road, a couple of picnic tables and a small lawn invite a stop and offer fine looks at the canal rockwork. The water shows but minimal movement, hinting at the original need for the towpath to move the barges from point to point. Cross-canal views find an unruly growth of trees and shrubs isolating the corridor. Often the canal channels a refreshing breeze.

Past Poolsbrook Road (7.3 miles) the corridor becomes more sun exposed; at road crossings the towpath typically opens up. As the canal widens to a pond, cross-canal views find scenic Poolsbrook Picnic Area, with its park benches and tables shaded by scenic willow and apple trees. Where the canal again narrows, a footbridge crosses to the picnic area.

A small trailhead parking lot serves towpath travelers at White Bridge Road (8.6 miles). The corridor itself remains little changed as the dense leafy border of the far shore continues. Past Bolivar Road, a scenic gape-board barn and a silo overlook the towpath.

At Lakeport Road (10.9 miles) search the southwest corner of the canal to find old cannery ruins. Cross the road bridge to reach the Chittenango Landing Canal Boat Museum (open daily 10:00 A.M. to 4:00 P.M. July and August; irregular hours other months). Find both indoor and outdoor exhibits, with three original dry-dock bays being rebuilt in original stone, replica sawmill and blacksmith buildings, and a mule-drawn steamboat and fine pictorial history.

The towpath narrows at Canaseraga Road at 12.5 miles. Hayfields and cornfields add to the serenity of the tour. East of Fuller's Bridge, cross from the northern towpath to the south shore at West Shore Railroad (14.9 miles). Where the trail meets Bebee Bridge Road, turn north (left), cross the bridge, and continue east along the northern towpath.

At 16.4 miles the canal parallels State Street into Canastota as the towpath now becomes a residential greenway. At Buck Street the towpath disappears; follow Canal Street east 0.3 mile, picking up the towpath past New York 13. On the north side of Canal Street, look for the Canastota Canal Museum, which houses canal artifacts and photos in a building on the National Register of Historic Places, circa 1874.

Where the towpath halts at North Court Road (19.5 miles), bear left, angling across the road to again pick up the northern towpath at the edge of a cornfield. Canal Road maintains a parallel course; the area remains rural, and more waterflow constructions mark the tour. By Cobb Street, leafy trees lace over the route for a scenic stroll.

After 22 miles the trail detours from the towpath, crossing Interstate 90 on an overpass. The towpath resumes only briefly before reaching the 2.2-mile travel gap at Durhamville (22.4 miles). End the tour here or pick up the trail on the north side of NY 31 at State Bridge. Another 11.4 miles of trail remain, passing through the rural countryside, first on the southern towpath, then crossing to the northern towpath at Lock 21 (31 miles), but the closeness of NY 46 intrudes.

October through April hikers may take the tour all the way east to the privately owned Erie Canal Village off NY 46, a re-created canal-era community. May through September, when the village closes its section of towpath for mule-drawn canal boat tours, end the hike at Fort Bull Road (35 miles).

48 Brookfield Swamp Loop

General description: This Beaver Creek State Forest circuit travels the wooded and meadow outskirts of Brookfield Swamp.

General location: In southeast Madison County, 1 mile north of Brookfield.

Special attractions: Hemlock-hardwood forest and conifer plantation, spring and summer wildflowers, wildlife sightings.

Length: 9.5-mile loop.

Difficulty: Easy to moderate.

Maps: Brookfield Trail System brochure.

Special concerns: None.

Season and hours: Spring through fall.

For information: New York State Department of Environmental Conservation, Region 7.

Key points:
- 0.0 Trailhead; hike west.
- 2.2 Cross Beaver Creek Road.
- 3.1 Cross Beaver Creek Road to Glenn Bacon Trail.
- 5.2 Bliven Road bridge.
- 6.4 First crossing of Fairground Road.
- 9.5 End loop at trailhead.

Brookfield Swamp Loop

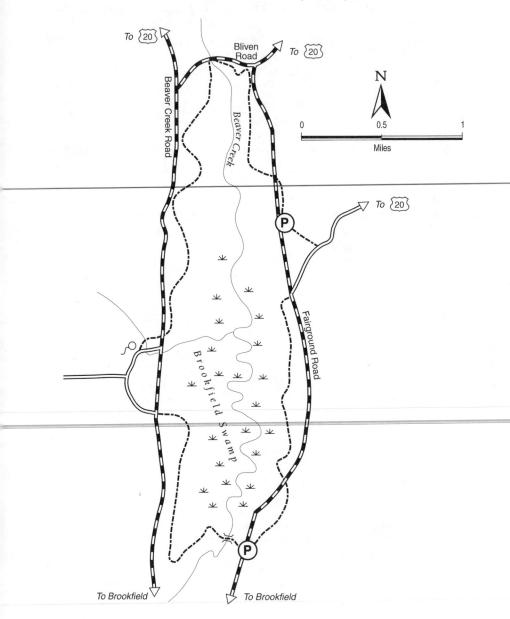

Finding the trailhead: From the junction of Fairground Road and Main Street (Skaneateles Turnpike) in Brookfield, go north on Fairground Road for 1 mile to find trailhead parking on the left. Arriving from U.S. Highway 20, turn south on Bliven Road between Bridgewater and Sangerfield, coming to a Y-junction in 1.4 miles. Bear left on Fairground Road and continue 3 miles to find the trailhead on the right, with parking for five vehicles.

The hike: Part of an extensive 130-mile trail system serving foot, horse, and snowmobile travelers, this well-marked circuit stays primarily on trail and closed woods roads linked by two short truck-trail segments open to vehicles, maximum speed 25 miles per hour. The rolling trail rarely comes in contact with Brookfield Swamp, centerpiece of the tour.

Hike the gravel track west from the parking lot for a clockwise tour. Scarlet tanager, woodchuck, and rabbit may number among the early wildlife sightings. Birch, alder, and shrubby deciduous frame the open trail. Keep to the gravel path, crossing the horse bridge over Beaver Creek; high railings protect horse and rider.

Pause on the bridge for the best view of Brookfield Swamp. Far-stretching views north and a more restricted view south present the attractive marsh. Dark-flowing Beaver Creek meanders through the broad swamp bottom, framed in turn by bog grass, wetland shrubs, and trees. Lilies and other aquatics decorate the shallow edge, and dragonflies buzz the surface.

A mowed swath continues the tour, with a scenic row of maple and black cherry trees toward the swamp, a tidy pine plantation to the left. Rock walls sometimes border the route, while wild strawberries offer tasty bites in June.

At the 0.8-mile junction turn right to traverse a low hemlock-clad ridge for a cool, shady passage. Oxalis and Mayflower decorate the floor. Descending the ridge, cross a small drainage dotted with false hellebore. An aspen stand and spruce plantation now vary the walk. Within the long grassy meadows dotted by pine and aspen, keep an eye out for turkeys.

Occasional engine sounds precede the crossing of Beaver Creek Road (2.2 miles) and the start of a truck-trail segment. Travel the semishaded dirt road uphill, bypassing a connector to the greater Brookfield Trail System on the left at 2.4 miles. At 2.7 miles turn left, entering the woods, bypassing a small rock-lined pond built for fire protection in the1930s. Descend and cross a side brook below the rock ruins of an old dam, and follow the levee to the right (downstream) along an old ditch.

Crossing back over Beaver Creek Road, follow the Glenn Bacon Trail, a mowed swath touring an open meadow corridor with full-skirted spruce, woody shrubs, hawkweed, daisy, buttercup, and various floral stalks. Before long the trail ascends sharply and steadily through mixed forest then levels to traverse another long meadow, coming to a tribute to Glenn Bacon, a horseman who advanced recreational opportunities in the area. A bench and picnic table overlook Brookfield Swamp and the wooded east ridge—a textured tapestry of mottled wetland, shrubs, leafy trees, and sharp plantation outlines.

Stay on the mowed track, alternately touring open field and spruce corridor. As the tour can be hot and humid, carry plenty of water. A bandanna for the head and insect repellent can bring some tranquility during bug

Beaver Creek and Brookfield Swamp, Beaver Creek State Forest.

season. The trail rolls as it approaches Bliven Road for a road-bridge crossing of Beaver Creek (5.2 miles). A few rural homes come into view.

On the opposite shore, the trail passes between meadow and plantation. In the mixed woods at 5.9 miles, a regal 4- to 5-foot-diameter white pine presides trailside. Soon the trail crosses Fairground Road, touring amid meadow and tamarack, bypassing the primary trailhead for equestrian users at 6.4 miles.

Remain on the east side of Fairground Road, ascending a grassy double-track in a cedar-hardwood forest. The trail tops out, meeting a truck trail at 6.9 miles; turn right, staying on the truck trail descending to Fairground Road (7.5 miles).

Angle left across the road and descend via foot trail, passing through meadow and crossing drainages. Past the tamarack seed orchard, a spruce corridor claims the tour. At 9 miles again cross Fairground Road for a brief swing along the wooded east slope, coming out opposite the parking area; cross the road and close the loop.

49 Glimmerglass State Park

Overview

In the heart of James Fenimore Cooper country, the wooded flank of Mount Wellington and the field, shrub, and woodland habitats of this state park shape the understated setting of Hyde Bay on Otsego Lake—the "glimmerglass" jewel of the area. Within this soothing backdrop, hikers enjoy short outings and subtle discoveries.

General description: Casual hikes explore lake cove, pond, woodland, and field habitats.
General location: 8 miles north of Cooperstown.
Special attractions: Historic estate, bird-watching, spring and summer wildflowers, fall foliage.
Length: Otsego Lake–Mount Wellington Hike, 3.5-mile loop; Beaver Pond to Woodland–Field Loop, 2.2 miles round-trip.
Difficulty: Both easy.
Maps: State park brochure.
Special concerns: Fee area.
Season and hours: Spring through fall.
For information: Glimmerglass State Park.

Key points:
Otsego Lake–Mount Wellington Hike:
0.0   Start near Hyde Hall; walk service road west.
0.3   Road fork; go left on lake loop.
0.9   Mount Wellington Trail junction; ascend left.
1.7   Lake overview.
3.4   Hyde Hall.
3.5   End at trail parking.
Beaver Pond to Woodland-Field Loop:
0.0   Beaver Pond Trailhead; start on wheelchair-accessible trail.
0.6   Shadow Brook covered bridge.
1.6   End loop at Shadow Brook bridge; backtrack to trailhead.

Finding the trailhead: From U.S. Highway 20 in East Springfield, turn south on Otsego County 31, following the signs for Glimmerglass State Park. In 3.9 miles turn right (west) to enter the park. From Cooperstown go 8 miles north on County 31 to reach the turn for the park entrance.

The hikes: For the **Otsego Lake–Mount Wellington Hike,** from the parking area west of Hyde Hall mansion, at the end of the public road, walk the closed service road west. A tight array of thin trees and big white pines chokes out early Hyde Bay–Otsego Lake views.

At 0.2 mile look for a roadside post and orange banding on the trees, the start of the Mount Wellington Trail, but delay taking it. Stay on the service road to complete the lake loop first. In 100 feet a gap offers an open view

Glimmerglass State Park

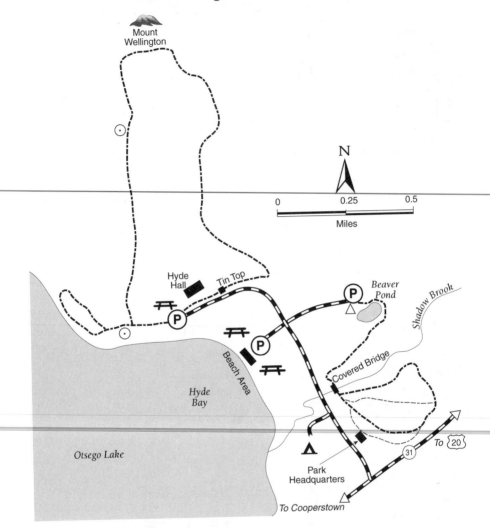

of the lake with attractive serial ridges beyond. The lake's sparkle inspired James Fenimore Cooper to dub it "Glimmerglass" in his popular tales about a frontier hero, "the Leatherstocking."

Where the service road forks, go left for a clockwise tour, rounding above the lakeshore. Morning sightings of deer may suggest an early start; lake views remain filtered. The loop's return travels slightly higher along the slope, passing beneath hemlock and birch trees.

Return to the roadside post (0.9 mile) and follow the orange route up the flank of Mount Wellington. The trail ascends the broad back of a side ridge for a comfortable tour. Mixed-age evergreens and hardwoods weave a high, full, and restless canopy. Where the ridge flattens, ferns grace the slope. Again, deer may be spied.

After a brief dip the ridge flattens before rounding the upper edge of the wooded slope, reaching a lake overview (1.7 miles). In summer trees filter much of the view. The trail now arcs back along the broad summit; moister areas hold distinct pockets of at least four fern varieties. Bold displays of five-finger fern particularly delight.

At 2.2 miles arrows point where the trail departs the plateau to wrap its way

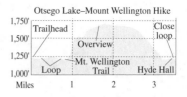

Otsego Lake–Mount Wellington Hike

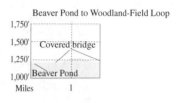

Beaver Pond to Woodland-Field Loop

downhill; still the big-diameter trees engage. In 0.5 mile the trail enters the sharpest descent of the tour. At 3 miles turn left along a utility corridor. Beware of the animal burrows masked by tall grasses, and watch for the next blaze that points downhill to the right.

Descend through a dense patch of big-leafed plants, reach the service road, and turn right, following the road between the twin gate cottages and beneath the domed arch of Tin Top. Cross the grounds of Hyde Hall mansion, formerly owned by Lieutenant George Clarke (a New York State governor from 1736 to 1744) and return to the parking area. The mansion, a dignified stone-block manor, is open for guided tours summer weekends or by appointment.

For **Beaver Pond to Woodland-Field Loop,** begin at the parking lot for the **Beaver Pond Trail,** opposite the entry to the park's main beach. The hike starts on the gated service road east of the lean-to, next to a privy. But first admire the shallow pond from the parking area, because a thick shrub border conceals it from the trail.

A mowed swath with added stonedust allows for wheelchair access where the trail curves right, rounding between picnic sites. The trail next travels the shrub-lined corridor between meadow and pond. Hawkweed, iris, buttercup, and clover sprinkle color. In winter the trail doubles as a cross-country ski trail.

At the Y-junction (0.4 mile) go left for the **Woodland-Field Loop,** now traversing a tallgrass field. The hike no longer is wheelchair-accessible. Pass through the Shadow Brook covered bridge (another remaining estate structure), and take the first left for a clockwise tour of the multilobed woodland-field circuit. Swallows nest in the bridge rafters.

Views of Shadow Brook quickly vanish. Where the trail passes through an open transition zone between field and woods, glimpse the rural neighborhood along the outer park. At 1 mile briefly enter a woodland pocket of big oaks, well worth slowing to get to know, and then proceed left at the upcoming junction. At the 1.2-mile junction, turn right for the selected woodland-field circuit; a left here expands the circuit, swinging an arc past the headquarters.

Hyde Hall, Glimmerglass State Park.

The trail, now a doubletrack, tours a gallery of magnificent old maples. Where the doubletrack bears right, continue straight on the mowed track to travel a young succession forest. The headquarters spur returns on the left. Return to the covered bridge at 1.6 miles and retrace Beaver Pond Trail to the trailhead.

50 Bowman Lake State Park

Overview

A quiet wooded setting, gentle terrain, and thirty-five-acre Bowman Lake are the hallmarks of this state park. Bordered by 11,000 acres of state forest land, the park contributes to a broad, open space for wildlife and a tranquil arena for hikers. The long-distance Finger Lakes Trail (FLT) passes through the park, and a fine nature trail encircles the lake.

General description: A pair of well-marked, rolling walks journey through natural hardwood stands and conifer plantations to visit a fire tower and explore the lake basin.
General location: 8 miles northwest of Oxford.
Special attractions: Lake setting, diverse hardwood forests, scenic rock walls, fire-tower access, bird-watching.

Bowman Lake State Park

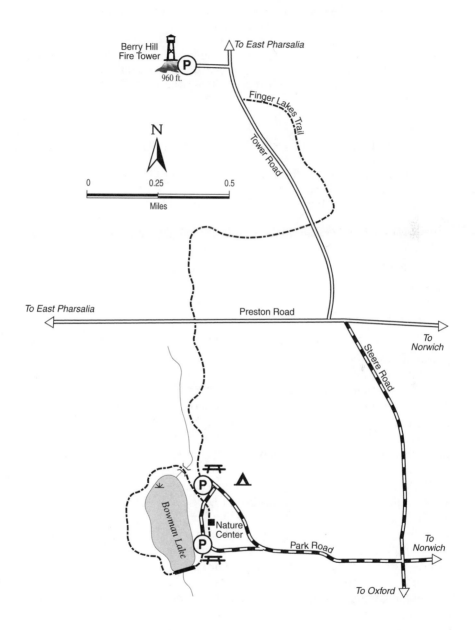

Length:	FLT to Berry Hill Fire Tower, 5.6 miles round-trip; Nature Trail, 1.3-mile loop.
Difficulty:	Both easy.
Maps:	State park brochure; Finger Lakes Trail Conference map, Sheet M24.
Special concerns:	Fee area. Expect some soggy stretches.
Season and hours:	Spring through fall, daylight hours. Nature Center: Friday evenings and weekends during summer.
For information:	Bowman Lake State Park.

Key points:

FLT to Berry Hill Fire Tower:

  0.0   Northernmost beach parking; hike FLT north.
  1.2   Cross gravel Preston Road.
  1.8   Cross gravel Tower Road.
  2.2   Follow Tower Road right.
  2.8   Berry Hill Fire Tower; return by the same route.

Nature Trail:

  0.0   Nature Center trailhead; hike north.
  1.1   Cross levee dam.
  1.3   Close loop at Nature Center.

Finding the trailhead: From the junction of New York 12 and New York 220 at the village green in Oxford, go 6 miles west on NY 220 and turn right (north) on Steere Road. In 1.4 miles find the park entrance on the left.

The hikes: To hike the **FLT to Berry Hill Fire Tower,** follow the signs through the park for BEACH PARKING and start at the northwest corner of the northernmost parking area. Look for the white blazes of the FLT heading north (right). Pass through woods, quickly meeting the park road. There turn left on a wide grassy swath to arrive at an FLT destination sign; bear right per the sign for Berry Hill Fire Tower.

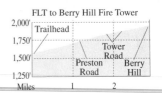

The trail travels a rich woods of hemlock, maple, yellow birch, and black cherry, following the small inlet brook upstream. Abundant lady fern, Mayflower, oxalis, and club moss create a vibrant contrast to the leaf mat elsewhere. Patterned fungi riddle logs and snags. Mouse and woodpecker share the woods.

Tiny meadows of ferns, false hellebore, grasses, moss, and forget-me-not enshroud the springs, while muddy pockets record the tracks of last night's wildlife. In an area of pines, pass a tree-painted mileage notice, remnant rock walls, and a trail register.

Ahead, a forest lane lined by big maple and black cherry trees gives way to a rolling tour through natural and planted woods. Cross over Preston Road and through a rock-wall egress for a scenic straightaway through a fern-lined

Fern frond, Bowman Lake State Park.

plantation. Gradually the forest includes more hardwoods, with maple and ash dominating the wetter areas.

At 1.8 miles cross gravel Tower Road, touring a red pine plantation; some of the plots show tidy rows. At 2.25 miles the FLT returns to Tower Road, following it to the right. Skirt a field and turn left on the side road at 2.6 miles to reach the fire tower and rustic cabin atop grassy Berry Hill.

The public may ascend the six-story tower, but the upper loft remains closed. Still the perch affords a fine overview of its south-central New York neighborhood—a landscape of low ridges, rolling fields, and wooded hills. Wild strawberries atop the hill suggest the site's name. Return as you came.

The red-marked **Nature Trail** starts at the nature center; look for a trail sign on the building's northwest corner. The trail heads north through the mixed forest of the developed park for a counterclockwise tour, thrice crossing park roads. Expect rocks, roots, and soggy stretches; rangers recommend that hikers inquire about trail conditions before starting.

In 0.2 mile skirt the western edge of the northern parking lot for the beach. Where the trail overlooks Bowman Lake, springtime hikers may spy Canada geese and their trailing young. At the northwest corner of the parking area, the red trail curves west into woods where red squirrels chide from the treetops.

Hemlock and tall deciduous trees weave a rich shade, while small drainages thread the woods. Pass some picnic sites and cross a footbridge over the rocky inlet; birch, ash, and beech favor this wetter site. At 0.5 mile reach a cattail shore where remnant footboards hint at a former interpretive site. Views still present the marshy shore, semisubmerged bullfrogs, and maple-willow edge. Find a length-of-the-lake view stretching to the earthen levee dam.

Ascend steeply from the lake and pass a remnant stone wall, traveling among congested spruce and moist meadow habitats. Woods roads briefly continue the tour before the marked trail climbs and contours the wooded west slope. Upon descent turn right on a woods road, rounding the lake closer to shore to cross the levee dam (1.1 miles).

Bullfrogs, sunfish fiercely protecting their cleared-gravel nests, and tadpoles animate the water, while a few irises grow along the levee shore. From the levee, signs point uphill to the right. Skirt the picnic area and return to the nature center (1.3 miles).

Capital-Saratoga Region

In this east-central New York region, with the capital complex at its core, hikers can retrace the march of the British in 1777; explore Helderberg Escarpment; visit field, forest, and wetland habitats; and venture to the Taconic Crest. Five major rivers thread through the region, and vistas sweep the Mohawk and Hudson valleys, the Adirondacks, Massachusetts, and Vermont. The region offers quiet nature strolls and vigorous hikes, with a range of tours in between.

51 Wilkinson National Recreation Trail

General description: An interpretive loop through fields and woods retraces the British march and visits sites where fortifications stood and battles raged during the Revolutionary War.

General location: Saratoga National Historic Park, 30 miles north of Albany.

Special attractions: Historical sites, interpretive boards, mixed woods, untamed fields, wildflowers, wildlife.

Length: 4.8 miles round-trip, including Breymann's Redoubt detour and Freeman Loop.

Difficulty: Easy to moderate.

Maps: Wilkinson Trail (WT) flier.

Special concerns: The park collects a nominal per-person fee from hikers, a per-vehicle fee for the auto tour. Upon payment, receive a trail pass good for seven days; keep it with you while hiking. Request a trail flier for the map and corresponding descriptions to the trail's lettered interpretive stations. The park service encourages hikers to wear bright colors during hunting season, October through November. Carry plenty of water.

Season and hours: Early April through November. Grounds open sunrise to sunset; visitor center open 9:00 A.M. to 5:00 P.M.

For information: Saratoga National Historic Park.

Wilkinson National Recreation Trail

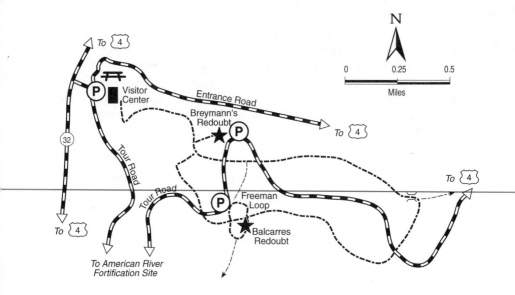

Key points:

- 0.0   Visitor Center trailhead.
- 0.7   Breymann's Redoubt/Benedict Arnold site.
- 0.8   Loop junction; go left.
- 3.2   Freeman Loop.
- 3.8   Close Freeman Loop.
- 4.2   Complete WT loop; bear left to visitor center.

Finding the trailhead: From Troy go 17.5 miles north on U.S. Highway 4 and turn left (west) to reach the Saratoga National Historic Park access road. Go 2.3 miles to the visitor center.

From New York State Thruway Interstate 87 south of Saratoga Springs, take exit 12 and follow the well-marked route to the park. It travels New York 67 east, U.S. Highway 9 north, New York 9P east, New York 423 east, and New York 32 north to enter the park in 12 miles; be alert for the frequent turns.

The hike: The two Battles of Saratoga fought in the fall of 1777 marked the turning point in the American Revolutionary War. Colonist victories over the British in this key area along the Hudson River

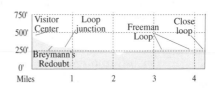

convinced the French that the Colonists could prevail. When France then declared war on Great Britain, the tide turned toward American independence. This national recreation trail (NRT) revisits those crucial battle scenes.

Cannon, Saratoga National Historic Park.

Exit the back door of the visitor center and turn right, passing cannons and memorials, as you cross the lawn to reach the trail kiosk in 500 feet. Beyond the kiosk, come to a junction and interpretive post A; bear left for the trail. White stakes with a WT and donated markers by the Friends of Saratoga Battlefield help keep hikers on course and locate interpretive sites.

The wide mowed track passes through a shrubby transition habitat; woods of planted pine, maple, oak, aspen, and fruit trees; and rolling untamed fields of thigh-high grasses and wildflowers. Islands of trees typically spot the fields. The National Park Service (NPS) deliberately manages this property to communicate the look of the land during the campaign of 1777. Only a few rooftops break the spell.

Downy woodpeckers telegraph their locations in the woods, while songbirds spread cheer in the field. The NRT occasionally crosses a horse trail and slips across the auto-tour route four times.

At 0.6 mile a spur to the left leads to Auto Tour Stop 7, Breymann's Redoubt. Converge on a paved walk to find interpretive boards, a pair of cannons, and posts outlining the site of the German breastwork. This crude log barrier that measured 200 yards long and 7 feet high was intended to protect the British right flank, but despite its imposing nature, Colonists overwhelmed the site, driving off the Crown forces on October 7, 1777. To find the Boot Monument, a tribute to Benedict Arnold, who received a leg wound while distinguishing himself in the fray, bear right on a paved lane descending from the redoubt.

Return to the Wilkinson Trail (0.8 mile) and turn left, quickly reaching the loop junction at post C; go left for a clockwise tour. Aster, Queen Anne's lace, goldenrod, and spotted knapweed interweave the autumn fields. Crossing the tour road for the first time (1.1 miles), pass through a pine corridor, reaching the Liaison Trail at post D. Continue straight ahead for the full tour; turn right on the Liaison Trail to shorten the loop by 2 miles.

The woods framing the Wilkinson Trail grow more mixed, with maple, oak, aspen, black cherry, elm, hornbeam, and hop hornbeam. The second road crossing soon follows. The trail now travels a wooded plateau between the Mill Creek and Great Ravine drainages. When the British marched along this route in 1777, old-growth trees 6 feet in diameter cloaked the highland. Today white-tailed deer commonly cross the path.

A couple of plank crossings precede the footbridge at post F (2 miles). Upon crossing the bridge, bear right; this open field would have been cultivated in the eighteenth century. Cross the tour road, still in field. Butterflies, crickets, and grasshoppers can divert the eye. The blooms of spring and the seedpods of fall bring a special beauty to the field.

Where the trail enters a deciduous stand at 2.25 miles, an autumn collage of leaves adds its own richness. Descend steeply, cross a ravine, and ascend the opposite slope to tour a low ridge clad in pine. Past post J, traverse a long open field. At the base of a rise cross over a horse trail, ascending to meet a paved walk at 3.2 miles. Go left to add a clockwise tour of the 0.6-mile Freeman Loop; the Wilkinson Trail bisects this loop.

This circuit and its spurs visit the John Freeman Farm and Balcarres Redoubt, noting the battles of September 19 and October 7, 1777. Visitors discover the posts outlining a British fortification that withstood the fiery American onslaught; a monument to a fallen American Captain; Bloody Knoll, named for the many casualties on October 7, 1777; and an obelisk and exquisitely crafted cannons. Interpretive panels, some with recorded messages, relate the history, while lilacs recall the farm. The Liaison Trail rejoins the tour at this site.

At 3.8 miles return to the loop's initial junction with the Wilkinson Trail and turn right. Cross back over Freeman Loop and pass through field and pine stand to make one last crossing of the tour road (4 miles). Beyond post N (the last of the interpretive sites), cross over a horse trail, reaching a T-junction with a mowed path. Go right, following the sign to the visitor center; to the left lies Barber Wheatfield, another battle site. Close the loop at post C in another 0.1 mile and bear left, retracing the first 0.6 mile to the visitor center (4.8 miles).

52 Taconic Crest Trail

Overview

The nearly 40-mile-long Taconic Crest Trail strings from southwest Vermont through New York to Pittsfield State Forest in Massachusetts. Taking the hike north from Petersburg Pass in New York showcases the trail's finest attributes. It travels hardwood forests, serves up multistate views, and visits a geologic oddity.

General description: A one-way hike from Petersburg Pass (on New York 2) to the New York 346 trailhead at the Hoosic River introduces the Taconic Crest and its neighborhood.

General location: At New York–Massachusetts border south of Vermont.

Special attractions: Multistate vistas, a snow hole, colorful fall foliage, solitude.

Length: 8.8 miles one-way.

Difficulty: Strenuous.

Maps: New York State Department of Environmental Conservation, Petersburg Pass Scenic Area flier (generally available at trail's start); The Taconic Crest Trail brochure.

Special concerns: No camping in Williams College Hopkins Memorial Forest or on private land. Use care crossing NY 2.

Season and hours: Spring through fall, daylight hours.

For information: New York State Department of Environmental Conservation (DEC), Region 4.

Key points:
- 0.0   Petersburg Pass trailhead; head north.
- 2.5   White Rock.
- 2.9   Snow Hole.
- 6.1   Prosser Hollow Junction.
- 8.8   End at NY 346 trailhead.

Finding the trailhead: From the junction of New York 22 and New York 2 (5 miles south of North Petersburg, New York), go 5.3 miles east on NY 2 to reach the large, open parking lot for Petersburg Pass Scenic Area on the right. The northbound trail starts across the highway.

Reach the trail's northern terminus off NY 346, 2.5 miles east of North Petersburg. The small developed trailhead is on the south side of the highway just before the Hoosic River bridge and the route's crossing into Vermont.

The hike: The hike north from Petersburg Pass has the advantage of being vehicle-free, allowing a serene look at the area. Along it, the Snow Hole suggests a good day-hike destination (5.9 miles round-trip with only a 300-foot elevation change).

Taconic Crest Trail

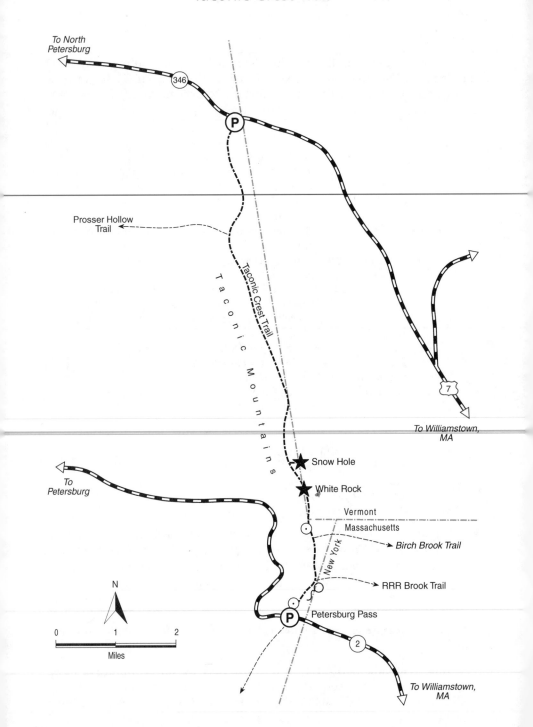

To North Petersburg

346

P

Prosser Hollow Trail

Taconic Crest Trail

T a c o n i c   M o u n t a i n s

7

To Williamstown, MA

★ Snow Hole

★ White Rock

Vermont

Massachusetts

→ Birch Brook Trail

New York

→ RRR Brook Trail

To Petersburg

N

0   1   2
Miles

P Petersburg Pass

2

To Williamstown, MA

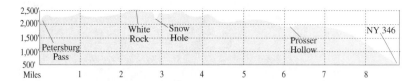

From the Petersburg Pass parking lot, cross to the north side of NY 2, taking one of the steeply ascending foot trails behind the TOWN OF PETERSBURG sign. In 250 feet these spurs meet the Taconic Crest Trail as it arrives on the right. Over-the-shoulder looks find Petersburg Pass and Mount Raimer. At 0.1 mile a spur leads to a western perspective overlooking a steep open slope to the valley below and the Adirondacks beyond.

The rolling trail travels 2,250-acre Hopkins Memorial Forest, contouring the Taconic's west flank and traversing the crest. It changes from tall, full-canopy forests of birch, beech, maple, black cherry, and oak to areas of low-stature trees with shrubby understories. In places, find a herald of June-blooming pink azalea.

At 0.7 mile proceed forward past the marked Shepherd's Well Trail to RRR Brook Trail. In places, the woods feature highly scenic candelabra-trunked trees, dipping low their shades of autumn. Elsewhere silver snags (victims of the pear thrip infestation of the late 1980s) draw eyes skyward. At times a chill air washes up the slope, invigorating leaves and travelers.

At 1.5 miles fountains of 3- to 4-foot-tall interrupted ferns claim the left side of the trail; the Birch Brook Trail heads right. Stay on the crest trail. As it makes a steady climb, the crest trail briefly crosses into southwest Vermont before returning to New York at White Rock (2.5 miles), a signed landmark. This site received its U.S. Geological Survey designation for the chunks of milky-white quartz scattered throughout the woods. Along the way, open berry fields present vistas of Petersburg Pass and the rolling New York terrain.

From White Rock drift east, descending into a forest of beech. At the marked Y-junction at 2.9 miles, leave the crest trail, detouring right for a 250-foot descent to the Snow Hole. This cavity in the ground has jagged, moss-covered chasm walls that meet in an ill-fitting bite. Explorers who enter the chasm discover cool air and snow and ice that linger into summer. This chill supports a boreal understory of hobblebush, club moss, and oxalis.

Area rocks wear names and dates from visitors from one hundred years ago, but the genuine etchings must be sorted from prankster and contemporary markings. A path overlooks the cavity and its cavelike end.

Return to the Taconic Crest Trail at 3 miles and turn right (north). Where the trail flattens, puddles can form and dictate bypasses. Disks have a fairly dependable spacing, so watch for them to stay on course. As the trail ascends, at 3.5 miles hikers will find disks marking a little-tracked path that arcs 0.2 mile along the eastern edge of the slope before returning to the main grade. Because this footpath offers just a single, narrow, clear-day view, hikers may choose to keep to main wide grade here.

Berlin Mountain, Taconic Crest Trail, an alternate destination south of Petersburg Pass.

A measured descent leads to the next woods road junction (4 miles). Proceed forward, ignoring the route that angles in on the right. An ascent then advances this rolling crest tour, taking the hiker past some showy black cherry trees in an otherwise birch-beech woods. A steeper descent follows, where loose rock and downward-pointed roots can steal footing.

As the ridgetop narrows, hikers catch glimpses down the east and west flank but no open views. The crest trail primarily hugs the east side. Where the ridge regains its height, enjoy a pretty grass-and-fern passage. The trail then dips west below the ridgetop to swing an arc right, returning to the crest at a junction (4.9 miles). Keep right, avoiding the unmarked woods road that heads left.

As you pursue the primary ridge route, gradually encounter blue DEC disks as well as the familiar white diamond markers. At 6.1 miles reach the Prosser Hollow Junction. The yellow disks to the left lead west to Prosser Hollow trailhead for an alternative 7.5-mile one-way tour. For the selected hike, proceed north on the Taconic Crest Trail to NY 346.

Maples, oaks, witch hazel, and striped maple add to the beech-birch woods. The hike still pursues the rolling woods road, tracing the crest. In 0.5 mile keep left, ignoring a trail angling back to the right. Where the crest route enters a big horseshoe bend on its descent at 6.8 miles, be alert for the multiple disk and diamond markers showing where hikers abandon the woods road to chase disks through the woods on a lightly tracked footpath. This addition of trail lacks the history of foot traffic but should improve with time.

The trail rolls up and over a huckleberry-clad hill to cross an old grade and start the biggest descent of this hike, now on an overgrown route. Its steepness, brushing grasses, and muddy spots can complicate travel, especially during rain. In places the mud can either steal footing or tug at engulfed boots. Insects can annoy at other times, but at least the trail's marking in this stretch is superior. Birdsong and sightings of fox, deer, grouse, and woodpecker help erase any hard feelings.

Another set of multiple markers at 7.5 miles sends the hiker left across and down the slope to where the trail crosses a gravel road. At about 8 miles the Taconic Crest Trail zigs right to pass through a transitioning meadow of knee-high vegetation. Some milkweed, ox-eye daisy, hawkweed, thistle, and fall-blooming wildflowers add to travel. At 8.2 miles reenter the forest, still descending as the crest drops to the Hoosic River Valley.

At 8.8 miles cross a brook via stones to emerge and end at the NY 346 trailhead, passing between the boulders at the parking lot's southwest corner. From the parking area view the next peak north above the Hoosic River and admire the rural scene.

53 John Boyd Thacher State Park

Overview

Boasts of this 2,300-acre park include 6 miles of the famous Helderberg Escarpment, one of the richest fossil-bearing formations in the world, dramatic cliffs, Mohawk–Hudson Valley panoramas, Indian trails and tales of Tory spies, waterfalls, and mixed woods. Short trails throw open the pages of the park.

General description:	Three easy hikes travel above and below the vertical limestone cliffs and through second-growth woods.
General location:	14 miles west of Albany; 17 miles southwest of Schenectady.
Special attractions:	Fossil-bearing limestone cliffs; vistas; historic Indian trade route and a Revolutionary-times paint mine; goshawk, rabbit, deer, and fox.
Length:	Indian Ladder Trail, 1 mile round-trip; Escarpment Trail, 2.5 miles one-way; Nature Trail, 1-mile loop.
Difficulty:	All easy.
Maps:	State park brochure.
Special concerns:	Vehicle entrance fee collected Memorial Day through Labor Day. Because the gates close promptly at dusk throughout the park, plan to be off the trails accordingly.
Season and hours:	Year-round, 8:00 A.M. to dusk. The Indian Ladder Trail is closed in winter.
For information:	John Boyd Thacher State Park.

John Boyd Thacher State Park

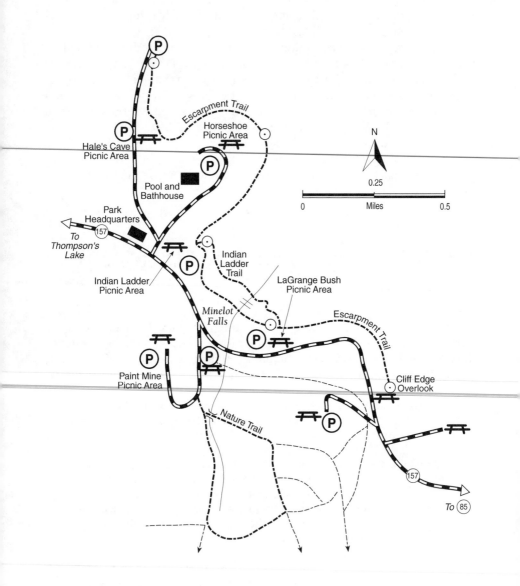

Key points:
Indian Ladder Trail:
  0.0   Trailhead at Indian Ladder Picnic Area.
  0.4   Minelot Falls.
  0.5   LaGrange Bush Picnic Area; backtrack or loop back on Escarpment Trail.
Escarpment Trail:
  0.0   Northernmost trailhead; hike south.
  1.2   Indian Ladder Picnic Area.
  1.7   LaGrange Bush Picnic Area.
  2.5   End at Cliff Edge Overlook.
Nature Trail:
  0.0   Trailhead; follow service road.
  1.0   Close loop at trailhead.

Finding the trailhead: The least-complicated approach is to take New York 85 west from Albany (NY 85 is exit 4 off Interstate 90) and follow it to New York 157 (about 10 miles). Go right on NY 157 and continue 4 miles into the park.

The hikes: The park's premier hiking trail, **Indian Ladder Trail,** wraps below the light-colored platy cliffs of Helderberg Escarpment between Indian Ladder and LaGrange Bush picnic areas. At Indian Ladder Picnic Area find the marked trailhead, taking the first right past the entry station.

This trail rounds the escarpment, where the Mohawk Schoharie constructed a shortcut to the valley by placing a sturdy notched trunk against the cliff for descending and scaling. Today stonework steps descend through a rock chasm, leading to a viewing platform and the start of an exciting, neck-craning tour at the base of the 100- to 200-foot-high cliffs.

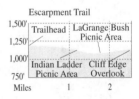

Outward vistas sweep the Mohawk–Hudson Valley, but the cliffs truly command with their bulges, overhangs, flutes, fissures, clefts, and hollows. Millions of years ago an uplift of limestone, sandstone, and shale followed by ages of erosion and weathering brought about the site's vertical fracturing, breakaway blocks, and ultimately these startling cliffs. Numbered signs identify key features. While some defacing exists, the park mostly succeeds in protecting this geologic treasure.

Cliff scallops and protrusions lend character on this north-to-east journey that traces a broad U-curvature. Outlets to underground streams, Outlet and Minelot Falls, and the wooded slope plunging to the valley floor further engage travelers. Nearing LaGrange Bush Picnic Area, beware of a low rock ledge. The return is as you came or via the Escarpment Trail.

221

Indian Ladder Trail, John Boyd Thacher State Park.

The thin footpath of the **Escarpment Trail** hugs the fenced escarpment rim, skirting the developed park. It travels from a turnout north of Hale's Cave Picnic Area to Cliff Edge Overlook.

Along its length, open overlooks and stolen glimpses across the rim's dense shrub cap bring about a new respect for the plummeting cliffs. Views feature the Mohawk–Hudson Valley and the escarpment arc. On clear days spy the distant ragged outline of the Adirondack High Peaks and Green Mountains.

A tangle of cherry, birch, cedar, sumac, and wild rose often isolates the trail, providing habitat for rabbits and songbirds; beware of poison ivy. At the end of the tour, find the best escarpment profiles; more boots travel the path between Indian Ladder and Cliff Edge Overlook. Ravens, hawks, and vultures soar below the rim. The aqua markers of the Long Path, a New York state through-trail, stamp part of the tour.

The **Nature Trail** (or **Forest Trail**) starts on an authorized-vehicles-only service road midway between Lower Paint Mine Picnic Area and the first parking lot for Paint Mine Picnic Area. Find the trailhead next to a roadside table.

The trail crosses a footbridge with upstream views of a pretty, stepped creek. A textured woods of maple, hickory, oak, hemlock, and white pine enfolds the tour. This trail also briefly advances the Long Path. After a climb from the creek, the Long Path heads left; the Nature Trail heads right.

Paper birch and aspen add to the mix, and at 0.3 mile the trail tops out. Posts from the former interpretive trail mark the way; stay right at each intersection, following foot trail and woods road. Lady's slipper, violet, clintonia, and Mayflower sprinkle the woods; red eft and frog favor the leafy-bottomed puddles. Upon crossing a drainage the trail meets the authorized-vehicle road; descend right, closing the loop.

54 Five Rivers Environmental Education Center

Overview

At this nationally recognized environmental education center, visitors, students, parents, and children examine habitat interrelationships while touring field, forest, meadow, and pond. Six self-guided nature trails explore the grounds. The center takes its name from the five major rivers flowing into the greater area: the Hudson, Mohawk, Sacandaga, Schoharie, and Hoosick.

General description: The easy loops provide opportunities for wildlife sightings and nature study.
General location: Capital District, just west of Delmar.
Special attractions: Bird-watching; spring and summer wildflowers; possible sightings of beaver, deer, turtle, frog,

bluebird, and Canada goose; small interpretive center.

Length:	Trails range from a fragment of a mile to 2 miles.
Difficulty:	All easy.
Maps:	Five Rivers Environmental Education Center brochure. Interpretive pamphlets are available at trailheads.
Special concerns:	Take necessary precautions for ticks, and carry insect repellent.
Season and hours:	Year-round (weather permitting), sunrise to sunset; interpretive center: 9:00 A.M. to 4:30 P.M. Monday through Saturday and 1:00 P.M. to 5:00 P.M. Sunday (closed major holidays).
For information:	Five Rivers Environmental Education Center (EEC).

Key points:

Woodlot Trail:

0.0 Start at southeast corner of parking lot.

0.2 End loop at parking lot.

Beaver Tree Trail:

0.0 Trailhead on south side of Game Farm Road; hike clockwise.

0.1 Pond overlook platform.

0.2 Pond overlook platform.

0.5 End loop at trailhead.

Wild Turkey Trail:

0.0 Trailhead right of maintenance building; hike north.

0.9 Loop junction; hike left.

1.1 Close loop; return south to trailhead.

North Loop Trail:

0.0 Trailhead left of maintenance building; hike north, bearing left.

0.2 Loop junction; head left.

0.5 Pass shelter and Big Pine Trail.

1.8 Close loop; turn left to return to trailhead.

Vlomankill Trail:

0.0 Trailhead past Goose Lane; descend to kill (stream).

0.7 Complete loop; backtrack to trailhead.

Old Field Trail:

0.0 Trailhead left of maintenance building; hike north, bearing right.

0.5 End at trailhead.

Finding the trailhead: From the junction of Albany County 52 (Elm Avenue) and New York 443 (Delaware Avenue) in west Delmar, go 1.4 miles west on NY 443 and turn right (north) on Orchard Street at a sign for the center. Go 0.4 mile and turn left on Game Farm Road, reaching the center entrance and parking lot on the right in 0.3 mile.

The hikes: All trails radiate from the interpretive building.

The wheelchair-accessible 0.2-mile **Woodlot Trail** heads east at the southeast corner of the parking lot. The loop travels boardwalk and wide, fine-gravel trail through a woodlot of young, skyward-shooting maple, ash, and beech. Flowering shrubs, wild grape, geranium, ferns, and Virginia creeper

Five Rivers Environmental Education Center

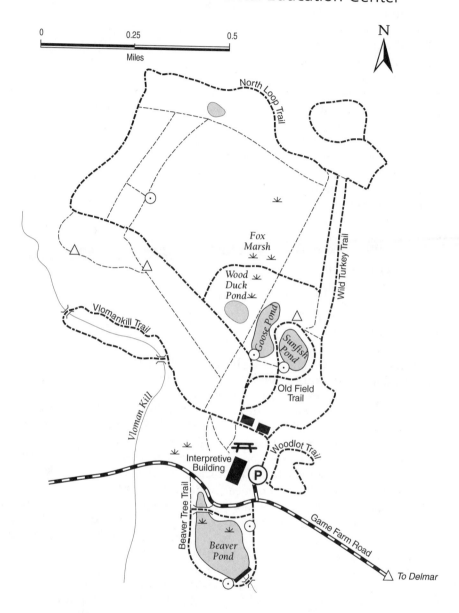

contribute to a dense mid- and understory. Butterflies and hummingbirds frequent the woodlot.

The popular 0.5-mile **Beaver Tree Trail** begins on the south side of Game Farm Road opposite the entrance. The tree-shaded route rings a rectangular man-made pond. Along it, deck overlooks, a spillway, and bridge offer up-close looks at the pond habitat. Duckweed and other water plants patchwork the pond's surface; cattails and purple loosestrife vegetate part of the rim. Ducks and geese rear their young, turtles sun on the logs, and beaver gnawings hint at the trail's name.

To reach Wild Turkey, North Loop, and Old Field Trails, hike north from the parking lot toward the maintenance buildings. Find the Wild Turkey trailhead to the right of the buildings, the other two trails to the left.

The 2-mile **Wild Turkey Trail** swings north through open meadow and field. Yellow, pink, and white wildflowers spangle the grassy areas; arrows may help guide hikers at junctions. At 1 mile the trail puts a loop on the hike, passing through forest near the north boundary. Second-generation hemlocks and a few big oaks punctuate the tour. Close the loop and backtrack to the hike's start. The different stages of meadow growth (either left wild to the whim of natural succession or cropped short) support various wildlife communities.

For the 2-mile **North Loop Trail** bear left, following the mowed track away from the trail's information board. At many junctions arrows help point out the North Loop Trail, but a number of unmarked mowed tracks can confuse. Because soggy stretches can discourage hikers, you may choose to walk the maintenance loop road instead. It visits most EEC habitats.

Early views stretch west to Helderberg Mountain. Rabbit, mourning dove, bluebird, and deer number among the early-morning sightings. Where the trail passes south of Goose Pond and Wood Duck Marsh, the turtles, frogs, muskrats, and herons cause fingers to point. Willows and cattails rim the open waters.

At the loop junction, bear left (west) for a clockwise tour. Encounter a shelter and a junction with the Big Pine Trail, just as the loop swings north. Along the middle third of the loop, the trail tours a dark, deep woods of hemlock, maple, beech, and oak. Some trees approach 18 inches in diameter.

Goose Pond, Five Rivers Environmental Education Center.

Waterplants, trillium, and jack-in-the-pulpit bring a blush of early spring. The North Loop Trail then swings east along the northern perimeter before paralleling the service road back south, crossing over it. Skirt Fox and Wood Duck Marshes to close the loop and return to trailhead.

Next door, the 0.5-mile **Old Field Trail** makes a figure-eight tour, rounding past Sunfish and Goose Ponds and through fields and second-growth woods. Abandoned fruit trees provide additional habitat. Again, the fields show different stages of succession; a picnic shelter lies off-trail. Old Field Trail ends next to the North Loop Trail information board.

The 0.75-mile **Vlomankill Trail** has the most remote trailhead. Hike north from the parking lot; turn west going past the maintenance buildings, North Loop and Old Field Trails, and Goose Lane (a maintenance road); and again turn north to find the marked trailhead. The trail descends fairly steeply, passing through hickory, maple, birch, and pine woods before arriving at Vloman Kill (a stream) and the loop. Cross the footbridge for a clockwise tour, journeying upstream and soon passing the Fordham's Crossing Trail, which heads left.

The Vlomankill Trail travels a hemlock-deciduous wooded flat threaded by the slow, murky waters of Vloman Kill. Erosion mars the banks. Greeting hikers at the second bridge crossing is a more picturesque water that spills over canted, layered rock, around grassy tufts, and through shallow horseshoe curves. A natural log dam accounts for the difference in flow between the two bridges. On snags look for the telltale pinhole drillings of sapsuckers. Virginia creeper and poison ivy scale and weave beneath the trees.

Catskills Region

At the southern heel of the state, this region brings together the chiseled beauty and lore of the Catskill Mountains, the cliff-and-crag realm of the Shawangunks, and the outlying wooded ridges parted by thin valleys. This is a countryside of kill and clove drainages, the land of Rip Van Winkle and Sleepy Hollow. Naturalist John Burroughs walked its reaches and drew from its inspiration.

Hikes explore forest, field, pond, sapphire lakes, and escarpment rim. Vistas sweep the Catskills, the Mohonks, and the Hudson Valley. This region also boasts one of the finest bird-watching areas in the state.

55 Little Pond Loop

General description:	This day hike stitches together Little Pond and Touchmenot Mountain, touring mixed forest, conifer plantation, and meadow habitats.
General location:	In the remote western Catskills, 14 miles northwest of New York 17/Interstate 86 at Livingston Manor.
Special attractions:	Little Pond, modest views, fishing, spring and summer wildflowers, fall foliage.
Length:	5.3-mile loop, including spur to Cabot Mountain.
Difficulty:	Moderate.
Maps:	New York–New Jersey Trail Conference map, Western Catskill Trails.
Special concerns:	Fee area. A few climbs require the use of hands.
Season and hours:	Spring through fall.
For information:	New York Department of Environmental Conservation, Region 4.

Key points:

0.0	Little Pond trailhead; follow yellow route.
1.7	Red-trail junction; detour left.
2.4	Beaver Kill Vista.
2.5	Cabot Mountain summit; backtrack to loop.
4.2	Touchmenot Mountain summit.
5.3	End loop above bathhouse.

Finding the trailhead: From New York 30 on the south shore of Pepacton Reservoir, 13.5 miles equidistant from Margaretville and Downsville, turn southeast on Beech Hill Road; go 6.3 miles and turn left on Beaver Kill Road (Ulster County 54). In 2 miles turn left on Barkaboom Road for 0.2 mile. Now turn left to find Little Pond entrance station in 0.8 mile. The loop starts near the bathhouse/shower facility above the pond.

Little Pond Loop

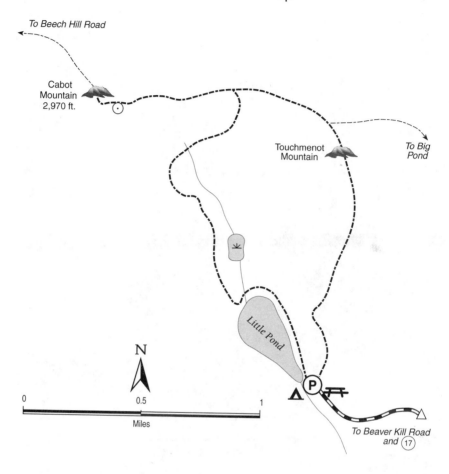

The hike: This hike explores the gentle western relief of the Catskill Mountains, swinging between Little Pond and Touchmenot Mountain, with a spur to Cabot Mountain.

Little Pond, a long lake with a small dam at its developed end, sits between low wooded ridges and holds stocks of pan-sized fish. The pond segment of the hike is most enjoyable before and after the summer vacation season.

For a clockwise tour follow the yellow-blazed trail between the bathhouse and the upper edge of the picnic area, rounding the east shore of Little Pond. Hemlocks push to the edge of the pond; oaks, birch, beech, and maple fill out the woods. Trillium, oxalis, clintonia, Mayflower, starflower, azalea, and mountain laurel pay tribute to spring. At the small drainages look for the

Frog catcher.

trail to arc deeper into the woods and for the growth of false hellebore and jack-in-the-pulpit. Isolated walk-in sites dot the wooded shore.

After crossing a rocky inlet brook at 0.5 mile, turn right to traverse the wooded bench overlooking the brook's steep ravine. Viburnum and ferns dominate the understory. Before long a beaver dam alters the brook; snags pierce the pond and even the lodge itself. Duckweed and a film of pollen coat the water as methane gas bubbles to the surface. A cacophony of croaking, knocking, drumming, and shrill notes fills the air.

Climb steadily, passing among stands of small-diameter trees, meadows of knee- to hip-high vegetation, and plantations of mature pine and spruce. From the meadows glimpse the area ridges. Near the upper end of an overgrown meadow, turn right, following the yellow markers through an area of young maple with a handful of ancient maples.

At 1.25 miles an egress in a beautiful rock wall leads to a more extensive grassy meadow with wild strawberries, a semihidden pond, an old rock foundation, and views of Touchmenot Mountain. Traverse the center of the meadow and cross a shale clearing before returning to a mixed-age woods. At the red-trail junction at 1.7 miles, go left to top Cabot Mountain; go right to continue the loop.

A detour left contours a similarly wooded slope of maple, birch, and beech, coming to the foot of Cabot Mountain and a fairly steep ascent. The moist slope supports nettles, ferns, waterleaf, violets, trillium, and jack-in-the-pulpit. Although steep, the thin footpath retains its earth. Amid the ledges and overhangs, expect to use your hands, and beware of the possible hail of loose rock from any hikers above you.

Traveling the wooded flat at the edge of the slope, look for the open ledge of Beaver Kill Vista at 2.4 miles. While leafy trees filter much of the view, Touchmenot Mountain, the Catskill ridges beyond Beaver Kill, and the glare of Little Pond still reward. Columbine dresses the rock, drawing hummingbirds to the hiker's feet. Past the vista point lies a wooded summit, flat with a lush fern floor.

Return to the 1.7-mile junction at 3.3 miles, staying on the red trail for a mildly rolling, shady walk to Touchmenot Mountain. Cross a rocky drainage and climb, finding wooded flats between the steep ledge ascents. At the junction at 3.8 miles, go right on the blue trail to close the loop at Little Pond. The red trail turns left for Barkaboom Road and Big Pond in 1 mile.

Continue the ascent of Touchmenot Mountain on the blue trail. Ledge overlooks allow for a forest appreciation but no outward views. Roll along the summit plateau before sharply descending at 4.3 miles. Mosses decorate the platy outcrops, ledges, and isolated rocks. Again use hands to ease descents. Once off the rocks, the trail charges straight downhill in a rich mixed forest. For the final 0.5 mile the descent eases; exit the woods above the bathhouse.

56 North–South Lake Loop

General description:	This Catskill Mountains loop travels the escarpment and wooded outskirts of North–South Lake, snaring views and passing cultural sites.
General location:	10 miles west of Catskill.
Special attractions:	Escarpment ledges, vistas, a monument and nineteenth-century hotel site, waterfalls, azalea and mountain laurel blooms, fall foliage.
Length:	10-mile loop, with destinations for shorter hikes.
Difficulty:	Moderate.
Maps:	Catskill Forest Preserve Camping, North–South Lake brochure; New York–New Jersey Trail Conference map, North Lake Area Catskill Trails.
Special concerns:	Fee area.
Season and hours:	Spring through fall.
For information:	New York State Department of Environmental Conservation, Region 4.

Key points:

0.0	Start at upper end of North Lake beach parking.
0.4	Artists Rock.
1.2	Sunset Rock.
2.2	Badman Cave/Rock Shelter Trail.
4.4	Haines Falls Road.
6.8	Inspiration Point.
9.0	Boulder Rock.
9.6	Catskill Mountain House site.
10.0	End loop back at North Lake Beach.

Finding the trailhead: From New York State Thruway Interstate 87, take exit 20 at Saugerties and go north on New York 32 to its junction with NY 32A (6 miles from the I–87 exit). Bear left on NY 32A, staying on it for 1.8 miles; there turn west on New York 23A. In 4.8 miles in Haines Falls, turn right on Greene County 18 for North–South Lake Campground, reaching the entrance station in 2.2 miles. Find the trailhead at the upper end of North Lake beach parking in another 1.6 miles; look for the blue blazes and sign for Artists Rock.

The hike: Although the loop travels the blue Escarpment and yellow Rock Shelter Trails ringing the North–South Lake area, it never approaches the lake.

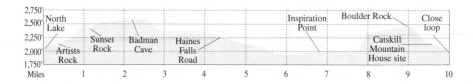

North–South Lake Loop

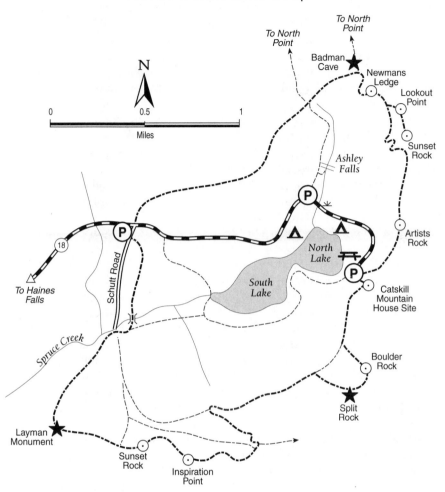

From the upper reaches of the beach parking lot, follow the blue trail left (north), rounding and ascending to Artists Rock; soon a yellow spur arrives on the left. Black oak, maple, pine, azalea, and mountain laurel decorate the brink as the broad sandstone ledges form natural avenues. The jut of Artists Rock extends a 180-degree Hudson Valley panorama; vultures sail below the point.

Ascend through forest, top the next ledge tier for a peek at North–South Lake (formerly two lakes), and then round below an immense conglomerate outcrop with cobbles eroding from the cliff. At 1 mile a 0.4-mile round-trip detour right leads to Sunset Rock for one of the finest vistas in the Catskills; the loop continues straight ahead.

On the detour visit the escarpment edge of Lookout Point for northeast views before reaching a series of plane-topped outcrops composing Sunset Point. Fissures measuring a foot wide and 20 feet deep isolate the rock islands. Views sweep across North-South Lake and its wooded basin to the swaybacked ridge of High Peak and Roundtop Mountain.

Resume the counterclockwise loop toward Newmans Ledge, ascending along a thin edge with a disturbing drop. Vistas span Rip Van Winkle Hollow to Rips Rock—after all, this is Knickerbocker and literature's Washington Irving country.

The trail then contours and ascends, tagging a junction below Badman Cave, shaped by an overhang and reached by a rock scramble. Leave the blue trail, now following the yellow Rock Shelter Trail straight ahead for a steady descent amid hemlock, spruce, and oak.

The descent grows rocky, traveling alongside the brook that drains to Marys Glen. Find the 3-mile junction near a 10-foot waterfall weeping from a rock overhang; bear right, staying on the yellow trail. The red trail descends to Ashley (or Marys Glen) Falls, a beaver meadow, and the campground. Spring peepers bring vitality to the glen in the evening hours.

Where the yellow trail draws even with the top of the 10-foot waterfall, veer left for the loop, descending to Haines Falls Road (4.4 miles). Rocks and roots riddle the trail, while a few maple old-timers grace the woods.

At Haines Falls Road angle left to reach and briefly walk Schutt Road. At 4.5 miles look for the blue Escarpment Trail (the loop), as it turns left off Schutt Road; this trail has sections of joint hiker-horse usage. Descend along the wide lane, touring hemlock-birch forest, passing segments of Colonial rock walls, and crossing an old railroad grade.

With a footbridge crossing of Spruce Creek comes the next junction (5.4 miles); turn right on the woods road, and soon after bear left on an earthen lane paralleling Spruce Creek downstream. A forget-me-not–clad bench separates the trail from the stream. Scenic rockwork marks Spruce Creek as the blue trail turns and ascends away.

Mountain laurel and azalea now fill the midstory with late-spring color and fragrance. With a descent along a rocky drainage, come upon a rock obelisk with a boulder crown. This monument honors firefighter Frank Layman, who lost his life in the fire of 1900. Round the obelisk to the left and in a few steps take a sharp left back uphill to the escarpment (6.4 miles). Vistas feature Kaaterskill drainage and the wooded ridge of High Peak and Roundtop Mountain.

Pass through a rock channel, and ascend and contour along the wooded escarpment. At 6.6 miles continue straight ahead for Inspiration Point, passing a second Sunset Rock. Beyond Inspiration Point obtain a view through the "V" of Kaaterskill Canyon at Hudson Valley. At 7.6 miles turn right on a woods road, reaching a junction; turn left to stay on the blue trail.

A rocky woods-road ascent between full borders of azalea, laurel, and oak leads to the next junction, where the blue trail heads right on a narrowed forest lane. Follow the signs to Boulder Rock, again turning right at 8.75 miles.

IN MEMORY OF
FRANK D. LAYMAN,
OF HAINES FALLS,
WHO LOST HIS LIFE ON
THIS SPOT AUG. 10, 1900,
WHILE WITH OTHERS
FIGHTING A FOREST FIRE
WHICH THREATENED TO
DESTROY THE HOMES AND
BUSINESS INTERESTS OF
THE PEOPLE OF THIS PLACE.
BY THOSE GRATEFUL
FOR HIS DEVOTED SERVICE
THIS MONUMENT IS ERECTED.

Layman Monument, Catskill Park.

Past Split Rock, where massive blocks have pulled apart from the escarpment face, find Boulder Rock, a naturally transported boulder that came to rest on the escarpment ledge. Bear left and meet the red trail. Here turn right to reach a clearing and sign at 9.6 miles that together recall Catskill Mountain House, a hotel that hosted presidents and dignitaries in the nineteenth century. Round left away from the sign, bearing right in 0.1 mile to come out at the open parking area above the beach at 10 miles.

57 Indian Head Mountain Loop

General description:	This loop rewards with a classic Catskills setting, vistas, and challenge.
General location:	In the Catskills, about 6 miles west of Saugerties.
Special attractions:	Vistas, the 500-foot cliffs of Indian Head, wildflowers, fall foliage, wildlife sightings.
Length:	7.5-mile loop.
Difficulty:	Strenuous.
Maps:	New York–New Jersey Trail Conference map, Northeastern Catskill Trails.
Special concerns:	Note that both parking and the start of the trail occur on private land; respect all posted notices to preserve the access privilege. Exercise caution on rocky climbs and descents. There is no camping above the 3,500-foot elevation.
Season and hours:	Spring through fall.
For information:	New York State Department of Environmental Conservation, Region 4 in Stamford.

Key points:

0.0	Prediger Road trailhead; follow red markers.
0.5	Loop junction; stay on red trail.
3.4	Outcrop ledge vista.
4.0	Indian Head Mountain.
5.0	Jimmy Dolan Notch/junction; follow blue trail right.
7.0	Close loop; backtrack left to trailhead.

Finding the trailhead: From the junction of New York 23A and Greene County 16 in Tannersville, head south on County 16 (Depot Street) for 5.5 miles; the road name changes several times. Turn right on Prediger Road for 0.5 mile, finding trail parking along the right shoulder only. Do not clog the road or block the private residence by parking on the left or too close to the trailhead. Leave enough space between parked vehicles for returning hikers to pull out safely. (An alternative trailhead that accesses the described route is the Steenburg Road lot, about 1 mile east of Prediger Road on County 16.)

Indian Head Mountain Loop

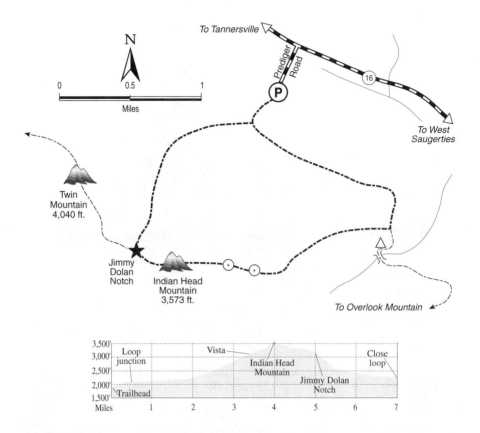

The hike: From Prediger Road follow the red markers away from the old cabin, passing through a stile and crossing a footbridge to enter a hemlock-deciduous woodland. Travel is on an often rocky woods road with a modest incline. At the 0.5-mile junction, the loop junction, continue straight on the red trail toward Devils Kitchen lean-to and Indian Head summit; the loop's return is via the blue Jimmy Dolan Notch Trail on the right.

Soon the old road of the red route tapers to trail width. Big maples and birch compose the canopy above a boulder-studded forest floor. Porcupine, deer, red eft, mouse, and toad draw attention away from the rolling trail. At 1.2 miles cross a thin creek; at 1.8 miles turn right on a woods road, coming to a signed junction. The blue markers straight ahead lead to Overlook Mountain. Remain on the red trail, which turns right and climbs toward Indian Head Mountain and destinations west.

This is true forest trail, at times rootbound and rock-studded, with the occasional crossing of a muddy drainage. A hemlock-deciduous forest houses the way. Some of the birch trees have impressive root systems. The pattern of ascent shows mild inclines interrupted by steep spurs. By 3 miles the

Forest on Indian Head Mountain, Catskill Park.

hemlocks drop from the mix, and spruce and fir have a spotty presence. Mossy rocks and ledges contribute to the mountain visuals.

At 3.4 miles, following a steep climb, hikers obtain an outcrop ledge where they can overlook a steep wooded slope to an exciting view that includes Roundtop Mountain, High Peak, Platte Clove, Plattekill Mountain, and the Hudson River Valley beyond Plattekill Clove. The wooded basin below holds a New York City Police Camp and small lake. Autumn presents a blended mosaic of colorful leaves and evergreen boughs.

The thin trail then contours the slope, extending views toward Overlook Mountain before the hike enters a rocky climb where hand assists are needed. A tight corridor of spruce and fir then ushers hikers to the next view (3.7 miles), where trees have been cut to open a window to Overlook Mountain, Ashokan Reservoir, Cooper Lake, Mount Tobias, Slide and Plateau Mountains, and the serial peaks and mountains filling out the image.

At 4 miles cross a small saddle for the final assault on Indian Head Mountain, which again requires some high-stepping and hand assists. Be careful on the ascent, especially under wet conditions or when burdened by a large pack. Vistas suggest breathers. At 4.4 miles pass the 3,500-foot elevation, topping the summit ridge. The trail then rolls along the top, crossing log walks over marshy sites.

The hike's vistas are gathered en route to the summit. The summit's reward is its fragile spruce-fir complex, a rarity on the East Coast and limited to the very high reaches. No camping is allowed here. After 0.4 mile the trail descends with a bold start and again can be rugged. Glimpses of Twin Mountain accompany the descent. Birch is now the primary tree.

At 5 miles reach Jimmy Dolan Notch and its trail junction. For the loop follow the blue trail right toward Platte Clove Highway. The red trail continues west to other Catskills destinations. A detour left (south) to the edge of the Notch offers a view out the "V" created by Twin and Indian Head Mountains toward Ashokan Reservoir and Slide Mountain Ridge.

The descent from the Notch remains steep, rocky, and sun exposed. Gradually the woods become more mixed and the trees bigger. At the drainage area at 5.4 miles, the descent eases and the trail curves right. Where hemlocks appear, find a dark woods. Later the trail follows a woods road for slope-contouring travel. At 7 miles cross the creek and close the loop back at the 0.5-mile junction. Turn left, backtracking to the trailhead. Remember to keep to the trail here as it crosses private land.

58 Overlook Mountain Hike

<table>
<tr><td>General description:</td><td>Suitable for a day outing or backpack, this hike mainly travels former woods roads through mixed forests, visiting a lake and an abandoned lookout tower.</td></tr>
<tr><td>General location:</td><td>In the Catskills, about 6 miles west of Saugerties.</td></tr>
<tr><td>Special attractions:</td><td>Vistas, lake, lean-tos, historic ruins, wildflowers, fall foliage, wildlife sightings.</td></tr>
<tr><td>Length:</td><td>13.4 miles round-trip, including spurs to Echo Lake and Overlook House ruins.</td></tr>
<tr><td>Difficulty:</td><td>Moderate.</td></tr>
<tr><td>Maps:</td><td>New York–New Jersey Trail Conference map, Northeastern Catskill Trails.</td></tr>
<tr><td>Special concerns:</td><td>Note that both parking and the start of the trail occur on private land; respect all posted notices to preserve the access privilege. Also heed posted camping closure at fire tower area.</td></tr>
<tr><td>Season and hours:</td><td>Spring through fall.</td></tr>
<tr><td>For information:</td><td>New York Department of Environmental Conservation, Regions 3 and 4.</td></tr>
</table>

Key points:

0.0   Trailhead; start on red trail.
2.1   Devils Kitchen lean-to.
4.9   Echo Lake.
6.9   Overlook House ruins.
7.5   Overlook Mountain; return to trailhead (13.4 miles).

Finding the trailhead: From the junction of New York 23A and Greene County 16 in Tannersville, turn south on County 16 (Depot Street) for 5.5 miles; the road name changes several times. Turn right on Prediger Road for 0.5 mile, finding trail parking along the right shoulder only. Do not clog the road or block the private residence by parking on the left or too close to the trailhead. Leave enough space between parked vehicles for returning hikers to pull out safely.

The hike: The southern approach to Overlook Mountain offers perhaps the most popular peak climb in the entire Catskills. This hike takes an alternative approach, arriving from the north. Although longer, it offers a comfortable

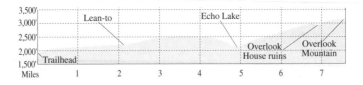

Overlook Mountain Hike

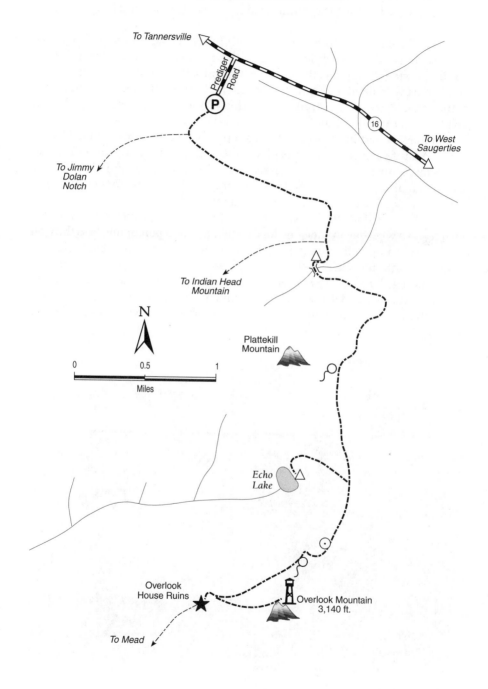

grade, a pleasant backdrop, points of interest, and fewer travelers; a detour en route finds charming Echo Lake. Despite the closure of the old lookout tower, side paths along the summit ridge help piece together the panoramic puzzle.

This hike shares its first 1.9 miles with Indian Head Mountain Loop (see the previous hike description). Follow the red markers away from the old cabin, passing through a stile and crossing a footbridge to enter a hemlock-deciduous woodland and travel a woods road. At the 0.5-mile junction continue straight on the red trail for Overlook Mountain. Before long, the old road tapers to trail width.

Big maples and birch weave the canopy above a boulder-studded forest floor. Wildlife can add elements of surprise. At 1.2 miles cross a thin creek; at 1.8 miles turn right on a woods road, coming to a signed junction. Follow the blue markers straight ahead for the summit; the red trail now turns right toward Indian Head Mountain and destinations west.

At 2.1 miles find Devils Kitchen lean-to, with privy and reliable creek source; on a weekday in June, the lone occupant was a porcupine. Pass through the lean-to camp and cross the creek footbridge for a steady ascent. Nettles, trillium, clintonia, starflower, and Mayflower contribute spring bloom.

Rounding the slope of Plattekill Mountain, pass a low stone bench and travel the semishaded brink of an old quarry, or perhaps a mill site with stone foundations. Here a footpath parts the vegetation of the old road, azalea brings

Overlook House ruins, Catskill Park.

its fragrant pink signature, and oaks join the mix. A wooded flat precedes the Echo Lake Trail junction at 4.2 miles.

Detour right, following the yellow trail along a former carriage road descending sharply to the lake and lean-to at 4.9 miles. The lean-to looks out at a grassy shore of Echo Lake. A 0.5-mile path rings the lake; above it looms the ridge of Overlook Mountain. In spring thousands of polliwogs blacken the shallows, while small toads seemingly cause the roadbed to percolate. This lake destination ideally serves novice backpackers.

Resume the trek to Overlook Mountain at 5.6 miles, again following blue markers and ascending along an escarpment edge for the next 0.25 mile. Mountain laurel, azalea, and pockets of beech trees adorn the way. A fuller forest follows. At 6.2 miles pass an unusual balanced rock on the right as rock ledges and overhangs now characterize the forest. Filtered views find Indian Head and Twin Mountains. Beyond is piped water for wetting the brow.

As the trail draws into the open near a signal tower, look for a junction (6.8 miles). Red markers point the way left to the summit. About 0.1 mile straight ahead, two huge concrete shells and other ruins hauntingly echo the bygone elegance of Overlook House, a classic nineteenth-century mountain hotel that once occupied this site. Built in 1878, the hotel fell to fire in the 1920s. The shell showing 1928 above its doorway represents an abandoned effort to rebuild. The road continues past the ruins downhill 2 miles to Mead.

From the signal tower the final 0.5 mile to the fire tower ascends via woods road. Side paths to the right top a ridge ledge for views to the south-southeast from Ashokan Reservoir to the Hudson River, peering down and out Lewis Hollow. The creased rocks shaping the left shoulder of the road also may call hikers over for a closer look.

The nine-story steel-framed lookout tower still stands, missing its lower flight of stairs. A picnic table welcomes a stay for lunch, but camping is prohibited near the tower. Spur trails pierce the ring of trees, reaching additional vistas. Looks south find Ashokan Reservoir, the Slide Mountain area, Cooper Lake, and Mount Tobias. Follow the wire corridor away from the tower to find outcrops with a western vantage; here views span Saw Kill drainage to Plateau, Sugarloaf, and Twin Mountains, with Hunter Mountain rising beyond Stony Clove Notch. Backtrack the series of red and blue trails to return to the trailhead.

59 Slide Mountain Loop

General description:	Traveling hemlock-deciduous and fir-birch forests, this popular trail tags the highest point in the Catskills and passes Burroughs Plaque and Curtis Monument.
General location:	16 miles southwest of Woodstock.
Special attractions:	Vistas, rare high-elevation fir forest, rock features, commemorative markers, fall foliage.
Length:	7 miles round-trip.
Difficulty:	Moderate to strenuous.
Maps:	Catskill Forest Preserve Camping, Woodland Valley brochure; New York–New Jersey Trail Conference map, Southern Catskill Trails.
Special concerns:	Due to the sensitive nature of this popular forest preserve peak, hikers need to play a protective and respectful role. Do not make this an annual trek, as it cannot sustain such heavy foot traffic, and keep your hiking party small. Avoid travel during and immediately following a rainstorm. If trails are wet keep to the red Wittenberg-Cornell-Slide Trail, a carriage road that can better handle the foot traffic; do not travel the delicate Curtis-Ormsbee Trail. Plan a day hike versus an overnight stay. If you do choose to camp, remember to protect this area's sensitive fir complex. There is no camping above the 3,500-foot elevation.
Season and hours:	Spring through fall.
For information:	New York State Department of Environmental Conservation, Region 3.

Key points:
- 0.0 Slide Mountain trailhead; cross river.
- 0.7 Loop junction; turn left.
- 2.7 Slide Mountain/Burroughs plaque.
- 4.2 Table Mountain vista.
- 4.9 Junction/trail builder monument; turn right.
- 6.3 Close loop; turn left to backtrack to trailhead.

Finding the trailhead: From the junction of New York 214 and New York 28 in Phoenicia, go west on NY 28 for 7.9 miles, reaching Big Indian. There turn south on Ulster County 47, go 9 miles, and turn left to enter the off-road parking area for Slide Mountain trailhead.

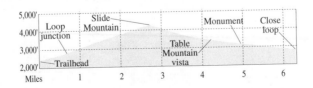

Slide Mountain Loop

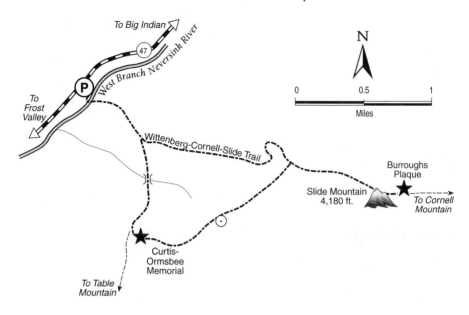

The hike: This hike strings together the yellow Phoenicia–East Branch Trail, the red Wittenberg-Cornell-Slide Trail, and the blue Curtis-Ormsbee Trail, for a rolling tour at the western extent of the Burroughs Range.

Rock-hop across the brook-sized West Branch Neversink River, following yellow markers for a rocky ascent. An open forest of maple, birch, and beech clads the slope. Where the trail reaches a woods road at 0.4 mile, follow it right, now contouring the boulder-studded wooded slope. Past a pipe providing water (treat trail sources), find the loop junction (0.7 mile). Turn left on the red trail for a clockwise tour, once again following a rocky woods road. Be careful not to turn an ankle.

Leafy branches lace over the ascending trail, offering a fragile shade while seasonal runoffs race across the route. The trail narrows and steepens, soon pulling above the 3,500-foot elevation. Fir, birch, and snags compose the skyline. Where the trail next contours the slope, it shows a trail width, with closely spaced firs shaping the aisle. Winds assail the ridge, and weather-watchers can delight in the rapid cloud changes. At 2 miles the blue trail to the right continues the loop; remain on the red trail to reach Slide Mountain.

The trail to Slide Mountain climbs steadily along the north edge of the ridge, remaining in the tightly clustered firs. Mayflower, clintonia, and moss touch green to the forest floor. At 2.5 miles a ledge to the left offers a view north-northeast from Overlook Mountain to Sugarloaf Mountain with Woodland Valley below.

Just ahead, the trail tops the open ledge of Slide Mountain (2.7 miles). Red markers point downhill to the right, where the trail rounds the foot of the cliff to view a plaque honoring John Burroughs, the early-day environmentalist and writer who introduced Slide Mountain to the world through his essays. The dramatic range arcing from Slide to Wittenberg Mountain carries his name.

On Burroughs's noted trek to this peak, he traveled cross-country from Woodland Valley, coming out just north of the summit. He arrived, ascending the slide of 1820; forest has since reclaimed the scar. During his sojourns he slept beneath the overhang next to which the plaque now rests.

From Slide Mountain views span across the spire-topped firs to an all-star lineup of Catskill peaks, including Wittenberg, Plateau, Twin, Indian Head, and Overlook Mountains. Cornell and Friday Mountains form bookends to Ashokan Reservoir.

Return to the loop junction at 3.5 miles and follow the blue-marked foot trail into a fir forest laced with birch and hobblebush. Before long, steep downhill spurs replace the mild descent. The forest grows more open and shrubby, with a meadowy floor. Stones aid the crossing of marshy sites, where the soft ground records the tracks of deer and the occasional print of a misplaced boot.

At 4.25 miles a short spur left leads to a ledge for a Table Mountain vista. With a couple more plunges, the trail offers views spanning the East Branch Neversink River. Some hand assists may be needed for the sharp descents that follow.

Soon the trail overlooks a rock island pulled away from the slope, before descending to skirt the massive rock. A road-sized gap parts the 12- to 15-foot-tall cliff faces. In places the crossbeds have eroded clear through. The trail now flattens for a comfortable shady-woods stroll to the 4.9-mile junction, site of the 3-foot-tall marble tribute to trail builders William Curtis and Allen Ormsbee, who designed the scenic blue trail just traveled.

Turn right on the woods road, following the yellow blazes back to the trailhead. While less rocky than the other woods roads advancing the loop, springs can muddy travel. After passing a small woods road on the left, cross a log bridge over a babbling headwater of the West Branch Neversink. Afterward, rocks prove invaluable for hopscotch travel along the soggy road. Close the loop, and at 6.6 miles turn left for a rocky descent to the trailhead.

60 Mohonk Mountain House– Mohonk Preserve

Overview

In the northern Shawangunks, these adjoining private properties offer hikers a diversity of trails varying in length, challenge, and attraction. Mohonk Mountain House, a national historic landmark and commercial resort, has served outdoor recreationists since 1869. Although access to the castlelike house (hotel) is restricted to paying guests, its regal exterior complements the Lake Mohonk setting.

Linked by an extensive network of trails, the woods and rock features of Mohonk Preserve extend the realm of discovery. Mohonk Preserve is the largest visitor/membership-supported nature preserve in New York State. Its mission is to protect the ridge for perpetuity.

General description: Three trails, each originating from a separate access point, introduce Mohonk Area splendor—one of inspiring cliffs, grand views, and fragile habitats.

General location: 6 miles west of New Paltz.

Special attractions: Vistas, dramatic quartz-conglomerate cliffs, spring wildflowers and flowering shrubs, fall foliage.

Length: Sky Top Hike, 1 mile round-trip; Bonticou Crag Hike, 4.2 miles round-trip (3.8 miles round-trip when varying the return, taking the Crag and Table Rock foot trails); The Trapps Loop, 5.25 miles round-trip.

Difficulty: Sky Top and The Trapps Loop, both easy. Bonticou Crag Hike, moderate.

Maps: Mohonk Mountain House and Mohonk Preserve trail maps.

Special concerns: These independent, privately owned properties each charge a per-person entry fee; the resort also charges a parking fee. A reciprocity has been struck, where payment for a day's hiking at one site buys same-day hiking privileges at the other. Weekday visits at the preserve cost less than weekend or holiday visits; pay fees at visitor center, gates, or self-pay stations. Users accept full responsibility for any risk, agree to follow the posted rules, and must wear an entry pass showing proof of both their payment and an understanding of these conditions. Hikers planning to walk any resort trails should phone Mohonk Mountain House beforehand to confirm that the trails will be open. The Mountain House and Lake Mohonk are accessible only to paying hotel guests. Find rest rooms at the preserve visitor center; portable toilets are available at Spring Farm Trailhead.

Season and hours: Spring through fall for hiking, sunrise to sunset.
Mohonk Preserve's Trapps Gateway Visitor Center:
8:15 A.M. to 4:45 P.M. weekdays; on weekends the
center opens at 9:00 A.M.

For information: Mohonk Mountain House; Mohonk Preserve.

Key points:
Sky Top Hike:
    0.0   Start near Mountain House putting green.
    0.4   Hayes Lookout.
    0.5   Sky Top/Albert K. Smiley Memorial Tower; return by same route.
Bonticou Crag Hike:
    0.0   Spring Farm trailhead; hike Spring Farm Road.
    0.7   Bonticou Road.
    1.2   Descend Bonticou Ascent Path.
    2.1   Crag escarpment vantage; return by same route or vary return.
The Trapps Loop:
    0.0   West Trapps trailhead; hike old turnpike southeast.
    0.2   Loop junction; follow Overcliff Carriageway left.
    2.6   Junction; follow Undercliff Carriageway right.
    5.0   Close loop; backtrack to West Trapps trailhead.

Finding the trailhead: From New York State Thruway Interstate 87, take exit 18 and go west on New York 299, passing through New Paltz and crossing over the Wallkill River bridge. Take the first right, turning onto Springtown Road; bear left at the fork in 0.5 mile. This is Mountain Rest Road. Follow it 3.4 miles to reach the Mohonk Mountain House gateway.

To hike Sky Top enter the gateway, pay the required fee for day visitation, and park in the large lot to the right of the gatehouse. Hikers then have the choice of hiking to the Mountain House and Lake Mohonk area via the Huguenot Trail or taking the shuttle bus (an additional fee).

To reach the start for the Bonticou Crag Hike, remain on Mountain Rest Road, proceeding another 0.9 mile. Turn right on Upper Knoll Road and drive 0.2 mile to the preserve's Spring Farm trailhead.

For Mohonk Preserve's Trapps Gateway Visitor Center and The Trapps Loop from I-87, go 7.2 miles west on NY 299, reaching the junction with U.S. Highway 44/New York 55. Go west on U.S. 44/NY 55 for 0.4 mile to locate the center and its parking on the right. The Trapps Loop can be accessed either from the center or from West Trapps Entry trailhead. Find its parking on the right 1.3 miles west of the center off U.S. 44/NY 55.

The hikes: For the shortest route to **Sky Top**, start at the putting green near the front of Mountain House and ascend past the conference building. This trail is closed during winter.

The trail transports visitors to a bygone era, crossing ledges, visiting rustic Victorian gazebos, and overlooking Mohonk Mountain House and Lake Mohonk. The castlelike Mountain House—an architectural collage of frame

Mohonk Mountain House–Mohonk Preserve

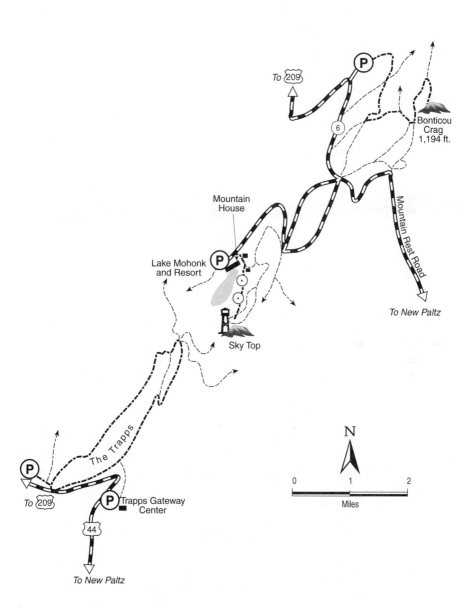

To 209

P

6

Bonticou
Crag
1,194 ft.

Mountain
House

Lake Mohonk
and Resort

P

Mountain Rest Road

To New Paltz

Sky Top

The Trapps

P

N

0   1   2

Miles

To 209

P Trapps Gateway
Center

44

To New Paltz

and stone structures with turrets, balconies, and gables—adds to the enchantment of the deep green lake and white cliff shore. An evergreen-deciduous forest with mountain laurel and berry bushes claims the slope.

By Hayes Lookout (0.4 mile) photographers attain a spectacular overview of Lake Mohonk, the Mountain House, the Hudson Valley, and Catskill ridges and peaks; the view excels when splashed with autumn red and yellow. The spur to Thurston Rock offers views at the far end of the lake and The Trapps.

Cross Sky Top Road and ascend the steps to arrive at the Albert K. Smiley Memorial Tower (0.5 mile), a regional landmark named for the founder of Mountain House. Huge stone blocks, a spiral staircase, and long thin tower windows contribute the tower's medieval charm; a 360-degree vista rewards the climb. Return as you came, or plot a loop return along the many interlocking trails and carriage roads.

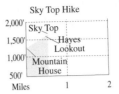

Sky Top Hike

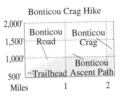

Bonticou Crag Hike

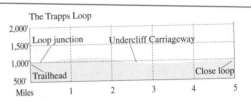

The Trapps Loop

The **Bonticou Crag** hike begins ascending via gated Spring Farm Road at the upper end of Spring Farm parking area; this dirt road is open only to authorized vehicles. Maples, oaks, hickory, red cedar, and sumac edge the route. Below stretches an open grassy slope that extends views west-northwest, dubbed "the million dollar view." After topping a knoll, the route then descends and keeps right, skirting historic farm structures and passing a toilet facility and rustic outdoor pavilion.

Because bikes and horses share the carriageways with hikers, be on the lookout for them around bends and on inclines. Some lovely old maples or a huge basswood, particularly pretty during bloom, can hold the gaze. Keep to the Spring Farm Carriageway, bypassing foot trails and crossing other carriage routes. Pass the blue Table Rock Trail at 0.2 mile and the red Crag Trail at 0.4 mile.

At 0.7 mile the hike follows Bonticou Road left toward the crag for a slope-contouring passage. Where both the red Crag Trail and Cedar Drive arrive on the left (1 mile), proceed forward on Bonticou Road, soon glimpsing the white rock of the crag beyond the trees.

Lake Mohonk and resort.

Reach the yellow-blazed Bonticou Ascent Path at 1.2 miles and descend left to emerge at a jumble of chunky boulders at the base of Bonticou Crag (1.25 miles), finding the blue Northeast Trail and the continuation of the yellow route. Avoid the yellow trail, which makes a rugged, rock-climbing assault on the summit. Instead follow the Northeast Trail left for a gentler backdoor ticket to Bonticou Crag.

At 1.7 miles go right, still following the blue Northeast Trail, passing between boulders and along the cliff to climb the wooded north slope. Top the ridge (1.9 miles), again meeting the yellow trail; this time follow it right. Traverse the summit ridge as it shows a burst of mountain laurel, low-stature trees, azalea bushes, a variety of wildflowers, and humped outcrops. Watch closely for the yellow blazes.

Upon attaining the escarpment ledge (2.1 miles), views include the crag overhang, wooded Guyot Hill, the Wallkill and Hudson river valleys, and the Catskill Mountains. Before exploring the white quartz-conglomerate rim, make a mental note of where the trail first reached the escarpment to speed your return.

Retrace your steps or vary the return, following the red Crag Trail downhill from the 1-mile junction. Together with the Table Rock Trail, this foottrail return will shorten the round trip by 0.4 mile.

The red Crag Trail offers a faster, steeper descent from the 1-mile junction. Pine, chestnut, and small hemlocks grow the roster of tree species shading the way. By 0.2 mile the Crag Trail drops off the ridge it followed to trace the upper slope. Cross Spring Farm Road at 0.3 mile (watch for cross-traffic), and quick on its heels cross unlabeled Cedar Drive. A sunny passage follows, tracing the edges of divided meadow slopes to Table Rock Trail. The meadow slopes open to views of the preserve and world beyond. Wildflowers decorate the meadows and attract butterflies. At 0.5 mile reach Table Rock Trail, near where it intersects Spring Farm Road. Follow Table Rock Trail left back to the parking area (0.6 mile), emerging via an unmarked rocky spur at the gate.

For **The Trapps Loop,** hike southeast from the end of the West Trapps Entry parking turnaround to reach the loop junction at Trapps Bridge. This 0.25-mile West Trapps Connector Trail follows part of the old turnpike; deciduous trees and mountain laurel frame its way. Pass the red Shongum Path on the left, before the bridge.

Ascend to bridge level, but do not cross it. Instead turn left to find The Trapps Loop junction at a signboard. Follow Overcliff left for a clockwise loop. The shale-surfaced carriage road contours the wooded slope for a gentle ascent, passing an impressive scatter of massive rock, a canted rock slab, and a small overhang. Rare gaps offer views across Coxing Kill.

Keep to the carriageway, rounding and descending to the other side of The Trapps ridge, once again touring an area of breakaway boulders beneath a cliff. Bypass the blue Sleepy Hollow Trail, and bear right as an unmarked carriageway arrives on the left.

Rhododendron Bridge (2.6 miles) marks a major junction. For the loop take the Undercliff carriage road to the right; the Laurel Ledge carriage road heads left. Across the bridge encounter Old Minnewaska carriage road and Oakwood Drive.

Undercliff again contours the woodland slope. Oaks, maple, birch, and hemlock compose the woods, with azalea and a few dogwoods displacing the mountain laurel. Wild geranium and jack-in-the-pulpit color the trail's sides. At 3.25 miles again bypass Sleepy Hollow Trail to find early leaf-masked views of The Trapps cliffs and hear climbers overhead.

Old-growth trees rise from the steep slope dropping away from the carriage road. Ahead find less impeded looks at the 200-foot white quartzite cliffs. Millipedes dot the overhangs, and boulder slabs continue to riddle the base. Forest gaps offer looks to the east-southeast and at a hairpin turn on U.S. 44/NY55 as the East Trapps Connector Trail arrives from the visitor center. Where the cliffs plunge to Undercliff carriage road in dramatic fashion, a memorial and a climbers kiosk introduce the early-day climbers who popularized the area and explain the conditions for climbing. Next round a shale slope to close the loop (5 miles); return to West Trapps trailhead (5.25 miles).

Hikers who opt to start from the visitor center likewise follow a 0.25-mile connector trail. The East Trapps Connector Trail joins the loop at the 4.5-mile mark. Turn left on Undercliff Carriageway for a clockwise tour, keeping the order of the hike.

61 Minnewaska State Park Preserve

Overview

A former resort and recent battleground between developers and environmentalists, this state park preserve presents a tranquil natural realm. The site boasts beautiful white-cliff escarpments, picturesque blue waters, and soothing forests—images to delight poet and photographer. Comfortable carriageways and foot trails travel the preserve for tours of varying length and discovery.

> **General description:** The selected carriageway circuit travels from Lake Minnewaska, around Lake Awosting, and across a Shawangunk escarpment rim for a rich and varied tour.
> **General location:** 10 miles west of New Paltz.
> **Special attractions:** Striking ledges and vistas, attractive mountain lakes, a waterfall, mixed woods, wildflowers, flowering shrubs.
> **Length:** 11.8 miles round-trip, including Rainbow Falls detour.
> **Difficulty:** Moderate.
> **Maps:** State park flier; New York–New Jersey Trail Conference maps, Shawangunk Trails-South and Lake Minnewaska Area.
> **Special concerns:** Fee area.
> **Season and hours:** Spring through fall, 9:00 A.M. to 7:00 P.M.
> **For information:** Minnewaska State Park Preserve.

Key points:
- 0.0   Trailhead; descend via red trail.
- 0.1   Lake Minnewaska; hike west on Upper Awosting Carriageway.
- 2.9   Rainbow Falls.
- 3.7   Lake Awosting; round counterclockwise.
- 8.2   Castle Point.
- 10.5 Kempton Ledge.
- 11.7 Close loop; ascend to picnic area.

Finding the trailhead: From New York State Thruway Interstate 87, take exit 18 for New Paltz and go west on New York 299 for 7.2 miles. At the junction with U.S. Highway 44/New York 55, go west on U.S. 44/NY 55 for 4.4 miles and turn left for the park. The trail starts from the picnic area at the end of the park road.

The hike: From the picnic area descend via the red trail to the Minnewaska lakeshore. At the northwest corner of the lake (opposite the swimming area), take the green Upper Awosting Carriageway west; a fine-grade

Minnewaska State Park Preserve

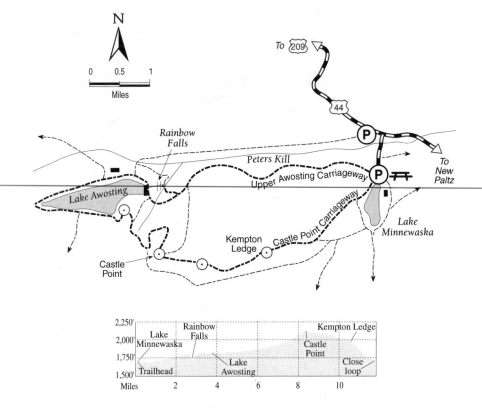

slate provides a smooth walking surface. Hemlock, maple, oak, beautiful white birch, and mountain laurel make up the woods.

The carefree stroll allows eyes and thoughts to roam; the occasional gap offers views north. Deer, grouse, and goshawk may slow strides. The trail shows a mild uphill grade more apparent to the eye than the body. The lure of the forest and song of the birds push aside any road noise. Cyclists may share the way.

At 0.7 mile pass an old orchard where the snarled trees still flower in spring and rusted pieces of farm equipment blend into the meadow. Along the way, side brooks sheet over outcrops draining to Peters Kill below, and color-coded foot trails branch away. Beneath a powerline, a flat gray outcrop suggests a stop.

Before long, scenic rock ledges with fern-and-grass-topped shelves border the way. At 2.6 miles the aqua-blazed Long Path emerges from a break in Litchfield Ledge. A detour right on Long Path leads to Rainbow Falls.

To view the falls descend through a deep woods of mature hemlock and beech, crossing a side drainage and Huntington Ravine. Rainbow Falls graces a side stream, plunging to the latter. Its rivulets pour from an overhang, embellishing a color-streaked cliff; a growing streamer of algae catches the water.

Return to Upper Awosting Carriageway (3.2 miles) and resume the hike west to Lake Awosting.

Gradually the terrain flattens. At the carriageway junction at 3.75 miles, turn right now following a black-blazed earthen carriageway for a counterclockwise tour of Lake Awosting. The dam presents an open lake view animated by ducks, geese, and shorebirds. Pinched at its middle, the huge lake shows scalloped coves, evergreen-deciduous shores, and slopes and ledges of white quartzite. Sweet pepperbush, azalea, and mountain and sheep laurel braid together in a showy understory display.

At 4.1 miles bypass a rangers cabin, staying above shore for overlooks and cross-lake views but no lake access. At 4.9 miles an open flat with an old foundation and broken bricks and glass hints at a bygone time. At junctions keep to the black carriageway.

At 5.25 miles the Long Path briefly shares the route; soon after, tour closer to shore. Monstrous hemlocks, pockets of sheep laurel, scenic pines, and lakeside outcrops add to the journey; side paths travel the small peninsulas. Past the foot trail to Spruce Glen and Murray Hill, find the swimming area with its lakeward white outcrop, bumpy with quartz and dotted by pines.

Stay on the black carriageway, drifting into woods at 6.4 miles. At 6.7 miles a spur leads to a ledge overlooking Lake Awosting; now turn away from the lake for good. At the upcoming junction go right on the blue carriageway, now hiking toward Hamilton and Castle Point Carriageways.

The trail alternately tours mixed woods interlaced with mountain laurel and stands of small bizarre-shaped pines accompanied by sheep laurel and

Upper Awosting Carriageway, Minnewaska State Park Preserve.

berry bushes. Periodic outcrops offer views. Glimpses of the white-gray cliff of Castle Point precede the junction at 7.5 miles. Go left on shale-surfaced Castle Point Carriageway, staying with the blue markers.

Pass beneath jutting overhangs and ledges for views spanning a deciduous-filled drainage to scenic Battlement Terrace. Ahead, top Castle Point Terrace, reaching Castle Point at 8.2 miles for a spectacular 180- to 200-degree vista sweeping west and south to Hamilton Point, Gertrude's Nose, Lake Awosting, the wooded rims and swells of the park, and the distant Hudson Valley.

With the descent, perspectives shift east, adding views of Sky Tower in the nearby Mohonks. Where the trail passes under a powerline, it drifts from the escarpment edge, touring a more varied woods. Top Kempton Ledge (10.5 miles) for overlooks of Palmaghatt Kill, the Hudson Valley, and an isolated outcrop of fluted cliffs. Pale green lichen blotches the smooth white stone, and deep fissures invade the terrace.

Follow the blue carriageway downhill, avoiding a spur turning right to Hamilton Carriageway. An open grassy area presents a Catskill view. Upon reaching Lakeshore Drive (the red carriageway rounding Lake Minnewaska), turn left to close the loop at the swimming area (11.7 miles), and return to the picnic area (11.8 miles).

Half the size of Lake Awosting, picturesque blue-green Lake Minnewaska reflects a partial shoreline of abrupt white cliffs with a talus base. Atop the white-cliff terrace sits the attractive stone building of the park office. Hemlock and pine interlace the deciduous trees of shore. Autumn's paintbrush puts a special flourish on this closing image of the tour.

62 Bashakill Wildlife Management Area

Overview

At this 2,175-acre wildlife management area (WMA)—more than half of which is freshwater wetland—a former railroad grade rolls out an avenue to relaxation and nature discovery. On the west side of Bashakill Marsh, snatches of the historic Delaware and Hudson Canal (1828 to 1898) offer additional exploration. A blockade halting soft-coal shipments from England gave rise to this 108-mile canal linking the domestic coal fields of Pennsylvania with Hudson River ports. A premier bird-watching site, the WMA attracts birders year-round and invites both daylight and evening watches.

General description: Part of the greater Long Path traversing New York State, this rail-to-trail travels the eastern edge of Bashakill Marsh, offering wildlife observation.
General location: Just south of Wurtsboro.
Special attractions: Largest freshwater marsh in southeastern New York; spring-nesting waterfowl and warblers, brooding

summer birds, and fall migrants; wetland and upland woods; observation towers; spring flora.

Length: 13 miles round-trip.
Difficulty: Easy.
Maps: Bashakill Wildlife Management Area brochure.
Special concerns: No amenities available; bring water. Expect some soggy stretches, and avoid during hunting season.
Season and hours: Year-round, twenty-four hours. In winter expect snow and unplowed lots to limit access. Although the WMA prohibits camping, night fishing, owl watching, and stargazing are acceptable nighttime activities at the refuge.
For information: New York State Department of Environmental Conservation, Region 3.

Key points:

0.0 Southern trailhead; hike north.
1.0 Observation tower.
2.2 Detour left to second tower.
3.7 Cross Haven Road to fourth trail access.
4.4 Lookout side loop.
6.0 New York 17/I–86 underpass.
6.5 Walker Lane in southeast Wurtsboro; backtrack.

Finding the trailhead: From New York 17/I–86, take exit 113 and go south on U.S. Highway 209 for 5.2 miles, turning left on Sullivan County 163/Orange County 61 for Otisville. Go 0.4 mile and turn left to round the WMA's east shore. In 0.1 mile find a fishing access; in 0.2 mile find the southern trailhead for the WMA's rail trail. Find its north end at the southeast outskirts of Wurtsboro.

The hike: From the southernmost access, the rail trail dead-ends to the south in 0.2 mile; the primary tour travels north, edging the marsh. In the morning, songbirds regale hikers and dew bejewels the vegetation. Woody vines droop between the trees that shape a thin border between the trail and wetland flat. Wetland often claims both sides of the rail levee. Duckweed, lily pads, loosestrife, clumps of arrowhead, algae, and flooded stumps and snags variously characterize the marsh. Cross-beams and footbridges ease drainage crossings.

Columbine, wild strawberry, wild geranium, violet, and more sprinkle color along the tour. Open sites offer fine marsh vantages and fishing access. In places the old rail ties ripple the trailbed or lie discarded to its side. Oriole, warbler, scarlet tanager, bluebird, green heron, grouse, osprey, vulture, and

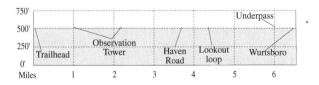

Bashakill Wildlife Management Area

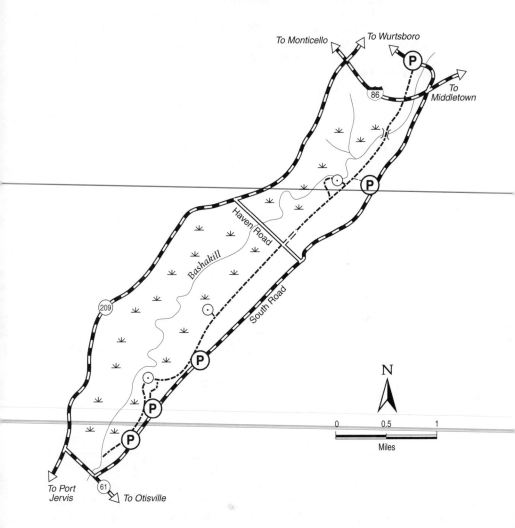

a wide variety of waterfowl lengthen the list of bird sightings. Woodchuck, muskrat, beaver, and white-tailed deer top the list for mammals.

At 0.5 mile find a junction and the second trailhead; with six trailheads to serve it, the rail trail readily welcomes hopscotch or car-shuttle travel. To the right a footbridge leads to the parking lot and a nature trail heads left. Curving between the two lies an overgrown segment of the rail trail. Veer left for the nature trail and observation tower; this spur rejoins the rail trail farther north, where it again clears for easier travel.

The nature trail shows a confusion of splits. At the first split the left fork dead-ends at a fishing access; the right fork advances the nature trail. Upon turning left for the first interpretive station, the trail again splits, with the left fork leading to a marshy point. The right split pursues the nature trail numbers to the tower (1 mile). White pines and oaks frame the single-story platform, which overlooks open water, treed islands, arrowhead, and lily pads; Canada geese navigate faint channels through the vegetation.

From the tower continue north along the marsh; bear left at the fork to return to the rail trail/Long Path (1.2 miles). A right at the fork continues the nature trail. Pine, hemlock, oak, mountain laurel, and azalea dress the return to the grade; yellow disks can mark the way.

Turn left (north) on the rail trail, finding a scenic aisle of white birch. Crossing a gap-toothed boardwalk and an area of embedded ties, reach the next parking area and a launch site at 1.6 miles. Ties again ripple the trailbed to the north as birch form a scenic arborway. At times red-winged blackbirds fiercely defend their nests, bombing geese that swim past. A vast field of loosestrife claims the marsh to the right, while arrowhead dominates the main marsh. The woody stems of the non-native loosestrife provide perches for blackbirds. Atop a snag sits an osprey nest, as another woodland tour begins.

Prior to an old gnarled maple at 2.25 miles, look for the overgrown path heading left to a second tower; beware—poison ivy intermingles with the grasses. Reach the tower in 200 yards for another overlook of the marsh mosaic. The northbound tour resumes with a bridge crossing. Skunk cabbage and false hellebore line the brook and riddle the wetland woods as the trail alternates between woods and marsh.

Birch-lined rail-trail, Bashakill Wildlife Management Area.

At 3.7 miles cross Haven Road; travel the gravel access road through the parking lot and round the gate to the north. This is the most popular access to the WMA and often overflows with birders' vehicles.

Pockets of horsetail reed now dot the trail. Past a scenic multitrunked pine at 4.4 miles, find a spur ascending a steep incline to the left labeled SIDE TRAIL TO LOOKOUT. Along it, tags identify some tree species. The tower view overlooks the meandering course of Bashakill. Follow the spur as it hooks past the tower to return to the rail trail. Soon after, find the footboard crossing to the next parking area.

Ahead, swampy passages mar the woods tour. At 5.3 miles pass below an area of private, abandoned houses. Footbridges over the split flow of Bashakill next mark off distance.

Sounds of NY 17/I–86 precede the underpass (6 miles), where Virginia creeper scales the tunnel's concrete walls. The rail corridor ahead shows an open cathedral, and turtles plop from the banks as hikers pass. At 6.5 miles the trail comes out opposite Walker Lane in southeast Wurtsboro. Although the Long Path continues north, return as you came.

Hudson Valley

This New York region celebrates the Hudson River—a vital transportation and recreation corridor, past and present. Rising above the broad water to the south find the striking Hudson Highlands and Bear Mountain/Harriman complex. The Appalachian Trail spends much of its 95-mile New York sojourn snaking through this region.

At the northeast extent of the region, the attractive Taconic skyline separates New York from Massachusetts and Connecticut. Tucked away at the Connecticut border find the nation's first Registered Natural Historical Landmark.

The Hudson Valley landscape is one of ridges, peaks, and valleys. Multistate vistas reward travelers. Mountain laurel, dogwood, and azalea endorse spring tours.

63 Taconic State Park

Overview

Snug in the southern Taconic Mountain Range, abutting 11 miles of the Massachusetts and Connecticut border, this New York state park boasts trails that blur state lines. Bash Bish Falls, which annually brings 100,000 visitors to the park, actually lies in Massachusetts but is best reached by this New York trail. The park's prized skyline route, the South Taconic Trail, meanders in and out of New York and Massachusetts with an equal disregard of borders.

General description:	Three hikes of varying difficulty begin at Bash Bish trailhead: an easy round-trip falls hike, a demanding full-day (or overnight) skyline hike, and a peak hike of average difficulty that may be car-shuttled.
General location:	East of Copake Falls, New York.
Special attractions:	Bash Bish Falls, mid-June to early-July azalea and mountain laurel blooms, skyline vistas of three states, overlooks of the autumn-painted Taconic Mountains.
Length:	Bash Bish Falls Trail, 1.5 miles round-trip; South Taconic Trail (South), 16.2 miles round-trip; South Taconic Trail (North), 4.2-mile shuttle or 7.4 miles round-trip.
Difficulty:	Bash Bish Falls Trail, easy; South Taconic Trail (South) strenuous; South Taconic Trail (North), moderate.
Maps:	Park trail flier (map not to scale); New York–New Jersey Trail Conference map, South Taconic Trail (includes contour lines).

Special concerns: Although this New York state park prohibits trailside camping within reach of the South Taconic Trail (South), Massachusetts has a first-come, first-served cabin and fifteen backcountry campsites (fee and permit required; contact Mount Washington State Forest, East Street, Mount Washington, MA). It is best for hikers to avoid the trails altogether during deer season, November–December in New York State and Massachusetts.

Season and hours: Spring through fall, dawn to dusk; state park campground: May 10 to October 31.

For information: Taconic State Park.

Key points:

Bash Bish Falls Trail:
- 0.0 Bash Bish trailhead; hike east (upstream).
- 0.7 Bash Bish Falls; return by same route.

South Taconic Trail (South):
- 0.0 Bash Bish trailhead; descend toward cabins.
- 1.2 Washburn Mountain view.
- 3.5 Alander Mountain ridge lookout site; continue south.
- 7.6 Pass Mount Frissell Trail.
- 8.2 Brace Mountain; backtrack South Taconic Trail to trailhead.

South Taconic Trail (North):
- 0.0 Bash Bish trailhead; cross New York 344.
- 2.6 Sunset Rock.
- 3.2 Sunset Rock Road (car-shuttle parking).
- 3.7 Prospect Hill; backtrack to appropriate trailhead.

Finding the trailhead: From Copake Falls go 0.7 mile east on New York 344 to reach Bash Bish trailhead on the right.

To spot a vehicle for the South Taconic Trail (North), take Cemetery Road north from Copake Falls and continue north on North Mountain Road. Go 1.4 miles from the intersection of Cemetery and North Mountain Roads and turn right on unmarked Sunset Rock Road, a seasonally maintained single-lane gravel road. Reach trailhead parking on the right in 1.1 miles.

The hikes: One can best appreciate the **Bash Bish Falls Trail** in the quiet off-season or in the early-morning hours midweek. Follow the closed service road east upstream above Bash Bish Brook for early overlooks of the sparkling stream coursing over bedrock. Hemlock and maple lace over the trail; boulders and rock slabs punctuate shore and waterway. Although deep pools invite, swimming is not allowed. At 0.75 mile stairs descend to a boot-polished schist outcrop offering an unobstructed view of the falls.

Bash Bish Falls, a split-character forked falls, spills in an energetic rush around a skyward-pointing rock wedge. An emerald pool enclosed by a crescent cliff and a bouldery outlet capture the water. The right fork shows a tiered veil broadening at the base; the left fork, a showery drop ending in a water slide. Downstream the gorge holds an exciting union of rock and water. Return as you came.

Taconic State Park

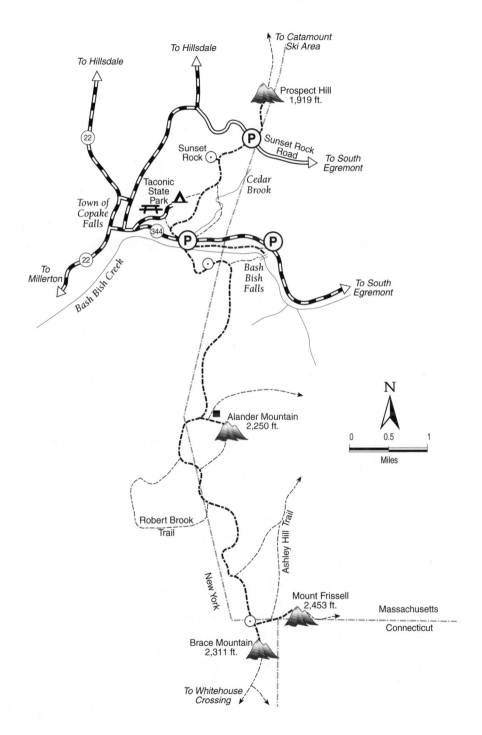

To Hillsdale

To Hillsdale

To Catamount Ski Area

Prospect Hill
1,919 ft.

22

Sunset Rock

P Sunset Rock Road

To South Egremont

Cedar Brook

Taconic State Park

Town of Copake Falls

344

P **P**

Bash Bish Falls

To Millerton

Bash Bish Creek

To South Egremont

N

0   0.5   1

Miles

Alander Mountain
2,250 ft.

Robert Brook Trail

Ashley Hill Trail

New York

Mount Frissell
2,453 ft.

Massachusetts
Connecticut

Brace Mountain
2,311 ft.

To Whitehouse Crossing

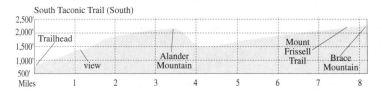

Bash Bish Falls Trail

South Taconic Trail (South)

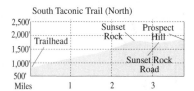

South Taconic Trail (North)

White blazes mark the entire length of the South Taconic Trail.

For the **South Taconic Trail (South),** follow the white markers along the limited-access road that angles downhill to the cabins, west of Bash Bish trailhead. Cross the bridge and go past the cabins before entering the wilds on a foot trail. A contouring ascent through mountain laurel, a sharp climb through a stand of 1- to 3-foot-diameter hemlocks, and a tour of a high-canopy maple forest and pine-oak area lead to a ridge junction at 1.1 miles.

Here a 0.2-mile round-trip detour via a blue spur trail finds a 180-degree western perspective with Washburn Mountain. The white South Taconic Trail continues its ascent in oak woodland and later a hemlock grove, soon bypassing a second blue trail. Save for a notch at 3 miles, the trail hugs the ridge. Pines appear now and again, and views flip to the east.

At 3.5 miles, prior to an old lookout site on Alander Ridge, look for a faintly painted blue marker atop a flat exposed outcrop. For the South Taconic Trail alone, continue straight ahead, staying with the white blazes.

For an Alander Mountain summit detour, descend left on the blue trail, coming to a saddle where an old but highly liveable cabin sits. The cabin offers a dry overnight wayside on a first-come, first-served basis; early summer azalea and laurel fancy it up. The blue fork descending past the cabin passes through Massachusetts's Mount Washington State Forest, eventually reaching the backpacker campsites; the blue fork ascending east tags Alander summit (0.3 mile from ridge junction) for a view.

Beyond the 3.5-mile junction the South Taconic Trail dishes up a fine 270-degree view with Massachusetts's Alander Mountain and Mount Frissell, Connecticut's Round Mountain, and New York's Brace Mountain and the

264

Bash Bish Falls, Mount Washington State Forest (Massachusetts).

westward stretching valley and foothills. An outcrop of wavy-patterned schist provides the vantage.

The trail, shaded by mixed oaks, maple, and beech, now drops away, sometimes steeply. Where it comes out at a former woods road, follow the woods road left, dipping to a drainage then ascending and bypassing an overgrown blue trail on the left.

A few white pines tower trailside, near the junction with the red-blazed Robert Brook Trail (5.2 miles). An occasional rock wall or waist-high ostrich ferns next decorate the South Taconic Trail. When the mountain laurels close ranks, a splendid floral aisle ushers hikers skyward in early summer.

At 6.7 miles a foot trail veers right, traversing a ridge outcrop for a western vantage before returning once more to the woods road and passing the Ashley Hill Trail. After the grade has eased, at 7.6 miles, a red trail descends left toward Mount Frissell and Tristate Point. The South Taconic Trail continues on the old woods road to Brace Mountain; go right where the roadbed forks.

A shrubby, open complex houses this moderate-grade route. At 8.2 miles a foot trail heads left topping Brace Mountain, where a 5-foot-tall cairn puts an exclamation mark on the hike. Views sweep the tristate area. Return as you came, or continue south to Whitehouse Crossing.

The **South Taconic Trail (North)** angles west across NY 344, following white blazes up a wooded slope to the left of Cedar Brook drainage. (A blue-blazed trail along the brook offers an alternative start but requires low water for fordings; it joins the trail description at 1.7 miles). At 0.2 mile turn left on a wide woods road and watch for the white markers pointing hikers uphill through a tight conifer stand.

At 0.5 mile join the red trail, ascending a much smaller woods road. From here to where the Cedar Brook Trail arrives at 1.7 miles, a series of color-coded trails arrive and exit; stay with the white blazes. Tall pine and maple offer shade, but with each burst of ascent, the trail opens up. The added sun brings out the park's earliest mountain laurel blooms. The upper reaches of the ridge again present a fuller forest of oak and maple.

At 2.5 miles exit a shrub corridor to find an unmarked spur leading left to Sunset Rock; the continuation of the South Taconic Trail follows the faint jeep track straight ahead. The side spur reaches westward-facing, humped-back Sunset Rock (elevation 1,788 feet) in 0.1 mile. Views take in the immediate valley farmland, with the Catskills and Hudson Valley some 50 miles distant.

Northbound, the South Taconic Trail flattens as it follows the grassy jeep track through an arborway of oak, pine, and thick mountain laurel. At 3 miles turn left for a mild descent along a neatly narrow woods path that comes out at Sunset Rock Road and the shuttle parking area at 3.2 miles.

For Prospect Hill, angle downhill across Sunset Rock Road and pass a spring-house ruins for a comfortable forest ascent through oak-maple woodland and a pine-shrub complex. Outcrops offer views west of farmland, east of mounts Everett and Darby, and south of Bash Bish and Alander Mountains.

Prior to a New York–Massachusetts boundary marker, turn left, topping Prospect Hill (elevation 1,919 feet) at 3.7 miles and bettering the view from Sunset Rock. Return as you came or to your shuttle vehicle.

64 Appalachian Trail

General description: This 2,155-mile national scenic trail from Maine to Georgia cuts across the southeast corner of New York State, rolling along ridges and dipping to roads. The New York leg takes an average of seven to ten days to complete.

General location: The trail swings between the Connecticut and New Jersey state lines.

Special attractions: Vistas, side trails, low-elevation mixed forests, historic stone walls, wildflowers, fall foliage.

Length: 95.2 miles one-way, with the northern 7.2 miles of trail slipping in and out of Connecticut.

Difficulty: Strenuous.

Maps: Appalachian Trail Conference (ATC), Appalachian Trail maps.

Special concerns: Hikers need to work out the logistics of carrying and obtaining adequate food and supplies, plan what to do in case of an emergency, and arrange for transportation at the end of the trail. Expect rocky, difficult conditions; strong map and compass skills ease travel. Stay alert for the white blazes, which occur at regular intervals. If you have hiked 0.25 mile without spying a blaze or other clue to the trail, backtrack to the last-spied blaze and reassess.

Season and hours: Spring through fall.

For information: Appalachian Trail Conference.

Key points:

0.0	Connecticut–New York border; hike AT south.
7.2	Hoyt Road (AT now remains in New York).
14.2	NY 22.
21.2	NY 55.
27.0	Interstate 84 overpass.
33.0	Taconic Parkway.
36.1	Shenandoah Mountain.
40.3	NY 301/Comstock Lake in Fahnestock State Park.
52.8	U.S. Highway 9.
58.6	Bear Mountain Bridge.
61.2	Bear Mountain.
65.6	Palisades Parkway.
77.4	NY 17/I–86.
83.5	Mombasha High Point.
85.5	Fitzgerald Falls.
89.4	NY 17A.
95.2	New York–New Jersey State Line.

Finding the trailhead: The Appalachian Trail crosses many New York state and county routes and traverses Fahnestock, Hudson Highlands, and Bear

Appalachian Trail

Mountain–Harriman State Parks. New York State through-hikers will find the northernmost road access to the Appalachian Trail at the New York/Connecticut 55–Hoyt Road intersection. Find the southernmost road access along New York 17A near Greenwood Lake.

The hike: The first trail in the nation to win national scenic trail designation, the Appalachian Trail (AT) salutes the mountain wilds of fourteen eastern states. Conceived in the early 1920s, this hiker filament rolls atop the ancient Appalachian Mountains, dipping to cross the important eastern river valleys. Most of the AT greenway has received permanent public protection; some 4,000 volunteers plus 200 public agencies maintain and oversee the trail.

For 95 miles through southeastern New York, the rolling tour passes through low-elevation deciduous woods and hemlock forests, traveling the state's low, rugged ridges and hilltops. The AT dips to cross brooks and drainages (often at road crossings), rounds lakes and ponds but with limited

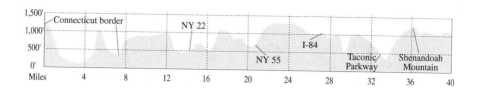

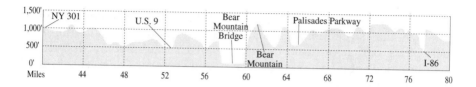

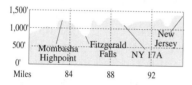

access, and gathers grand views, including the Hudson River Valley, the Taconics, the Catskills, the Shawangunks, the Hudson Highlands, and the Manhattan city skyline.

Open to foot travel only, the white-blazed AT advances primarily via foot trail, with some sections of abandoned woods road. The trail does travel developed roads where it descends to cross Bear Mountain Bridge over the Hudson River. The trail can be rocky and steep; expect to use your hands from time to time for steadying, climbing, and easing yourself over rocks. Beware of rattlesnakes. Tight passages such as the "Lemon Squeezer" in Harriman State Park add interest to the tour. As the protected greenway can be narrow, keep to the trail to avoid straying onto private land.

Despite some fifteen lean-tos along or just off the trail, a tent is standard equipment. Because these first-come, first-served waysides cannot be reserved, chancing that you will be the first to arrive and claim a lean-to for the night is both unwise and an unnecessary wilderness risk. When pitching a tent, camp in an established site to minimize environmental harm.

On a north-south tour, the AT sashays between New York and Connecticut for the first 7.2 miles before committing to New York's watch for the next 88 miles. As it travels the rich hardwood forests of Hammersley Ridge in Pawling Nature Reserve (owned by The Nature Conservancy), a few marshy sites mark the tour. Early views feature the rolling countryside of Dutchess County.

The 7-mile leg between New York 22 and New York 55 finds an open view from West Mountain. Much of the way, large oaks and fields characterize the tour. The southern 2 miles of this segment travel within a quarter mile of a nuclear-fuel testing site, now cleaned up and cleared for unrestricted use. But for hikers who feel uneasy about the land's past, an alternate blue trail travels a roadway, avoiding this stretch.

South of Interstate 84 the AT gathers open views from Depot Hill, traversing rock ledges while rolling along the wooded ridge. The undulating trail remains along ridge or slope, topping Stormville and Hosner Mountains for views of the Catskills, Shawangunks, and Hudson Highlands. Historic stone walls recall an earlier time.

South of the Taconic Parkway, cross Shenandoah Mountain, entering Clarence Fahnestock Memorial State Park. An overlook applauds the shimmery platter of Canopus Lake before the trail descends to round the wooded slope and ridge of the west shore. The AT only reaches Canopus Lake level where the trail crosses New York 301.

Ahead, briefly follow the bed of an 1862 narrow-gauge railroad used to transport ore. Hemlock groves, swamps, and ridgetop views advance and vary the AT. Blueberry patches and mountain laurel bring seasonal flourish.

At Denning Hill, the New York City skyline assumes its place in the panorama. While traversing the Hudson Highlands, enjoy spectacular Hudson River views. The tour is rugged but the rewards great. A steep, grueling descent leads to Bear Mountain Bridge for the Hudson River crossing.

The popular Bear Mountain–Harriman State Park recreation complex next hosts the AT. It was here in 1923 that the first section of the newly built Appalachian Trail was christened and opened to walking. Park trails meeting the AT allow day-hike loops.

Pass through the developed area of Bear Mountain Park with its Trailside Museum and Zoo, picnic area, swimming pool, and lake. A hearty ascent follows, topping Bear Mountain at Perkins Memorial Tower (1,305 feet). Travelers secure vistas from Bear, West, and Black Mountains before skirting Island Pond. The terrain remains steep and rugged as the trail continues to collect peaks and vistas.

About 10 miles north of the New Jersey state line, Fitzgerald Falls—a hemlock-shaded 25-foot waterfall spilling down a rocky cleft—wins its share of admirers. New York's send-off to the AT comes at Bellvale Mountain, where ledges reward with views of Greenwood Lake and Ramapo Hills.

Because spatial constraints necessarily limit the detail of this description, through-trail hikers and AT day hikers should contact the ATC (see Appendix D) for official maps and point-to-point guides. Entire books have been devoted to this premier trail and to the New York–New Jersey trail component alone. Check at your local library, bookstore, or backpacker/outfitter store.

65 Breakneck Ridge Trail

General description:	In Hudson Highlands State Park, this trail makes a rugged ascent from near river-level to roll along a knobby ridge, gathering vistas and reaching a lookout.
General location:	East side of the Hudson River, 4 miles south of Beacon.
Special attractions:	Hudson River and Shawangunk and Catskill Mountain vistas; old fire lookout tower; mixed forest; mountain laurel and spring and summer wildflowers.
Length:	9.6 miles round-trip.
Difficulty:	Strenuous.
Maps:	New York–New Jersey Trail Conference map, East Hudson trails.
Special concerns:	Expect some hand-over-hand rock scrambles, and wear boots that protect ankles. High winds and rain increase risk factor for the rocky ascent.
Season and hours:	Spring through fall.
For information:	Hudson Highlands State Park.

Key points:

0.0 Tunnel trailhead; climb tunnel embankment to west slope.
1.5 Pass Breakneck Bypass Trail (the return).
4.2 Devils Ladder.
4.7 South Beacon Tower; backtrack to Breakneck Bypass Trail.
8.9 Head left on Wilkinson Trail.
9.6 End at Tunnel trailhead.

Finding the trailhead: From the New York 301–New York 9D junction in Cold Spring (8.5 miles north of Bear Mountain Bridge), go north on NY 9D for 2 miles to find the trailhead and parking for two vehicles just north of the tunnel on the west side of the highway. Find additional parking 0.1 mile north on the left and the Breakneck Bypass trailhead 0.2 mile north on the right. Because this state park corridor is minimally marked, be alert for paint blazes signaling that the trail starts.

The hike: For a northbound ridge tour, follow the white-blazed trail south from the trailhead, passing through a narrow tree corridor at the north end of the NY 9D tunnel. Almost immediately the trail reveals a "go for it" character with a rigorous rocky ascent of the tunnel embankment and the steep

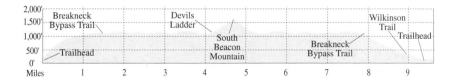

Breakneck Ridge Trail

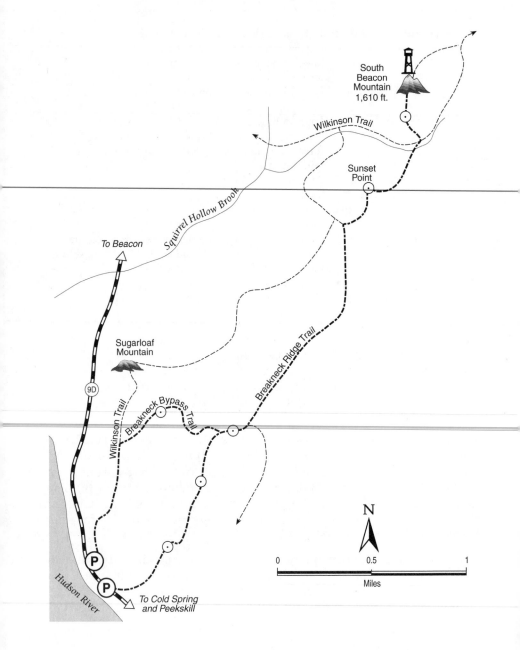

South
Beacon
Mountain
1,610 ft.

Wilkinson Trail

Sunset
Point

Squirrel Hollow Brook

To Beacon

Sugarloaf
Mountain

9D

Wilkinson Trail

Breakneck Bypass Trail

Breakneck Ridge Trail

N

0   0.5   1

Miles

P

P

Hudson River

To Cold Spring
and Peekskill

Hudson River from Breakneck Ridge, Hudson Highlands State Park.

west flank of Breakneck Ridge. Sumac, birch, viburnum, and grasses intersperse the rock, though they may go unnoticed because the climb takes utmost attention. Initially, beer cans, bottles, and graffiti mar the stage.

With a few directional changes, attain the rocky shoulder of the ridge for views of the river, Pollepel Island, Storm King Mountain across the way, and Palisades Interstate Park to the south. The ascent now follows the ridgeline, adding looks at the steep drainage shaped by Breakneck Ridge and Mount Taurus.

For the next spurt of ascent, hikers have the option of following the white "X" alternative route, which adds a few steps by rounding versus scaling the imposing rocks ahead. At 1 mile comes the first vista knoll as the trail rolls from bump to bump, traversing the ridge north. Oaks, maple, ash, and birch compose the woods. The passage between knobs varies from relatively flat to steep notch descents. A fuller woods claims the dips, and grouse and deer can disrupt one's reverie. Views build as the trail progresses.

At 1.5 miles the red Breakneck Bypass Trail descends left, offering a saner return to the trailhead, but first continue the trek north. The next rise holds a 360-degree view of the Hudson River, the valley communities, the Interstate 84 bridge, and South and North Beacon mountains. Upon descent, the blue trail arrives on the right to share the ridge route. Patches of mountain laurel interlace the mixed forest.

At 3.2 miles the blue trail departs left as the white trail enters a brief forested ascent, tagging Sunset Point—a rock outcrop ringed by low oaks. A flatter tour follows before a sharp descent to Squirrel Hollow Brook, which generally carries enough water to dampen a bandanna.

Cross the brook and briefly merge with the yellow Wilkinson Trail (4.1 miles), a woods road. Follow it right for a short distance and then break away left for a demanding ascent via Devils Ladder; white arrows point the way up this steep rocky slope. A past fire swept this site; young birch and big-toothed aspen head the succession species reclaiming the slope. The trail then grades into woods before emerging into the open at South Beacon Tower (4.7 miles).

Whether one chooses to mount the old lookout tower or not, the view atop the breezy ridge rewards, trumping all previous ones. Take in the river, the ridge, and nearby peaks as well as the distant flat ridge of the Shawangunks and more ragged outline of the Catskills.

Although the white trail continues north, retrace your steps to the Breakneck Bypass at 7.9 miles and follow its red-blazed route down the deciduous-wooded west flank. Mountain laurel gains a stronghold, while viburnum and huckleberry weave a complement. At times the descent is markedly steep. After following a thin seasonal drainage, reach an outcrop (8.4 miles) with limited river views and a good look at Sugarloaf Mountain.

Before long, meet the woods road of the yellow-marked Wilkinson Trail, and bear left, following it downhill to NY 9D. Big tulip trees and dogwoods decorate the lower slope. The trail comes out on the east side of the highway at 9.4 miles; turn left (south) to reach the additional trail parking in 0.1 mile and to close the loop at the tunnel in 0.2 mile.

66 Bear Mountain Loop

General description:	A demanding all-day or overnight loop rolls through steep wooded terrain, topping Bear and West Mountains and offering views of the Lower Hudson River area.
General location:	The northeast corner of the Bear Mountain–Harriman State Park complex, 18 miles south of Newburgh.
Special attractions:	Vistas, Perkins Tower, lean-to, historic area, mountain laurel and dogwood blooms, fall foliage.
Length:	9.7-mile loop.
Difficulty:	Strenuous.
Maps:	State park flier; New York–New Jersey Trail Conference map, Harriman Park–North Half.
Special concerns:	Fee parking.
Season and hours:	Spring through fall.
For information:	Harriman State Park.

Bear Mountain Loop

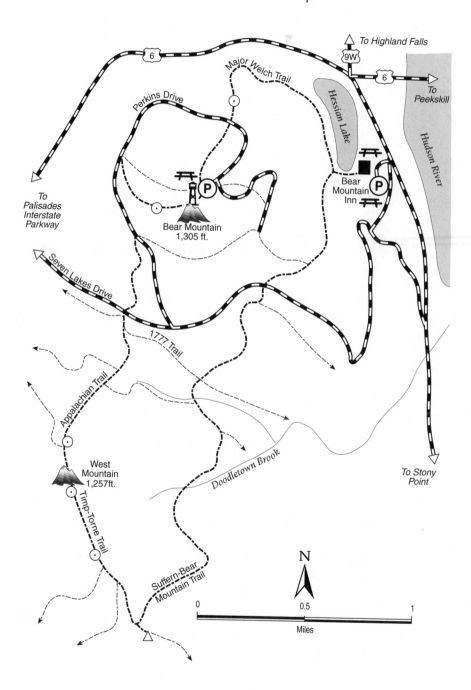

To Highland Falls

9W

6

To Peekskill

Hudson River

Hessian Lake

6

Major Welch Trail

Perkins Drive

P

Bear Mountain Inn

P

Bear Mountain
1,305 ft.

To Palisades Interstate Parkway

Seven Lakes Drive

1777 Trail

Appalachian Trail

West Mountain
1,257ft.

Timp-Torne Trail

Doodletown Brook

To Stony Point

Suffern-Bear Mountain Trail

N

0   0.5   1
Miles

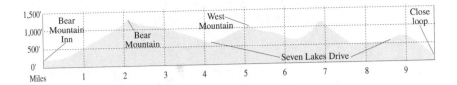

Key points:
- 0.0 Bear Mountain Inn; head west to Major Welch Trail.
- 2.2 Perkins Tower/Bear Mountain summit.
- 4.2 Cross Seven Lakes Drive.
- 5.1 West Mountain.
- 8.7 Cross Seven Lakes Drive.
- 9.7 Close loop at southwest corner of Hessian Lake.

Finding the trailhead: From the Bear Mountain toll bridge over the Hudson River, go south on U.S. Highway 9W for 0.4 mile; turn right to reach the fee parking lot at Bear Mountain Inn.

The hike: This counterclockwise loop samples several prized trails: the Major Welch (red), the Appalachian and 1777 (both white), Timp–Torne (blue), and Suffern–Bear Mountain (yellow).

From the south side of Bear Mountain Inn, head west to reach and follow the Major Welch Trail north; it follows an asphalt path on the west shore of developed Hessian Lake. This popular path serves walker, jogger, and hiker. A rich forest shades the route, while an outcrop offers a lake overlook. Near the north end of the lake, follow the red-marked footpath to the left, ascending the north flank of Bear Mountain.

With steep spurts, the trail climbs and contours the maple-oak clad slope; rocks and roots sometimes foul footing. After a mile the trail charges straight up, takes a switchback, and finds a host of mountain laurel. The trail now travels on or along granitic outcrops, soon overlooking the wooded hills to the Hudson River. Views build north and east, including an up-river look at Bear Mountain Bridge.

Cross Perkins Drive and continue climbing and topping outcrops. Within an oak and laurel picnic grove, cross a paved lane to again reach Perkins Drive near the summit; turn right for Perkins Tower (2.2 miles)—an attractive five-story 1930s stone tower that is still staffed.

Next follow the red trail, descending the outcrop ledges to the southeast below the tower. This rugged, vista-packed tour enwraps the oak-huckleberry slope, rolling between terraces of granite ledges and tilted outcrops, adding views south and west.

At 3 miles cross the road and follow the white-blazed Appalachian Trail (AT) left, staying along the road shoulder for the next 0.5 mile. Turn right, touring an open woods of maple, oak, and box elder. Grasses claim the forest floor.

At 3.8 miles an outcrop offers looks at West Mountain, the next destination. The AT then descends steeply through rock-studded woods to cross Seven Lakes Drive (4.2 miles) and follow the historic 1777 Trail for 0.1 mile. The

1777 Trail retraces the path taken by the British when they stunned the colonists by overtaking two crucial forts along the Hudson River, a strategic supply line during the Revolutionary War.

Turn right at a pine plantation to ascend amid a tall, full forest parted by snags. Follow a woods road left for 0.2 mile to pick up the foot trail on the right for a more serious ascent. Over-the-shoulder looks find Bear Mountain and the Hudson; snags and young trees claim the upper slope. Atop West Mountain, outcrops invite travelers to catch their breath, measure their accomplishment, and take in the view.

Angle left atop the summit ridge to merge with the blue Timp–Torne Trail for a rolling tour, tagging the high point at 5.1 miles. Where the trail dips to the other side of the ridge, find a 180-degree view west. An old fire zone claims the upper reaches of West Mountain, with young birch taking the lead in plant succession. Eventually the trees will reclaim the view; meanwhile, hikers enjoy vistas every 0.1 mile or so.

After attaining a grand 270-degree view of Black Mountain, West Mountain ridge, Bear Mountain, and the river, stay on the blue trail, which bears left, leaving the AT at 5.8 miles. Soon the yellow Suffern–Bear Mountain Trail merges, and the joint blue/yellow trail rolls across the ridge, passing from regenerating forest to one of small-stature oak.

Where the route bends left (6.3 miles), the blue and yellow trail part company. A detour right on the blue trail finds an attractive stone lean-to atop an outcrop in 0.1 mile. It serves up a spectacular view of the Hudson River, The Timp, High and Little Tor, and the Manhattan skyline on clear days.

Dogwood blooms, Harriman State Park.

The yellow trail continues the loop, with a rolling descent among the laurel. After topping a bump on the flank of West Mountain, the trail descends steeply to cross and parallel Doodletown Brook downstream; birch and beech line the brook. At 7.7 miles turn left on a woods road bypassing a marshy bottomed forest. Then turn right, still following the yellow blazes as the route crosses a small rise and side brook.

At the woods road at 8.1 miles, turn right, following the 1777 Trail only to take a quick left on a second woods road for a beautiful tour through mature woods resplendent with dogwood blooms in the spring. Magnificent, big tulip trees and entangling vines also are spied.

At 8.6 miles follow the earthen trail, striking uphill to cross Seven Lakes Drive. The tour now follows a shady woods road paralleling an unobtrusive utility line. Mountain laurel replaces the dogwood as the route descends and contours, once again meeting the white-blazed AT. Continue forward, following the yellow/white blaze scheme, contouring on a broken asphalt path above the skating rink and administration building. At 9.7 miles close the loop at the southwest corner of Hessian Lake.

67 Pine Meadow Lake Loop

General description: This rolling, meandering circuit travels the milder reaches of Harriman State Park, touring woodland, topping hills, and skirting brook, lake, and swamp.
General location: 5 miles north of Suffern.
Special attractions: Mixed woods, rock features and ledge vistas, historic ruins, bird-watching, mountain laurel and azalea blooms, fall foliage.
Length: 13.2 miles round-trip.
Difficulty: Moderate.
Maps: New York–New Jersey Trail Conference map, Harriman Park–South Half.
Special concerns: Expect muddy passages, especially in early spring and following rains. A precarious rocky descent off Diamond Mountain requires caution and the use of hands.
Season and hours: Spring through fall. Reeves Meadow Visitor Center (and rest room): Memorial Day through Labor Day.
For information: Harriman State Park.

Key points:
0.0   Reeves Meadow trailhead; hike north.
1.6   Pine Meadow Brook footbridge/loop junction; head right (upstream).
2.4   Dam and Pine Meadow Lake vista.
5.4   Panther Mountain.
10.6 Diamond Mountain.
11.6 Close loop; backtrack to trailhead.

Pine Meadow Lake Loop

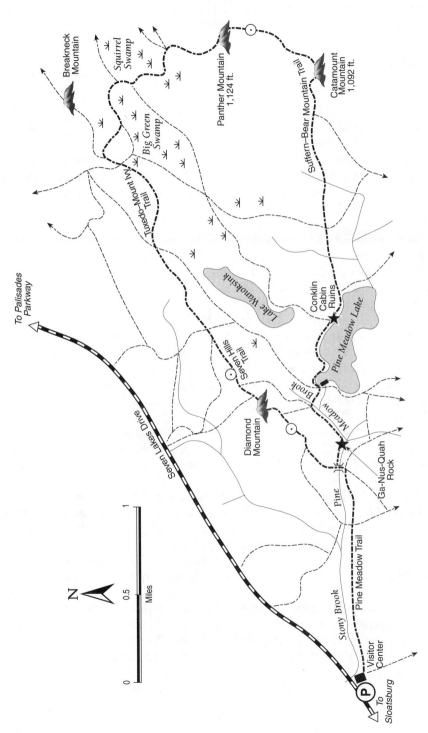

Finding the trailhead: From New York State Thruway Interstate 87, take exit 15 and go north on NY 17/I–86 for 2.1 miles, passing through Sloatsburg. Turn right on Seven Lakes Drive and go 1.5 miles to find Reeves Meadow Visitor Center on the right and additional parking 500 feet past it on the left.

The hike: On the east side of the visitor center, hike north past the water spigot to pick up an old woods road entering the woods on the right. A red-on-white

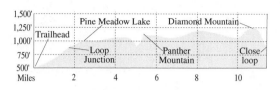

blazing pattern marks the rocky Pine Meadow Trail as it parallels Stony Brook upstream. Stony Brook is an attractive, bouldery waterway, edged by mossy rocks, draped by branches, and accented by cascades and pools. Hemlock, oak, maple, birch, and beech weave the canopy. Morning hikers may spook deer.

At 0.4 mile the trail bears right uphill through forest, remaining on a wide rocky trail threaded by small drainages. On the slope, mountain laurel contributes to a full midstory. At 1.2 miles a white-blazed trail briefly shares the route; 500 feet ahead, bear left at the fork.

Tulip trees and box elder appear helter-skelter in the forest as the trail now continues upstream along quiet-spilling Pine Meadow Brook, a headwater fork of Stony Brook. Where the trail grows soggy, rocks become allies instead of obstacles and violets sprinkle color. Where the blue Seven Hills Trail merges from the right, find a small fireplace.

Cross the Pine Meadow Brook footbridge at 1.6 miles. On the opposite shore, the red and blue trails divide, forming the loop. Stay with the red Pine Meadow Trail, following it upstream (right) to Pine Meadow Lake for a counterclockwise tour. The trail bypasses a scenic moss-and-fern-dressed boulder before reaching trailside Ga-Nus-Quah (Giant Stones) Rock, a room-sized boulder overlooking Pine Meadow Brook where it pours through an outcrop and boulder gorge.

At 2.2 miles a side loop to the left finds a stone foundation with a rusting pipe. Ahead, where the red trail travels the wooded north shore of Pine Meadow Lake, remnant pipeline and an old holding pond echo back to the days of the Civilian Conservation Corps camps.

Upon reaching Pine Meadow Lake, hikers may choose first to detour right 200 feet to the dam for an open lake vista. Elsewhere along the lake, the thick mountain laurel isolates the red trail from the boxy boulder shore. In unlike ways, azalea or a free-swinging brier can capture hiker attention as the lake trail passes the ruins of Conklin Cabin, which dates to 1778. At 3.3 miles before the inlet, the trail swings left away from Pine Meadow Lake for a meandering tour through a maple-oak woodland; red blazes continue to point the way.

Stony Brook, Harriman State Park.

With a brook crossing, find swampy stretches that again suggest hopscotch travel from rock to rock. Azaleas favor these moist reaches. At 4.7 miles the Pine Meadow Trail halts at the yellow Suffern–Bear Mountain Trail; follow the latter left to continue the loop. A steep descent precedes the ascent of Panther Mountain, a scooped hilltop with twin peaks. Outcrops along the first summit provide the lone views east and south. The quiet terrain rolling away from the hill offers no clue that New York City lies but 30 miles away.

Descend from the second summit to enter a full forest, rich with mountain laurel. Oriole, grouse, turkey, towhee, blue jay, and tanager add to a roster of bird sightings. The trail rolls from rise to brook, arriving at an overgrown woods road, the red-blazed Tuxedo–Mount Ivy Trail. Again an old fireplace marks the junction; go left for the loop.

The trail now skirts Squirrel and Big Green Swamps, with only filtered looks at the shrub-filled bottomlands. Where the trail meets a woods road between the two swamps, bear right; cross a footbridge and continue left through a mountain laurel showcase in June. Be alert for the red blazes.

At the junction at 8 miles with the white Breakneck Mountain Trail, stay with the red trail as it curves left. Off the hilltops, the forest shows little change. Cross a gravel road and look over the lower end of Big Green Swamp, which shows areas of phragmites (feathery-headed marsh grasses) and open water. The trail then climbs, traveling the flat rock outcrops of a small rise. As this section of the hike receives less foot traffic, watch for markers.

At 9.9 miles, beyond a woods road, find the blue Seven Hills Trail and follow it left for the close of the loop; the trail is again better defined. With a brief woods road link, the rolling foot trail passes through woods, overlooks the watery-arm profile of Lake Sebago, and resumes straight ahead at a junction with the yellow trail (10.5 miles). A white trail then shares the way, traversing Diamond Mountain with its striated granites and scrub trees.

Stay on the blue trail to complete the tour; brief, complicated descents lead to and from an open outcrop ledge, offering a grand view across the treetops and out Pine Meadow Brook drainage. Think through each descent, and be watchful of the thin ledges. Use your hands as needed, but look before you reach because snakes do exist in this park.

Where the trail comes out at Pine Meadow Brook, turn left (upstream) to close the loop (11.6 miles). Cross the footbridge and turn right, retracing the initial 1.6 miles back to Reeves Meadow Visitor Center.

68 Mianus River Gorge Wildlife Refuge and Botanical Preserve

Overview

Unlike the awe-inspiring sandstone-shale gorges of New York State's Finger Lakes Region, the steep ravine of Mianus River Gorge captivates with a dark-woods enchantment. Spared the fate of the ax because of its steep character, the preserve boasts one of the few intact stands of old-growth forest in the East.

This 750-acre preserve represents the pioneer land project of The Nature Conservancy (TNC), managed by Mianus Gorge Preserve, Inc. The site bears the distinction of being the nation's first Registered Natural History Landmark with the U.S. Department of Interior.

General description:	A generally carefree stroll travels downstream along the Mianus River, exploring gorge and rim, but the terrain is rolling, which can be troublesome for some seniors.
General location:	On the New York–Connecticut border, 10 miles southeast of Mount Kisco, New York.
Special attractions:	350-year-old hemlocks, cascades, wooded gorge (ravine), historic quartz-feldspar quarry.
Length:	5-mile loop (add about 0.5 mile if you walk all the side spurs).
Difficulty:	Easy to moderate, depending on the hiker's health.
Maps:	Preserve trail guide.
Special concerns:	Donation suggested. No pets, smoking, or picnicking and no wheeled vehicles (mountain bikes or strollers). Obey all posted rules and closures.
Season and hours:	April through November, 8:30 A.M. to 5:00 P.M.
For information:	Mianus Gorge Preserve.

Key points:

- 0.0 Trailhead; hike red trail east.
- 0.5 Safford Cascade spur.
- 0.6 Junction A; bear left on red trail.
- 1.1 Junction B; stay on red trail.
- 2.0 Royal Fern Glen.
- 2.5 Bargh Reservoir/"Point C"; backtrack to blue return trail.
- 5.0 End at trailhead.

Finding the trailhead: From the Bedford Village green, go 0.8 mile east on New York 172 (Pound Ridge Road) and turn right on Stamford/Long Ridge Road. In 0.5 mile turn right on Miller's Mill Road, cross the bridge in 300 feet, and turn left on Mianus River Road. Find the trailhead on the left in 0.6 mile.

Mianus River Gorge Wildlife Refuge and Botanical Preserve

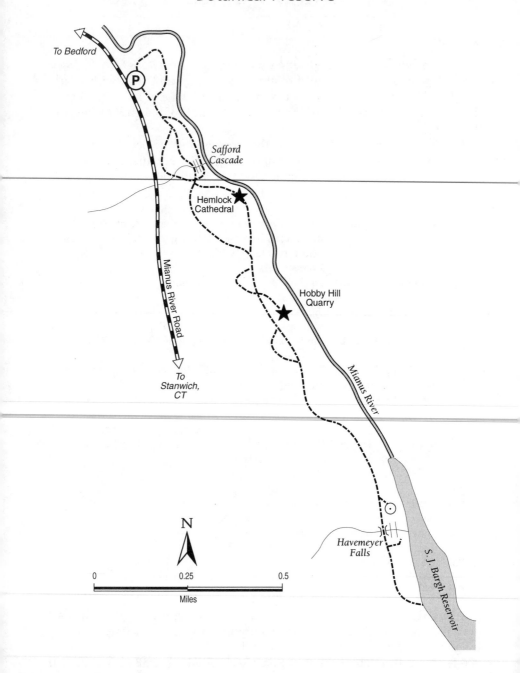

From the Merritt Parkway (Connecticut 15) in Connecticut, take exit 34; go north on Connecticut 104 (Long Ridge/Stamford Road) for 7.2 miles, and turn left on Miller's Mill Road, crossing the bridge and turning left for the preserve.

The hike: The preserve has color-coded trails and lettered junctions to aid travel. The red "outgoing" trail is the official entryway to the preserve and leads to all side spur discoveries. The

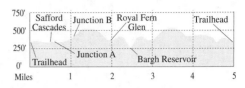

blue trail holds the return and opportunities to shorten the loop.

Round the left side of the information shelter to follow the red Brink of the Gorge Trail east toward the river for a downstream tour. Soon the well-marked 3-foot-wide trail skirts a memorial bench overlooking the shallow, quiet-spilling 20-foot-wide Mianus River—more brooklike than riverlike in character.

Hugging the shore, the trail tours a leafy hollow with showings of fern, poison ivy, skunk cabbage, and false hellebore. Painted, snapping, and spotted turtles may be spied along the river; box tortoises in the woods. A huge white pine stands guard where the trail ascends. Oak, maple, hickory, pine, and snags dress the higher slope. A rock-slab footbridge spans a drainage brimming with skunk cabbage.

At the first signed junction keep left, following the outgoing red trail. At 0.5 mile go left on the green spur to travel closer to the river and visit Safford Cascade.

Downstream from Safford Cascade, stone-step across the brook. The split, lacy stream spills around and over scenic moss-capped rocks. Even when reduced to a mere weep, the mossy site retains its charm. The trail then parallels the brook upstream to junction A (0.6 mile); bear left to resume the red tour. The blue trail presents an opportunity to shorten the loop and return to the trailhead.

As the trail contours the slope, above it stretches a Colonial rock wall that separates the upland agricultural land; below rests the narrowest point of the gorge. Orange-and-black beetles feed on conchs, and ferns flourish where the sunlight penetrates the forest. With an ascent, the trail enters the majestic beauty of Monte Gloria with its 100-foot-tall, 350-year-old hemlock monarchs. Oak, beech, maple, and tulip trees fill out the forest.

Past the plaque honoring preservationist Gloria Hollister Anable, find junction B (1.1 miles); stay left to travel to the end of the preserve. Ahead, a 0.2-mile round-trip detour leads left to Hobby Hill Quarry, mined with the use of mule carts in the 1800s and excavated by Native Americans some four thousand years ago. Sparkles of mica and bits of quartz and feldspar precede the quarry, which shows but a small depression in the slope, time-softened by moss and fern. No collecting is permitted.

The downstream tour resumes, traversing 250 feet above the river and overlooking the steep gorge slope. Beautiful big beech and tulip trees and

Forest canopy, Mianus River Gorge Preserve.

more of the Colonial rock walls add to travel. At 2 miles the trail bypasses a vernal pool giving life to Royal Fern Glen, after which a spur to the left leads to a rock outcrop and leaf-framed view of S. J. Bargh Reservoir, a long widening of the river with a scalloped shore. Mountain laurel accents the vista site.

Back on the red trail and down the hill, cross the stone bridge over the tributary that feeds to Havemeyer Falls; take an immediate left to descend to this attractive 15-foot seasonal waterfall. Its waters spill to a pool the color of dark ale before racing downhill to the awaiting reservoir. An island of moss and fern isolates the lacy streamers.

The red trail halts along the bank of Bargh Reservoir (at 2.5 miles); private lands lie to the south. Return, following the blue trail, which shares portions of the red trail but clings to the upper wooded slope, smoothing out the dips. The return route bypasses the big trees, touring second-growth woodland and old agricultural land to emerge back at the parking lot near the trailhead (5 miles).

Long Island

Completing the lineup of New York State regions, this island domain at the southeast extreme serves up its own prescription for outdoor fun. Stretching from Gateway National Recreation Area to Montauk Point, Long Island brings together rare pine barrens; seaward, bayshore, and Long Island Sound beaches; ghost forests; dune and swale habitats; spring-fed rivers; and a rare pine swamp. At-risk piping plovers and least terns nest on the island's barrier and bay beaches. Fox, deer, owl, and osprey may also enliven a tour. Despite its proximity to Manhattan, the island boasts a surprising wealth of natural discovery.

69 West Pond Trail

General description: At Gateway National Recreation Area, this simple interpretive loop within the Jamaica Bay Wildlife Refuge introduces the wildlife and natural habitat of West Pond, Jamaica Bay, and the island's outwash plain.

General location: In New York City, southwest of John F. Kennedy International Airport.

Special attractions: Some 330 bird species, with warbler migration (April/May), shorebirds (July/August), raptors (September through November), and winter waterfowl (March through early April); outstanding New York City vistas; nesting terrapins (June/July); flowering shrubs and wildflowers.

Length: West Pond Trail: 2-mile loop. Seasonally hikers may add a 0.5-mile round-trip on the Terrapin Trail spur.

Difficulty: Easy.

Maps: Gateway National Recreation Area brochure, which includes the West Pond Trail map.

Special concerns: Regardless of the hour of their visit, hikers are required to carry a free visitors pass while touring the refuge trails. Contact the visitor center to secure a pass. Hikers planning an early-morning visit should obtain the pass on the preceding day. No bikes, no pets.

Season and hours: Year-round, sunrise to sunset. Visitor center: 8:30 A.M. to 5:00 P.M. daily.

For information: Jamaica Bay Wildlife Refuge.

West Pond Trail

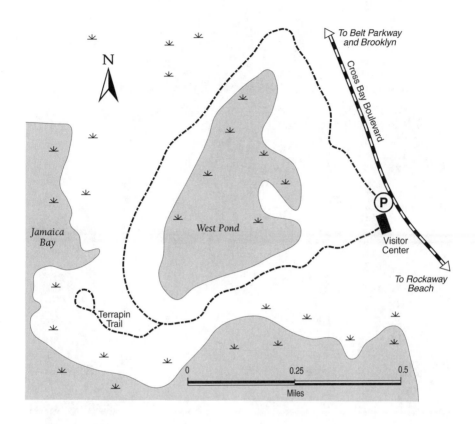

Key points:
- 0.0   Trailhead at visitor center; hike wide gravel trail left.
- 0.5   Seasonal Terrapin Trail.
- 2.0   End at visitor center.

Finding the trailhead: From the Belt Parkway in New York City (Brooklyn), take exit 17S and go south on Cross Bay Boulevard for Gateway National Recreation Area. In 3.5 miles turn right for the visitor center and trailhead.

The hike: Protected by Rockaway Peninsula, the islands forming Jamaica Bay Wildlife Refuge make up a vital habitat and sanctuary for native and migratory wildlife. West Pond Trail encircles one of the impoundment ponds protected originally as a New York City park and now as part of the national park system.

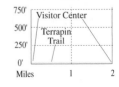

From the back door of the visitor center near a registry for bird sightings, hike the wide gravel path heading left; the path to the right is the Upland

Swallow birdhouse, Jamaica Bay Wildlife Refuge.

Nature Trail. A flowering shrub and vine thicket borders the pond trail; beware of poison ivy.

The occasional interpretive sign, bird and bat nesting boxes, osprey nesting platforms, and frequent benches enhance travel. The circuit gradually dishes up views of Jamaica Bay with its mudflats, saltwater marsh, and open water. Views of West Pond feature its dense rim and crooked-arm peninsula of phragmites (tall marsh grass). Cross-bay views find the Manhattan skyline. The refuge is an enigma—a natural island in an oh-so-urban wild.

With the change of seasons comes a change in residents. Warblers claim spring, snowy egrets occupy the refuge June through August, shorebirds dominate in July and August, and snow geese and migrating raptors reign in October/November. Throughout the year a vibrant harmony of melodic and raucous notes rides the coastal breeze, with trills, honks, squawks, pipings, and plaintive screeches. Kestrel, ibis, red-winged blackbird, tern, gull, goose, duck, heron, cormorant, vireo, and thrush suggest repeat visits.

The shrub corridors grow more broken as an outwash plain hosts the tour. Its desert soils give rise to cactus and yucca, which bloom in June. At 0.5 mile find the Terrapin Trail, closed during nesting season (June 1 through August 1); opt for this tour only when appropriate. Its sandy path passes between a shrub border and the outwash plain overlooking the riprap bank of a mudflat toward low estuary islands. At times a frenzy of shorebirds crisscross the mudflat in search of food.

This side spur, which forms a loop at its end, also adds a view of the Empire State Building before overlooking a pretty bay curvature. Backtrack to the West Pond Trail and go left to resume the clockwise tour. Nearshore snags overlay the water, providing cormorants a convenient drying post.

The periodic roar of an airplane amplifies the serenity of the refuge. In spring Canada geese waddle the paths with their young. Occasionally the guarding parent will urge hikers on their way with a hostile hiss. Eventually the broad, channeled estuarine marsh distances the trail from the open-water bay, as the tour alternates between shrub and plain.

Bypass the barn owl box, keeping to the main track of the loop. As the trail approaches Cross Bay Boulevard at 1.5 miles (2 miles with spur), turn right on the gravel lane to return to the visitor center; a doubletrack heads left. This last section of trail holds the first shade of the hike. Bypass a drinking fountain and a birder's blind to end back at the visitor center at 2 miles (2.5 miles with spur). Evening primrose, bouncing Bet, and salt-spray rose edge the route.

70 Rocky Point Natural Resources Management Area

Overview

For the price of one dollar, New York State purchased this 5,100-acre pine barrens and oak-wooded parcel formerly used by Radio Corporation of America (RCA) for transatlantic broadcasting. Now only the concrete footings of the transmission towers remain. The northern reaches of this natural resources management area (NRMA) mildly roll, while the southern extent stretches out flat. Rocky Point Road slices the preserve into east-west halves.

The color-coded hiking trails crisscross sandy woods roads and firebreaks, some of which double as mountain bike or horse trails. Independent trail systems serve each user.

General description:	A relaxing circuit explores the NRMA's pine barrens and oak woodland habitats.
General location:	Rocky Point, Long Island.
Special attractions:	Pine barrens; spring wildflowers; wildlife sightings of deer, songbird, woodpecker, box turtle.
Length:	10.9 miles round-trip.
Difficulty:	Easy.
Maps:	Rocky Point Natural Resources Management Area trail map.
Special concerns:	Access by permit only; for free permit and map, request in person or in writing (two weeks in advance) from New York State Department of Environmental Conservation in Stony Brook. In written requests state your name, address, and intended activity, and specify Rocky Point NRMA.
Season and hours:	Year-round, but the NRMA is closed to hiking during the January deer season, and it is best to avoid during the hunts of November and December.
For information:	New York State Department of Environmental Conservation, Region 1 (Stony Brook Office).

Key points:
- 0.0   Whiskey Road trailhead; hike north.
- 0.5   Loop junction; bear right.
- 2.9   Sand Hill.
- 4.5   Cross Rocky Point Road.
- 8.7   Cross back over Rocky Point Road.
- 10.4   Complete loop; return to trailhead.

Finding the trailhead: From the junction of Rocky Point Road (Suffolk County 21) and New York 25A in Rocky Point, go south on Rocky Point Road for

Rocky Point Natural Resources Management Area

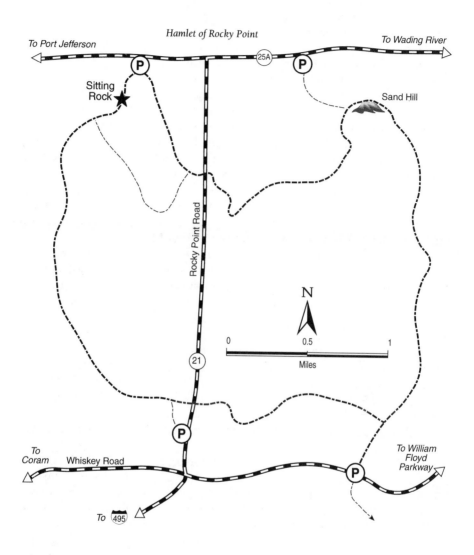

2.5 miles, then turn east on Whiskey Road. In 1.1 miles turn north to enter the trail parking lot.

The hike: Cross the stair stile, entering the NRMA and follow the footpath north into a pine stand. Initially, red trail markers and Paumanok Path symbols mark the way. Within 100 feet oaks and huckleberry fill out the forest. At 0.5 mile is the loop junction; bear right for a counterclockwise tour, staying along the red trail. The blue trail concludes the tour.

The loop now parts company with the Paumanok Path (a burgeoning 100-mile-long trail traversing Long Island's pine barrens from Rocky Point to Montauk Point). The flat-

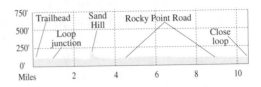

ness of the tour and the sameness of the forest lull one into a relaxed, almost trancelike state. Crossing over woods roads and passing firebreak clearings, the trail reaches and ascends Sand Hill, topping it at 2.9 miles.

The hill likely owes its start to a stream that flowed over a glacier, depositing silt over time. When the glacier receded at the end of the Ice Age, this modest hill remained. Curve left over the sandy summit, which lacks views, to again find the red trail. It descends steeply for 0.1 mile and then turns left. The yellow trail straight ahead rolls over the next rise to reach a trailhead on NY 25A.

The well-marked loop continues through oak woodland, crossing fire grades and woods roads, with pines once more winning a place in the forest. Throughout the tract, bountiful ferns announce recently burned areas. Although fire regenerates the pine forest, an encroaching civilization looks upon fire with fear and disapproval. Therefore, setting aside large intact tracts of pine barrens becomes key to the habitat's survival. Pine barrens once covered 250,000 acres of Long Island; now only a third of the barrens remains. The primordial forest most likely comprised oak, chestnut, and hickory.

At 4.5 miles a narrow foot path leads to the crossing of Rocky Point Road and the western half of the preserve, where oak woods and huckleberry bushes claim the tour. At the junction at 4.6 miles, continue straight on the red trail.

The gently rolling route passes through firebreak field and pine-oak woods, nearing the NRMA boundary before emerging at an open flat with concrete walks and roads, an old foundation, and an untamed border of maple, chokecherry, dogwood, and poison ivy. Skirt the site, following the paved route to the right.

At 5.4 miles, where the abandoned avenue forks, go left for the loop, once again finding the white blazes of the Paumanok Path. To the right lies NY 25A with its fast food eateries, should hikers want to grab a burger or soft drink. Rounding the foundation flat, keep an eye out for the blue-blazed path on the right; it continues the loop.

The trail now passes through a varied woods of red cedar, ash, cherry, oak, and pine, with an understory of grass, Virginia creeper, fern, and poison ivy. At 5.6 miles find a pair of rocks, identified as SITTING ROCK on the NRMA map. The lone rocks for the tour, they do indeed suggest a seat.

At 5.9 miles a 0.5-mile yellow trail journeys left to Lookout Point for an uninspired woods view overlooking a firebreak corridor. The loop follows the blue trail, encountering more road and trail crossings. Ant mounds riddle the forest.

Where the trail bottoms out, it again travels a pine stand with an open cathedral and only patchy shade. Long straightaways characterize travel. Scarlet tanagers capture attention with their brilliant color, while cinquefoil and

Fern forest floor, Rocky Point Natural Resources Management Area.

violet bring spring to the porous sand. After 8.3 miles taller oaks fill out the forest. At the junction at 8.7 miles stay on the blue trail as it crosses back over Rocky Point Road.

The trail continues much as it has through pine barrens, returning to the loop junction at 10.4 miles. Turn right on the red trail, retracing the 0.5-mile spur back to Whiskey Road.

71 David A. Sarnoff Pine Barrens Preserve

Overview

This 2,056-acre preserve features classic pine barrens, wetlands, and kettle depressions. Suffolk County 104 divides the preserve into east-west tracts, with the larger part west of the highway.

General description:	A loop trail explores each tract of the pine barrens. Discoveries include the subtle changes in pine-oak mix, size, canopy, and tightness of forest.
General location:	Long Island, just south of Riverhead.
Special attractions:	Pine barrens, arid meadows, wildlife ponds, kettle depressions, bird-watching.
Length:	Western Loop, 5.4 miles round-trip; Eastern Loop, 3.6 miles round-trip.
Difficulty:	Easy.
Maps:	David A. Sarnoff Pine Barrens Preserve trail map.
Special concerns:	Access by permit only; for free permit and map, request in person or in writing (two weeks in advance) from New York State Department of Environmental Conservation in Stony Brook. In written requests state your name, address, and intended activity, and specify David A. Sarnoff Pine Barrens.
Season and hours:	Year-round, but the barrens preserve is closed to hiking during the January deer season, and it is best to avoid during the hunts of November and December.
For information:	New York State Department of Environmental Conservation, Region 1 (Stony Brook Office).

Key points:
Western Loop:

0.0	Suffolk County 63 trailhead.
0.2	Frog Pond.
0.5	Loop junction; go left.
4.9	Complete loop; backtrack to trailhead.

David A. Sarnoff Pine Barrens Preserve

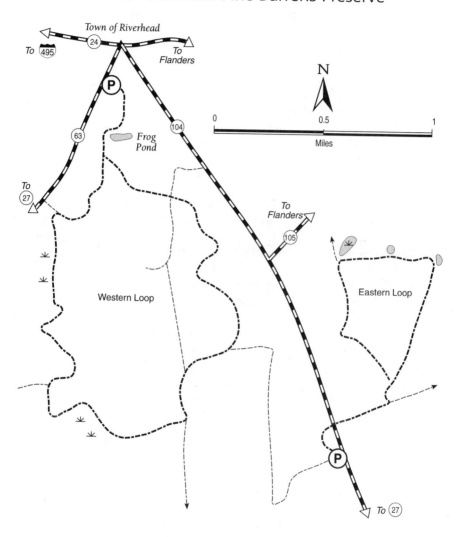

Eastern Loop:
- 0.0   Suffolk County 104 trailhead; hike north.
- 0.3   Cross County 104.
- 0.9   Loop junction; turn left.
- 2.7   Complete loop; backtrack to trailhead.

Finding the trailhead: For the Western Loop, from the New York 24 rotary in South Riverhead, take Suffolk County 63 south for 0.2 mile, finding off-road parking on the east side of County 63. For the Eastern Loop, from the NY 24 rotary go south on County 104 for 2.2 miles, finding off-road parking on the west side of the highway.

The hikes: Both loops aptly present the natural features and aesthetic qualities of the pine barrens preserve.

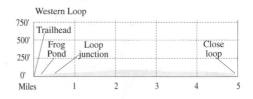

The **Western Loop** (red trail) bears right, edging an open, paved flat, and stays right, traveling an oak-huckleberry complex toward Frog Pond (0.2 mile), an oval water adorned by lily pads and overhung by red maples. Bullfrogs serenade in raucous harmony, while a flicker may betray its hole.

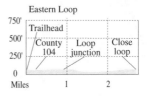

A tight order of pines next claims the way. Disk markers appear at regular intervals, with signs at key junctions. At 0.5 mile is the loop junction; go left for a clockwise tour, traveling a pine-oak woods with bearberry and the occasional lady's slipper calling attention to the porous sand floor.

After a mild incline the trail turns left at 0.75 mile, passing through an area of small-diameter pines not more than 20 feet high. By 1 mile the open trail travels the northern edge of an arid wildflower meadow to cross a paved road. Angle slightly right, keeping toward the woods rim of the meadow. Swallows may emerge from the birdhouses to dart after insects.

At 1.2 miles turn left, reentering woods. Oaks come and go from the mix as open flats, crossroads, and concrete footings and cables from the abandoned radio antennas mark the tour.

At 2 miles the loop turns right as a yellow access trail heads left toward County 104. At 2.25 miles turn left on a sandy woods road, then take a second left onto a smaller woods lane. At 2.5 miles the loop follows a foot trail to the right, skirting a kettle depression barely visible beyond the trees and shrubs. In the kettle, gray birch appear.

At the remains of an antenna at 3.2 miles, go left, still rounding the kettle depression to the left. Descending at 3.4 miles, be alert for where the loop turns right onto a narrow, easy-to-miss foot trail.

The trail ventures into a second kettle depression, touring a complex of tall shrubs, highbush blueberry, laurel, and azalea. At the 3.5-mile junction continue straight for the loop. The trail mildly rolls and sashays, drawing out of the moist kettle habitat to sign off the tour in a classic pine barrens. Bear right at 4.6 miles and again at 4.8 miles to close the loop at 4.9 miles. Retrace the first 0.5 mile to return to your vehicle.

The **Eastern Loop** begins on the west side of County 104, rounding to the right of an old foundation and heading north through an open area. Follow the white blazes and yellow disks. At 0.1 mile follow the footpath to the right through a pine woods that burned in the 1990s and shows the face of renewal. At 0.2 mile bear left, passing through head-high scrub oak and scattered pines to cross County 104 at 0.3 mile; exercise caution in crossing.

298

Now the straight-arrow hike passes through pine barrens, showing an undertangle of blueberry, huckleberry, sweetfern, and bearberry. At 0.8 mile go left to reach the loop; the white-blazed Pine Barrens Trail (part of the long-distance Paumanok Path from Rocky Point to Montauk Point) continues straight. At the loop junction at 0.9 mile, go left, following the blue markers for a clockwise tour.

At the start lush, elbow-high huckleberry bushes and tall pines and oaks crowd the trail. Gradually the lush stand yields to a drier, more open pine barrens. At 1.5 miles cross an avenue of broken pavement to follow another straight-arrow lane.

Be alert when approaching a seasonal wetland pond rimmed by dense vegetation at 1.7 miles; here the loop turns right off the woods lane. Although marked, the blue disk sits inside the woods some 30 feet from the trail and is easily missed.

The trail now skirts the southern wooded edge of the pond, bypasses and overlooks a second pond, and then edges a third one. Scrub oak fills out the midstory, and dwarfed laurel appears in the mix. Past a small open pine flat, bear left at the trail junction. Tall oaks ease back into the ranks, but the corridor again opens up as the loop draws to a close at 2.7 miles. Retrace the initial 0.9 mile back to the trailhead.

72 Connetquot River State Park Preserve

Overview

Color-coded primary and unmarked secondary trails explore this 3,500-acre state park preserve. Previously the site served as a private trout and hunting reservation for an elite sportsman's club, whose membership included such names as Tiffany, Vanderbilt, Belmont, and Carnegie. Distinguished guests included Ulysses S. Grant, Daniel Webster, and General Sherman. A fish hatchery, restored gristmill, and rustic buildings recall the preserve's past. River, ponds, mixed hardwood-evergreen forests, and pine barrens engage travelers.

General description:	A long, lazy loop travels former carriage roads and trails through this unique natural area.
General location:	Long Island, west of Oakdale.
Special attractions:	Trout fishing; fish hatchery, ponds, and river; historic lodge and restored gristmill; pine barrens; deer, swan, fox, osprey, heron, hawk, and box turtle.
Length:	9.8 miles round-trip.
Difficulty:	Easy.
Maps:	State park preserve flier.

Special concerns: Access permits required; request in writing two weeks in advance. Indicate name and address, intended activity (hike, fish, horseback ride), number in party, and intended date of visit; include a legal-sized self-addressed envelope. Permit and identification must be in possession while touring the preserve. No smoking, no pets.

Season and hours: Closed Monday year-round, Monday and Tuesday, October through March. Hours: 6:00 A.M. to sunset.

For information: Connetquot River State Park Preserve.

Key points:
0.0 Entrance station trailhead; hike northeast.
0.1 Main Pond/spillway.
2.0 Fish hatchery/Deep Water Pond.
4.3 Collins junction; bear right.
5.5 Cordwood Road.
8.8 Slade Pond.
9.5 Complete loop near Main Pond; turn left.
9.8 End at entrance trailhead.

Finding the trailhead: From Oakdale on New York 27 (Sunrise Highway), go 1.4 miles west and turn north, entering the park. Eastbound traffic must make a U-turn in Oakdale, as there is only westbound access.

The hike: This tour links the red, blue, and green trails, swinging a north-south loop the length of the preserve.

From the entrance station hike northeast along the park road, coming to a barricade. To the left are the yellow and green trails; the road straight ahead launches both the red and blue trails. Follow the red/blue markers past the historic shingle-sided buildings, including the Main House, an 1820s tavern that served as clubhouse from 1866 to 1973. Bear right, crossing the spillway between Main and Lower Ponds. Above the spillway sits the restored Nicoll Gristmill, circa 1760.

Canada geese graze the lawns and ply the ponds alive with fish. No wonder anglers covet the preserve's thirty-two allotted fishing sites; do not intrude on their designated spaces. You might even spy an osprey with a large trout in its talons—another satisfied sportsman.

The ponds show an attractive mixed-deciduous rim, with pine trees overlooking the leafy tops. Brook Road (a dirt road) continues the loop, touring a wetland woods of oak, red maple, sweet pepperbush, poison ivy, and jack-in-the-pulpit. Pungent skunk cabbage invades the standing water. From the east shore of Main Pond, cross-pond views reflect the gristmill.

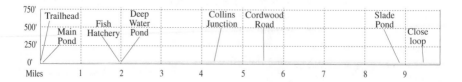

Connetquot River State Park Preserve

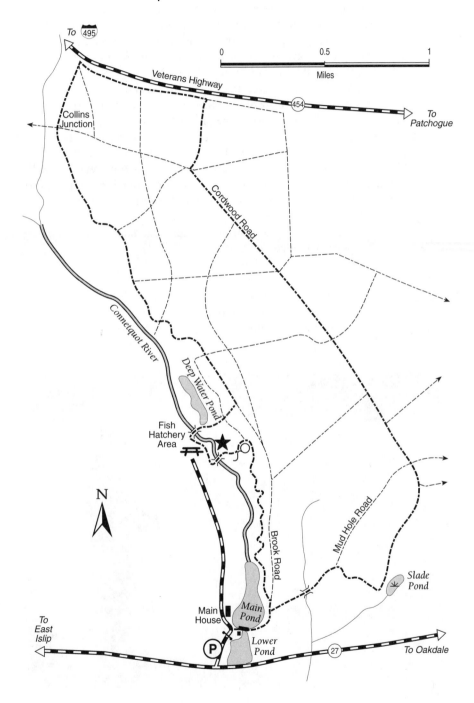

At 0.5 mile the red and blue trails part company but follow parallel routes. Because the red trail passes closer to Main Pond and the river, follow it. Tall pitch pines brush the blue sky, and highbush blueberry borders the trail. By fishing site 8 detect the river's influence on upper Main Pond. Like the three other major rivers draining Long Island (the Nissequogue, Carmans, and Peconic), the Connetquot springs from an aquifer beneath the pine barrens, a habitat being decimated by development.

Keep to the red trail. Deer, garter snake, red fox, and hawk commonly divert the eyes. According to preserve regulars, foxes have grown comfortable with their preserve immunity and commonly venture forth in daylight.

At 1.6 miles bypass wells bringing water to the surface. As the red trail nears the fish hatchery, arrows point travelers clockwise on a brief interpretive trail; plaques explain the natural history. Cross the river below the hatchery. Water starwort thickens the water, while a black-crowned heron may wing to safety. At the hatchery rest rooms, a drinking fountain, and picnic table serve travelers.

The loop now follows the blue trail north along the shore for a short distance to cross a pair of bridges over the river and the lower end of Deep Water Pond. At Brook Road (2.3 miles) turn left (north), touring an oak woodland.

Opposite a closed area at 3 miles, continue straight ahead—now on the green trail, part of the Greater Greenbelt Trail that traverses Long Island. At Collins Junction (4.3 miles) bear right, following the green markers toward the noise

Main Pond, Connetquot River State Park Preserve.

of Veterans Highway and the park's north boundary. Here the Greenbelt Trail leaves the park; turn right on the blue trail for the loop.

A younger, congested woods with low-growing shrubs now frames this sunny tour that parallels Veterans Highway, just 100 yards away. At 5.5 miles turn right, following Cordwood Road through the preserve's pine barrens—woody thickets of scrub oak, runty pitch pine, and dense shrub—a veritable tinderbox. The hike's wide, shadeless roads suggest firebreaks; carry water, and wear sunglasses and a hat. At junctions, keep to Cordwood Road and the blue trail.

After 6.4 miles the barrens show full-sized oaks versus scrub oak and gradually lose the thicket midstory. At the crossroads with Mud Hole Road (8.2 miles), continue straight ahead, returning to a full mixed-deciduous and pine woods. At 8.6 and 8.8 miles bear right, keeping to Cordwood Road. A detour left at 8.8 miles finds Slade Pond in 100 feet. Water starwort riddles the pond, coloring it green; trees and shrubs crowd the rim. At 9.2 miles bear left, passing through a wetland woods to close the loop at Main Pond within sight of the gristmill. Retrace your steps to the parking lot (9.8 miles).

73 Fire Island National Seashore

Overview

This circuit travels between Smith Point and Watch Hill, exploring a 7-mile stretch of Fire Island—a 32-mile-long barrier island protecting Long Island's south shore from the punishing Atlantic. The toe of the seaward dune attracts nesting piping plover and least terns; April through August, maintain a respectful distance. The back bay and dune swale compose Otis Pike Wilderness Area, the only federally designated wilderness in New York State. Flowering beach plum, beach heather, and wild rose accent a springtime return through dunes.

General description:	An all-day loop hike explores the sandy beach of the national seashore and the back bay and dune swale of Otis Pike Wilderness Area. When starting at Smith Point Ranger Station, find the end of the loop along the site's 0.8-mile boardwalk interpretive trail.
General location:	Fire Island, off the south shore of Long Island.
Special attractions:	Nesting piping plovers and least terns; migrating waterfowl, songbirds, raptors, and butterflies; deer, rabbit, and fox; primary dunes, blowouts, swales, thickets, and salt marsh; beach plum and beach heather; Atlantic Ocean and Great South Bay views; interpretive trail; visitor centers.
Length:	14.2-mile loop, with opportunities to shorten the hike at established boardwalk crossings.

Difficulty:	Moderate.
Maps:	Fire Island National Seashore brochure.
Special concerns:	Rangers recommend that wilderness area hikers register at Smith Point Ranger Station, alerting the staff to their presence in this little-used area. Heed closures for nesting piping plovers and terns, and be sensitive of the primary dunes, crossing only at designated stairways and boardwalks. As mosquitos are common, carry repellent. Amid vegetation, be alert for poison ivy and deer ticks (Lyme Disease carriers). These ticks may exist year-round, so take precautions. Find drinking water at Smith Point and Watch Hill. Toilets can be found at visitor centers (when open) and seasonally at Old Inlet.
Season and hours:	Year-round; Smith Point Ranger Station, year-round; Watch Hill Visitor Center, July and August.
For information:	Fire Island National Seashore.

Key points:

0.0	Smith Point Ranger Station; descend to beach.
2.0	Old Inlet.
3.6	Viewing deck atop dunes.
7.1	Watch Hill/Burma Road; head east.
11.0	Viewing deck/picnic shelter (first seen at 3.6 miles).
12.6	Old Inlet.
13.9	Boardwalk interpretive trail; go either way.
14.2	End loop at ranger station.

Finding the trailhead: On Long Island at Shirley, take exit 58S from New York 27 (Sunrise Highway) and go south on New York 46 (William Floyd Parkway) for 5 miles, crossing over the bridge to reach Fire Island National Seashore and Smith Point Suffolk County Park. As the national seashore offers parking for handicapped users only, park at Smith Point County Park, a fee area. A ferry operating out of Patchogue, New York, accesses the Watch Hill area for an alternative approach to the national seashore.

The hike: For an east-to-west beach stroll, descend the seaward-stretching boardwalk at Smith Point Ranger Station and turn right on the 150-foot-wide strand. The fine, light-colored crystalline sand tosses back the sun as the thunderous waves break in strings. Energy spreading along the wave crests and churned foam sliding up the beach captivate onlookers.

Fire Island National Seashore

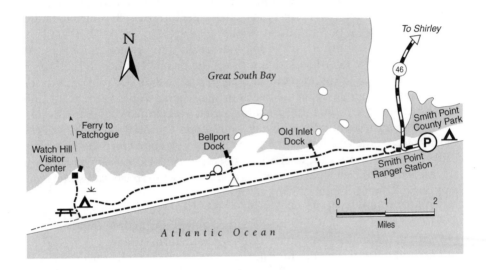

As the official wilderness area extends only from the toe of the primary dune north to Great South Bay, the ocean beach falls outside the protective designation, leaving it open to some beach driving. Expect to see tire tracks, save for the last week in May and during the entire month of June, when the National Park Service closes the beach to all vehicles for the protection of nesting birds.

Along the beach, staggered posts mark off the nesting sites; grant the birds a wide berth so as not to interfere with nesting. The lower beach typically offers easier walking with tide-compressed sand; where walkable, the upper beach holds discoveries of wind patterns, lacy insect signatures, and bird chirps. At 1 mile a gap in the primary dune offers a glimpse north at Great South Bay.

At 2 miles a stairway leads to Old Inlet, offering the first opportunity to shorten the loop. Here hikers find a boardwalk linking beach and bay, an attractive T-shaped dock on the bay, and seasonally open toilets and showers.

For a full day's hike, continue west along the beach. To shorten the loop to about 4 miles, hike north on the Old Inlet boardwalk. Partway find the faint track of Burma Road (a nature-reclaimed jeep road that predates the wilderness) as it intersects the boardwalk. Hike east on Burma Road, traveling at the back side of the dune, returning to Smith Point.

Along the oceanfront, clam shells, skate egg cases, sea-polished pebbles, and horseshoe crabs toyed with by gulls call to beachcombers. The cant to the ocean grows more pronounced, tiring calf muscles. The dunes now fluctuate from a few feet to 20 feet high.

Atop the dunes at 3.6 miles, a slat-roofed deck overlooks the beach. Owned by the village of Bellport, this site offers travelers a shady resting stop and another turnaround point. Follow the boardwalk toward the bay to find the dune trail as it bisects the boardwalk. Turn right to return to Smith Point, touring back bay and dune swale.

For this hike continue west along the beach; terns swoop the waves. At 7.1 miles find the boardwalk that crosses the primary dunes to the Watch Hill area and campground, both hidden by the rise. A slat-roof lean-to for shade, a rest room/changing facility, showers, phone, drinking fountain, and snack bar serve travelers. In July and August lifeguards oversee the beach.

From the campground boardwalk, find sandy Burma Road at the base of the seaward dune and follow it east away from camp to close the loop. The trail alternately tours loose sand or overgrown track, passing through a shrub swale with beach plum, beach grass, sweet pepperbush, salt-spray rose, and poison ivy. Springtime brings a blush of color.

At the 7.8-mile fork bear left, continuing east across the dune-protected area. Caches of tall, feathery-headed phragmites, springtime puddles pulsing with toads, and a lush, green estuary characterize the trek.

Dip into a sandy bowl (8 miles), then top its rim for a bay overlook and the merest peek at the ocean. The trail then levels, traversing areas of beach grass and beach heather, sandy plains, and pockets of pitch pine; beware of poison ivy and brier, common beneath the pines.

Where the trail curves toward the beach at 10 miles, it travels the loose sand of a secondary dune, skirting blown-out depressions. Wooden debris,

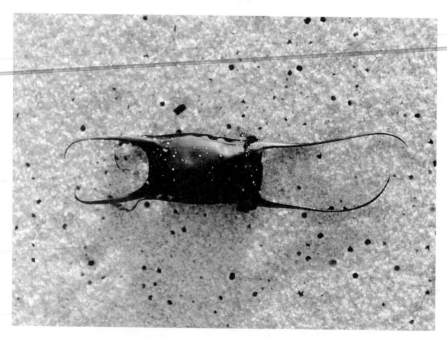

Skate case, Fire Island National Seashore.

an old cable route, and seashells are possible sightings, but the shifting sand frequently alters the canvas.

At 10.7 miles an old well feeds a circle of green. At 11 miles bypass the picnic shelter owned by Bellport Village, crossing over its boardwalk. The sandy track now rolls up rims and through bowls, soon traversing a broad coastal plain. The small bay island and cottage off Old Inlet command the view. At 12.6 miles cross over the boardwalk at Old Inlet.

The track becomes more grassy, and shrubs reappear as the trail draws a straight shadeless line back to Smith Point Ranger Station. It arrives at the boardwalk interpretive trail near post 12 (midway); go either way to end at the ranger station (14.2 miles).

74 Mashomack Preserve

Overview

Covering the southeastern third of Shelter Island, this 2,000-acre preserve of The Nature Conservancy (TNC) encompasses a maritime environment of tidal creeks, woodlands, fields, swamps, freshwater ponds, and 10 miles of stirring but inaccessible coastline. Four interlocking color-coded trails, a short barrier-free Braille trail, and the 1-mile wheelchair-and-stroller-friendly Joan Coles Trail introduce the site. A fine nature garden displays some of the common vegetation.

General description:	A 12-mile round-trip travels each of the four interlocking loops in their entirety, backtracking on itself only once at the 0.7-mile stretch between junctions 3 and 4.
General location:	East End Long Island.
Special attractions:	Natural osprey nesting colony, a rare pine swamp, dogwood blooms, vistas, colorful fall foliage.
Length:	12 miles round-trip.
Difficulty:	Easy.
Maps:	Preserve trail map (available at visitor center).
Special concerns:	Reached by ferry service. Suggested donation to TNC. Keep to the trail and obey posted rules. As TNC has marked the trails for only one direction of travel, follow the flow pattern indicated on the preserve map to avoid losing your way.
Season and hours:	Year-round, daily except Tuesday; seven days a week in July and August. Hours: 9:00 A.M. to 5:00 P.M. (9:00 A.M. to 4:00 P.M. October through March). Visitor center: summer and weekends only.
For information:	Mashomack Preserve or The Nature Conservancy, South Fork–Shelter Island Chapter.

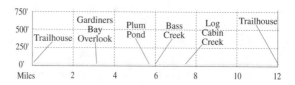

Key points:

- 0.0   Trail House trailhead; head east via red trail.
- 3.1   Gardiners Bay Overlook.
- 5.6   Plum Pond Overlook.
- 6.0   Wildlife blind, Bass Creek.
- 7.5   Wildlife blind at Log Cabin Creek.
- 12.0   End at Trail House.

Finding the trailhead: From North Haven take the South Ferry to Shelter Island and go 1 mile north on New York 114, turning east to enter the preserve. Arriving from the North Ferry out of Greenport, follow NY 114 south 3 miles to the entrance.

The hike: All trails share a common start near the Trail House (the preserve visitor center). The 0.2-mile barrier-free boardwalk tours the native plant garden, woods, and a freshwater kettle, while the color-coded trails head east off the entry road into a rich woodland of mixed oak, red maple, hickory, beech, dogwood, and black locust. The Joan Coles Memorial Trail is accessed near the end of the red trail.

A rare pine swamp, recognized for its uniqueness by the New York State Department of Environmental Quality, occupies this western edge of the preserve. Rimmed by swamp azalea, water willow, and highbush blueberry, the site's pines spring from a floating mat of sphagnum moss.

Nearing a service road at 0.3 mile, bear right per the red arrow. The trail then merges with a wide woods lane, rounding to a gazebo overlooking Miss Annie's Creek—a tidal marsh bay with sandy strands and a treed island. Views stretch south, overlooking Shelter Island Sound and the South Ferry crossing.

At junction 1 (0.8 mile) bear right for the yellow, green, and blue trails; the red trail hooks left, returning to the visitor center. A boardwalk continues the tour, crossing a salt meadow extension of the marsh; keep an eye out for the osprey nesting platform. After crossing a management road, pass amid twisted oaks and an open field before descending to junction 2 (1.2 miles). Here the yellow trail heads left to close its loop, the blue trail heads straight, and the green trail bears right.

Follow the blue-marked trail through a field to explore the largest of the preserve loops, soon entering a shady beech-climax woods. At 2.2 miles bear left per the markers and again bear left in another 0.1 mile. At 2.6 miles the blue trail turns right, following a semishaded woods road as it curves east toward the bluff rim for a sunnier tour.

At 3.1 miles a bench overlooks Gardiners Bay and Island, and at 4.1 miles a triple-trunked beech presides trailside. As the blue trail travels the outskirts

Mashomack Preserve

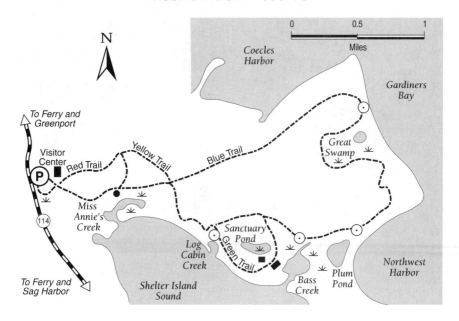

of Great Swamp, dense with phragmites (tall, feathery marsh grass), a foot trail briefly replaces the woods road; keep to the rim. Bullbrier entangles the woods as the open trail rolls south, trading looks at Gardiners Bay for looks at Northwest Harbor. Dogwoods accent the tour.

At 5.6 miles reach the Plum Pond Overlook with its fine Northwest Harbor view. Plum Pond may be masked by a leafy shroud. The trail then rounds above a kettle depression, bearing right and coming to a wildlife or birder's blind. Set back in the woods and camouflaged by phragmites, the blind overlooks the upper estuary of Bass Creek. From inside the blind look left to spy a sapsucker-drilled trunk; holes ring the trunk's circumference every few inches.

Where the blue trail tags the green loop at junction 4 (6.6 miles), bear right to stay on the marked trail and follow the flow pattern indicated on the preserve map. The trail passes through mixed woods and crosses a service road to reach junction 3 (the head of the green trail loop) at 7.3 miles.

Bear left to add the green loop; going right returns to the visitor center. The green loop passes through a diverse woodland, overlooks the blue waters of Smith Cove, and at 7.5 miles reaches a blind looking out at Log Cabin Creek.

Ahead, turn right on the management road, passing through the staff residence area, with its wood-shingled buildings, groomed lawns, shade trees, tidal ponds, and freshwater Sanctuary Pond. The buildings are off-limits to the public.

Shelter Island beach, Mashomack Preserve.

The road becomes a doubletrack as it reenters woods, skirting the Bass Creek estuary. With an upland woods ascent, the hike returns to junction 4 at 8.8 miles. Go left, retracing the tour between junctions 4 and 3.

Once again at junction 3, follow the green trail, ascending the steps to the right to return to the visitor center. Scenic oaks shade a bench and suggest a pause as the trail traverses a coastal bluff. Below the trail sits a pristine, thin pebble beach reserved for wildlife (off-limits to the public). Upon crossing the management road, pass through woods and fields to reach junction 2 (10.3 miles).

Take the right fork of the yellow trail, tracking the yellow and red arrows back to Trail House. After crossing the management road at 10.9 miles, bear right on the wood-shavings path of the red trail. It quickly turns left on a closed roadway for the return to the visitor center; plaques identify the diverse roadside vegetation.

75 Hither Hills State Park

Overview

On Long Island's east end, this 1,755-acre state park brings together a superb lineup of offerings: walking dunes and "phantom forests"; a pristine mile of Atlantic beach; the cobbled, remote Napeague Bay shore; Goff Point, where piping plover, tern, and oyster-catcher nest; and an interior region of pine barrens, dune heath, and maritime grassland. Semiformal trails explore bay, spit, and dune. Paumanok Path, the long-distance route linking the barrens habitats between the Rocky Point Natural Resources Management Area and Montauk Point, traverses the park's inland realm for an easy-to-follow tour. For other hikes through the woods and barrens, consider joining a guided walk led by a local hiking club.

General description:	Two hikes introduce the park's prized habitats. One explores the dunes and phantom forest; the other, the bay shore and inland oak woodlands and pine barrens.
General location:	7 miles east of Amagansett.
Special attractions:	40-foot dunes, buried forests, seashells, a native cranberry bog, wild plums, bird-watching.
Length:	Walking Dunes Trail, 1-mile loop; Napeague Shoreline–Paumanok Path Loop, 14.5-mile loop (13.5 miles when nesting season closes off Goff Point).
Difficulty:	Walking Dunes Trail and Napeague Shoreline–Paumanok Path Loop, easy to moderate.
Maps:	State park map (request at campground).
Special concerns:	Obey all posted closures. It is best to avoid Goff Point during nesting season (late May through June) and to give seals ample space when they haul out on the Atlantic beach in winter. Expect some beach driving along Napeague shore (vehicle access is by special permit in designated areas). On the Walking Dunes Trail, the shifting canvas of sand can alter course.
Season and hours:	Year-round (hot and humid hiking in summer).
For information:	Hither Hills State Park.

Key points:
Walking Dunes Trail:
    0.0   Trailhead; hike east.
    0.8   Napeague Harbor Beach; turn left.
    1.0   End loop at trailhead.
Napeague Shoreline–Paumanok Path Hike:
    0.0   Trailhead; hike harbor shore north.
    1.2   Neck of Goff Point; round point. (Cross neck late May through June.)
    7.4   Rocky Point.

Finding the trailhead: From Amagansett go 6 miles east on New York 27 (Montauk Highway) and turn north on Napeague Harbor Road to find the Paumanok Path on the right in 0.4 mile (no parking). The shared trailhead for Walking Dunes and Napeague Shoreline is at road's end, in another 0.3 mile. Sand drifts limit parking to a handful of vehicles. Do not block the limited vehicle access to the beach. For Atlantic beach access, from Amagansett drive 7.2 miles east on NY 27 and Old Montauk Highway, turning south to enter Hither Hills State Park, a fee area.

The hikes: For the **Walking Dunes Trail,** be sure to pick up the interpretive brochure (seasonally stocked at the trailhead) that corresponds to the numbered posts. Head east (right) off the end of Napeague Harbor Road, following a sandy path into a maritime corridor of mixed oak, beach grass, beach plum, pitch pine, bearberry, and poison ivy. Next enter the rare zone of shifting sand that "walks" over trees 30 feet tall. This sensitive landscape calls for respectful appreciation—no dune play.

At a three-prong fork take the central path, passing through an oak-fringed blowout. Where the trail again forks, go right for the prescribed counterclockwise loop, avoiding the well-tracked assault on the dune straight ahead. Notice how only the crowns of the nearby oaks clear the burying sand. With a gust of wind, the sands go walking.

The trail contours and gradually ascends the dunes, with first forest and then wetland sweeping away to the right. Minerals can streak the dunes purple or black; beach grass and beach heather vegetate the tops. As the dune curves noticeably northwest, angle to the top of the dune for a grand Walking Dunes–Hither Hills State Park overview, with Napeague Harbor and Bay, the sandy spit of Goff Point, and Gardiners Island.

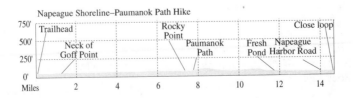

Hither Hills State Park

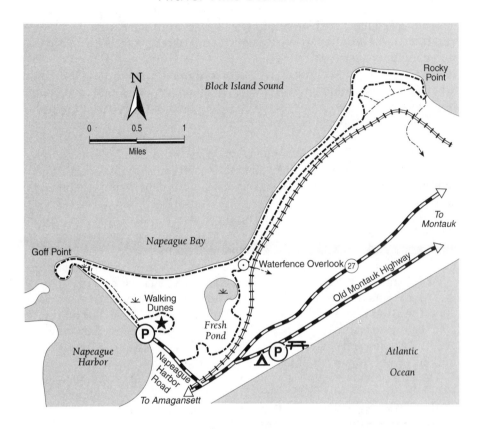

The trail then descends to the western bowl and phantom forest; survey the bowl for the snags that record past forests overtaken and ultimately killed by the sand. Next up, this counterclockwise tour rounds a native cranberry bog; stay to its left. Passing through bayberry, aim for the wide sand track ahead and follow it over a rise and into the next bowl to reach the harbor beach (0.8 mile). Turn left to return to the vehicle and close the loop.

The Napeague Shoreline–Paumanok Path Loop explores Napeague Harbor, Goff Point, and the Napeague Bay shore east as far as Rocky Point. In places tire tracks may steal from the harbor and bayshore wildness, but generally the tour does not disappoint. Late May through June, hikers should forgo rounding Goff Point and instead cross to the bay at the neck of the spit at 1.2 miles. The hike concludes via the Paumanok Path or via the jeep grade backing the bayshore beach.

From the end of Napeague Harbor Road, follow the Napeague Harbor shoreline north, traveling an avenue of pinkish-orange sand and cobbles. Terns, gulls, herons, and egrets make carrying binoculars worthwhile. A scattering of open-hinged scallops may record the recent passing of a turnstone.

At the neck of Goff Point (1.2 miles), a broad flat draws feeding piping plovers and resting terns; sit quietly and watch their antics. Waterspouts betray the presence of clams. When appropriate, continue north around the spit, but keep below the high-tide line because oyster-catchers, piping plovers, and terns have nesting territories; netted enclosures protect the highly vulnerable plover nests.

By 1.5 miles round the sand-and-pebble shore at the head of Goff Point, where gulls congregate, cormorants string off shore, and slipper and orange jingle shells collect in stringy deposits. The hike leaves Goff Point opposite Skonk Hole, a wet depression at 2.2 miles.

At the start of the bay tour, a breach in the dune offers a look south at a maritime grassland of beard and switch grass, with beach plum adorning the dunetop in showy spring finery. Rounded cobbles and shells form a crunchy thoroughfare. Again, slipper shells abound, with caps of pink, white, and green seaweed.

Before long, looks east find the pilings of a shellfish bed and distant Rocky Point. By 3.6 miles the beach shows more sand; over-the-shoulder views admire the curve of Goff Point. Gradually the dune gives way to a 25-foot bluff with an abrupt slip face; colonies of swallows nest in the solid seams.

At 4.3 and 4.7 miles boulders scatter the beach, suggesting a dry seat. As the hike begins to round Rocky Point at 5.9 miles, cobbles once again dominate the strand, and a cliff rises above the beach. At 7.4 miles attain the point before bayshore travel ends at Dyer's Landing (7.5 miles). Eastern views of Fort Pond Bay and Culloden Point cap off the bayshore segment. Now watch for and follow the foot trail heading uphill to the right.

The hike quickly meets a road where it follows the blazed Paumanok Path right. The route is regularly marked with white blazes or Paumanok Path markers. Travel oak woodland, tangled with brier and wild grape. At 7.8 miles is a Y-junction; head right. Openings and spurs to the right present views of Block Island Sound; spurs left lead to Old North Road.

At the T-junction at 8.2 miles, head right toward shore, but turn left before actually tagging it. The brushy coastal thicket of the marine terrace advances travel. At the next T-junction, a short detour right leads to a Sound overlook; the Paumanok Path heads left, again swallowed by an oak woodland. A shady, pleasant meander follows.

Forest changes occur with the appearance of maple, hickory, basswood, and other species. At 9 miles meet and follow right Old North Road. Comfortable and tree-draped, Old North Road pleasantly pieces together the Paumanok Path segments. At 9.4 miles a 0.1-mile spur heads right to the Notch and an uninspired view; continue forward. At the upcoming road junction, a right leads to Quincetree Landing; keep to the Paumanok Path, which later turns right off Old North Road to pass closer to shore atop cliffs or coastal slope. Although the path dips to shore level, it never tags shore.

By 10.7 miles the hike is back in oaks and passing parallel to a railroad track, usually hidden from view by the dense forest. At the crossroads at 11.5 miles, a 0.5-mile detour to the right finds Waterfence Overlook, with its fine vantage and spur trails to the beach. For the Paumanok Path alone,

Long Island Sound shore, Hither Hills State Park.

proceed forward, drifting farther from shore. Keep an eye out for blazes guiding you through junctions. Box turtles can be spied.

At the four-way junction at 11.9 miles, Paumanok Path heads left, rounding Fresh Pond and passing through forest. A 100-foot detour to the right leads to the pond's shore. Fresh Pond is a large, open bass pond rimmed by sweet pepperbush and high-canopy forest. The next crossroads offers another opportunity to access the pond.

By 13.5 miles pitch pines make an appearance and eventually gain dominance. Sounds from NY 27 creep into the peacefulness of the hike. At 14.2 miles meet Napeague Harbor Road and turn right to end at the Shoreline Trailhead (14.5 miles).

During nesting season, high tides, or strong winds, a jeep trail paralleling the Napeague Bay shore offers a way to vary the loop. This jeep trail veers east at the northern edge of the Walking Dunes (0.2 mile north of the end of Napeague Harbor Road) and remains within 0.1 mile of the bayshore for much of the way. Breaches in the dune suggest natural passageways between jeep trail and bayshore.

Appendix A

Hiker's Checklist

Not every item on the following checklist will be needed for every trip, so customize the list, taking into account your needs and comforts, the duration of the outing, weather, and the unexpected. Use this list as an organizing tool for planning, packing, and minimizing oversights. Feel free to pencil in items that you find critical to a successful trip.

Ten Essentials

- [ ] extra food
- [ ] extra clothing
- [ ] sunglasses
- [ ] knife
- [ ] fire starter
- [ ] matches in waterproof container
- [ ] first-aid kit and manual
- [ ] flashlight
- [ ] map(s) for the trail
- [ ] compass

Clothing

- [ ] lightweight underwear
- [ ] long johns
- [ ] under socks
- [ ] wool boot socks
- [ ] long pants and shorts (or convertible pants)
- [ ] long-sleeve shirt
- [ ] T-shirts
- [ ] wool sweater or shirt
- [ ] wool hat and gloves
- [ ] visor or cap

- [ ] rain gear
- [ ] warm coat or parka
- [ ] belt
- [ ] bandanna
- [ ] swimsuit or trunks
- [ ] hiking boots
- [ ] wading shoes

Personal Items

- [ ] contacts or eyeglasses
- [ ] comb
- [ ] toothpaste and brush
- [ ] biodegradable soap/towelettes
- [ ] towel
- [ ] nail clipper and tweezers
- [ ] facial tissue or handkerchief
- [ ] toilet paper and trowel
- [ ] sunscreen and lip balm
- [ ] insect repellent
- [ ] wallet and keys
- [ ] emergency medical information
- [ ] watch

Gear

- [ ] water bottles
- [ ] pack(s)
- [ ] tent, with required poles and pegs
- [ ] ground cloth
- [ ] sleeping bag and foam pad
- [ ] stove and fuel
- [ ] pots and eating utensils
- [ ] can opener
- [ ] rope
- [ ] stuff bags
- [ ] large trash bags for emergency shelter for self or gear
- [ ] plastic bags for trash
- [ ] zip-seal bags for foodstuffs
- [ ] aluminum foil

Food

- [ ] three meals, plus snacks for each day out
- [ ] extra food for delays
- [ ] salt/pepper
- [ ] vegetable oil
- [ ] drink mixes

Health and Safety Items

- [ ] medications
- [ ] antibacterial solution
- [ ] emergency blanket
- [ ] water pump or purification tablets
- [ ] whistle
- [ ] pencil and paper
- [ ] picture wire for emergency repairs

Miscellaneous

- [ ] mosquito netting
- [ ] binoculars
- [ ] camera and film
- [ ] guidebooks
- [ ] identification books
- [ ] fishing gear and valid license

Appendix B

Further Reading

Appalachian Hiker II by Ed Garvey. Appalachian Books.

Backpacking One Step at a Time, Fourth Edition, by Harvey Manning. Random House.

The Basic Essentials of Map and Compass by Cliff Jacobson. ICS Books.

Be Expert with Map and Compass by Bjorn Kjellstrom. Charles Scribner's Sons.

A Child's Introduction to the Outdoors by David Richey. Pagurian Press Limited.

The Complete Walker III by Colin Fletcher. Alfred A. Knopf.

Country Walks Near New York by William B. Scheller. Appalachian Mountain Club.

A Field Guide to the Birds by Roger Tory Peterson. Houghton Mifflin Co.

Fifty Hikes in Central New York by William P. Ehling. Backcountry Publications.

Fifty Hikes in the Hudson Valley by Peter Kick, Barbara McMartin, and James M. Long. Backcountry Publications.

Fifty Hikes in Western New York by William P. Ehling. Backcountry Publications.

Finding Your Way in the Outdoors by Robert L. Mooers, Jr. E.P. Hutton Co., Inc.

Guide to Adirondack Trails: Central Region, by Bruce C. Wadsworth. Adirondack Mountain Club, Inc.

Guide to Adirondack Trails: Eastern Region by Betsy Tisdale. Adirondack Mountain Club, Inc.

Guide to Adirondack Trails: High Peaks Region edited by Tony Goodwin. Adirondack Mountain Club, Inc.

Guide to Adirondack Trails: Northern Region by Peter V. O'Shea. Adirondack Mountain Club, Inc.

Guide to Adirondack Trails: Northville-Placid Trail by Bruce Wadsworth. Adirondack Mountain Club, Inc.

Guide to Adirondack Trails: Southern Region by Linda Laing. Adirondack Mountain Club, Inc.

Guide to Adirondack Trails: West-Central Region by Arthur W. Haberl. Adirondack Mountain Club, Inc.

A Guide to Field Identification: Wildflowers of North America by Frank D. Venning. Golden Press.

Guide to the National Wildlife Refuges by Laura and William Riley. Collier Books.

Mountaineering First Aid, Third Edition, by Martha J. Lentz, Steven C. Macdonald, and Jan D. Carline. The Mountaineers.

Mountaineering Medicine by Fred T. Darvill. Wilderness Press.

Natural New York by Bill and Phyllis Thomas. Holt, Rinehart and Winston.

New York Walk Book, Fifth Edition, by the New York–New Jersey Trail Conference. Anchor Books, Doubleday.

Official Guide to the Appalachian Trail in New York and New Jersey by the New York–New Jersey Trail Conference. The Appalachian Trail Conference.

Rock Scenery of the Hudson Highlands and Palisades by Jerome Wyckoff. Adirondack Mountain Club.

Short Nature Walks on Long Island, Seventh Edition, by Rodney and Priscilla Albright. The Globe Pequot Press.

The Shrub Identification Book by George W. D. Symonds. William Morrow and Company.

Travel Light Handbook by Judy Keene. Contemporary Books.

Wild Country Companion: The Ultimate Guide to No-trace Outdoor Recreation and Wilderness Safety by Will Harmon. Falcon Publishing, Inc.

Wilderness Basics: The Complete Handbook for Hikers and Backpackers, Second Edition, by the San Diego Chapter of the Sierra Club. The Mountaineers.

Appendix C

Where to Find Maps

For trail maps produced by the managing agencies, contact the information source listed in each trail summary. Find the complete address and phone number in Appendix D.

For copies of United States Geological Survey topographic quadrangles (USGS quads), check at libraries, at most backpacking and mountaineering stores, or at specialty maps and publications stores. A state index will help you identify the name of the quad(s) that cover the area you are seeking.

Or contact the United States Geological Survey Map Distribution Center, Box 25286 Federal Center, Building 41, Denver, CO 80225, for a New York State index and a price list for the maps.

Maps produced by the New York–New Jersey Trail Conference, Adirondack Mountain Club, or Appalachian Mountain Club typically are available at backpacker and mountaineering stores or for direct order from the organization. For an order blank and price list, contact the respective organization:

New York—New Jersey Trail Conference, 232 Madison Avenue, New York, NY 10016; (212) 685–9699.

Adirondack Mountain Club, 814 Goggins Road, Lake George, NY 12845-4117; (518) 668–4447.

Appalachian Mountain Club, 5 Tudor City Place, New York, NY 10017; (212) 986–1430; or the Appalachian Trail Conference, P.O. Box 807, Harpers Ferry, WV 25425-0807.

For information on ordering the Finger Lakes Trail Conference maps, contact the Finger Lakes Trail Conference, P.O. Box 18048, Rochester, NY 14618-0048; (716) 288–7191. These simple line-drawing maps show the trail, key routes, towns, public lands, and landmarks; paired with each is a point-to-point description, indicating the progressive mileage.

Appendix D

Land Management Listings

Adirondack Trail Improvement
Society
P.O. Box 565
Keene Valley, NY 12943
No phone number for general information

Allegany State Park
2373 ASP, Route 1, Suite 3
Salamanca, NY 14779
(716) 354-9121

Appalachian Trail Conference
P.O. Box 807
799 Washington Street
Harpers Ferry, WV 25425-0807
(304) 535-6331

Beaver Lake Nature Center
8477 East Mud Lake Road
Baldwinsville, NY 13027
(315) 638-2519

Bowman Lake State Park
745 Bliven Sherman Road
Oxford, NY 13830
(607) 334-2718

Buttermilk Falls State Park
RD #10
Ithaca, NY 14850
(607) 273-5761

Chautauqua County Visitors Bureau
P.O. Box 1441
Chautauqua, NY 14722
(800) 242-4569; (716) 357-4569

College of Environmental Science
and Forestry
State University of New York
6312 State Route 28N
Newcomb, NY 12852
(518) 582-4551

Connetquot River State Park Preserve
P.O. Box 505
Oakdale, NY 11769
(631) 581-1005

Finger Lakes National Forest
Hector Ranger District
5218 State Route 414
Hector, NY 14841
(607) 546-4470

Finger Lakes Trail Conference
P.O. Box 18048
Rochester, NY 14618-0048
(716) 288-7191

Fire Island National Seashore
120 Laurel Street
Patchogue, NY 11772
(631) 289-4810

Five Rivers Environmental
Education Center
New York State Department of
Environmental Conservation
56 Game Farm Road
Delmar, NY 12054
(518) 475-0291

Glimmerglass State Park
1527 County Highway 31
Cooperstown, NY 13326
(607) 547-8662

Harriman State Park
Palisades Interstate Park Commission
Bear Mountain, NY 10911
(845) 786-2701

Hither Hills State Park
50 South Fairview Avenue
Montauk, NY 11754
(631) 668-3781

Hudson Highlands State Park
Route 9D
Beacon, NY 10512
(845) 225-7207

Iroquois National Wildlife Refuge
1101 Casey Road
Basom, NY 14013
(716) 948-9154

Jamaica Bay Wildlife Refuge
Floyd Bennett Field
Building 69
Brooklyn, NY 11234
(718) 318-4340

John Boyd Thacher State Park
RD 1, Box 238, Route 157
Voorheesville, NY 12186
(518) 872-1237

Letchworth State Park
1 Letchworth State Park
Castile, NY 14427
(716) 493-3600

Mashomack Preserve
P.O. Box 850
79 South Ferry Road
Shelter Island, NY 11964
(631) 749-1001

Mianus Gorge Preserve
167 Mianus River Road
Bedford, NY 10506
(914) 234-3455

Minnewaska State Park Preserve
P.O. Box 893
New Paltz, NY 12561
(845) 255-0753

Mohonk Mountain House
Lake Mohonk
New Paltz, NY 12561
(845) 255-1000

Mohonk Preserve
P.O. Box 715
New Paltz, NY 12561
(914) 255-0919

The Nature Conservancy
Central and Western New York Office
339 East Avenue, #300
Rochester, NY 14604
(716) 546-8030

New York State Canal Corporation
200 Southern Boulevard
P.O. Box 189
Albany, NY 12201-0189
(800) 422-6254

New York State Department of
Environmental Conservation,
Region 1
Building 40 SUNY
Stony Brook, NY 11790-2356
(631) 444-0273

New York State Department of
Environmental Conservation,
Region 3
21 South Putt Corners Road
New Paltz, NY 12561-1696
(914) 256-3098

New York State Department of
Environmental Conservation,
Region 4
1150 North Westcott Road
Schenectady, NY 12306
(518) 357-2450

New York State Department of
Environmental Conservation,
Region 4
65561 State Highway 10, Suite 1
Stamford, NY 12167-9503
(607) 652-7365

New York State Department of
Environmental Conservation,
Region 5
Route 86
P.O. Box 296
Ray Brook, NY 12977-0296
(518) 897-1200

New York State Department of
Environmental Conservation,
Region 6
State Office Building
317 Washington Street
Watertown, NY 13601-3787
(315) 785-2261

New York State Department of
Environmental Conservation,
Region 7
1285 Fisher Avenue
Cortland, NY 13045
(607) 753-3095

New York State Department of
Environmental Conservation,
Region 8
6274 East Avon–Lima Road
Avon, NY 14414
(716) 226-2466

Old Erie Canal State Historic Park
RD #2, Andrus Road
Kirkville, NY 13082
(315) 687-7821

Paul Smiths Visitor Interpretive
Center
P.O. Box 3000
Route 30
Paul Smiths, NY 12970
(518) 327-3000

Saint Lawrence County Planning
Office
48 Court Street
Canton, NY 13617-1194
(315) 379-2292 (weekdays only)

Saratoga National Historic Park
648 Route 32
Stillwater, NY 12170
(518) 664-9821, extension 224, for
information desk

Taconic State Park
Valley View Road, Box 100
Copake Falls, NY 12517
(518) 329-3993

Taughannock Falls State Park
P.O. Box 1055
Trumansburg, NY 14886
(607) 387-6739

Tifft Nature Preserve
1200 Fuhrmann Boulevard
Buffalo, NY 14203
(716) 896-5200

Watkins Glen State Park
P.O. Box 304
Watkins Glen, NY 14891
(607) 535-4511

Wellesley Island State Park
44927 Cross Island Road
Fineview, NY 13640
(315) 482-2722

Whetstone Gulf State Park
RD #2, Box 69
Lowville, NY 13367
(315) 376-6630

Glossary

Car-shuttle hikes. Typically these are linear routes for one-way travel that allow for a drop-off and pickup arrangement or for the spotting of a second vehicle at trail's end.

Woods roads. These dirt, grass, or rocky roads or faint road depressions represent old logging, mining, or farm routes that through time have fallen into disuse. Reclaimed for trails, most are closed to vehicle travel, although some may allow snowmobile or mountain bike use. We have attempted to alert readers to where woods roads are open or closed to vehicle use.

Truck trails. These maintained dirt roads are intended for and do receive vehicle travel; most allow a maximum speed limit of 25 miles per hour.

Service roads. These routes have minimal traffic, open to official vehicles only.

Forest lanes. These routes typically are narrower than a woods road yet wider than a trail, serving foot and horse travelers.

Carriageways or cart paths. In the past these well-groomed, well-graded routes offered comfortable travel for guests staying at the state's historic nineteenth-century mountain inns. Today, closed to vehicles, these routes may serve foot, horse, and/or bike travel; prior to a visit, check with the managing agency for acceptable use.

Jeep trails. These doubletrack routes typically serve foot and horse travelers. Most are no longer drivable.

Corduroy. This side-by-side alignment of logs, boards, or branches provides dry passage over soggy trail segments or delicate meadow sites.

Help Us Keep This Guide Up to Date

Every effort has been made by the authors and editors to make this guide as accurate and useful as possible. However, many things can change after a guide is published—trails are rerouted, regulations change, techniques evolve, facilities come under new management, and so on.

We would love to hear from you concerning your experiences with this guide and how you feel it could be improved and kept up to date. While we may not be able to respond to all comments and suggestions, we'll take them to heart and we'll also make certain to share them with the authors. Please send your comments and suggestions to the following address:

The Globe Pequot Press
Reader Response/Editorial Department
P.O. Box 480
Guilford, CT 06437

Or you may e-mail us at:

editorial@globe-pequot.com

Thanks for your input, and happy travels!

About the Authors

Over the past two decades the Ostertags, outdoor veterans, Rhonda (a writer) and George (a photographer), have collaborated on more than a dozen recreational guidebooks and have sold thousands of articles on topics of nature, travel, and outdoor recreation. With the second edition of *Hiking New York*, they again pointed their toes east. Trails have been rewalked and the agencies pestered for detail. The information has been fully updated with new information blocks and a couple of surprises thrown in.

George, born and raised in Connecticut, brings to the project his childhood enthusiasm for the region tempered by a reflective eye. Rhonda, a westerner, brings fresh perspective.

Other titles by this team include *California State Parks: A Complete Recreation Guide* and *100 Hikes in Oregon*, both with the Mountaineers, and *Hiking Southern New England, Hiking Pennsylvania*, and *Scenic Driving Pennsylvania*, all FalconGuides.

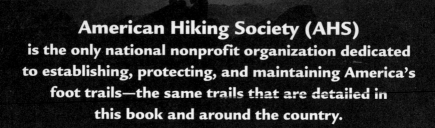

American Hiking Society (AHS)
is the only national nonprofit organization dedicated
to establishing, protecting, and maintaining America's
foot trails—the same trails that are detailed in
this book and around the country.

**As a trail user, your support of AHS is important to ensure
trails are forever protected and continually maintained.**

Join American Hiking Society today and you will learn about trails to hike, their history,
their importance, and how you can help protect them. American Hiking Society is:

A strong voice. With increasing threats to our treasured open space and wilderness,
American Hiking Society exists to actively represent hikers' interests to safeguard these
areas. To protect the hiking experience, AHS affects federal legislation, shapes public
lands policy, collaborates with grassroots trail organizations, and partners with federal
land managers. As a member of AHS, feel assured that while you are hiking, AHS is
going *the extra mile* for you.

A helping hand. With more than 200,000 miles of trails in America, AHS steps in with
needed maintenance for trail managers and hiking clubs. Through our Volunteer Vaca-
tions program, we provide more than 24,000 hours of trail work annually to help preserve some of the most scenic places in America. As an AHS Member, you can take
advantage of this opportunity to give back to the trails that you use and love.

A critical resource. Each year, crucial trail funding continually falls behind trail
maintenance demands. Your favorite trail will **not** be next, thanks to American Hiking
Society! Our National Trails Fund annually awards financial grants to local and
regional hiking clubs for land acquisition, volunteer recruitment, and trail maintenance.
As you support AHS, you share in the satisfaction of helping grassroots trails clubs na-
tionwide.

Join TODAY!   **American
Hiking
Society**

1422 Fenwick Lane · Silver Spring, MD 20910 · (301) 565-6704
www.AmericanHiking.org · info@AmericanHiking.org